D1220069

Women at Work

VOLUME II

Women at Work

VOLUME II

INTERVIEWS FROM

the PARIS REVIEW

WITH A PREFACE BY

Emily Nemens

AND ILLUSTRATIONS BY

Joana Avillez

PARIS REVIEW EDITIONS

New York

Paris Review Editions
544 West 27th Street, New York 10001

Library of Congress Control Number: 2018959897

ISBN 978-1-732-81550-6

Printed by the Sheridan Press in Hanover, Pa.

First Edition

1 3 5 7 9 10 8 6 4 2

Designed by Jonathan D. Lippincott

Special Thanks to Lauren Kane and Matt Levin

Contents

Preface

One of my first tasks upon arriving in New York this summer as the new editor of *The Paris Review* was to pick twelve interviews for the second volume of the Women at Work series. I looked back to the first volume, which was the first book to be issued under the renewed imprint of Paris Review Editions, now an in-house line of beautifully designed and illustrated limited-edition books. In that volume, published in 2017, I found Dorothy Parker's 1956 conversation about her fiction and Claudia Rankine's Art of Poetry interview from sixty years later. Reading them—and often rereading them, as I am one of a large cadre of writers who turn to the Writers at Work series for advice and inspiration—I considered how to proceed in assembling a companion volume. Nothing of literary editing is formulaic, but a set of parameters did emerge: here was an anthology of women's voices from across the magazine's history, here were women writing around the globe. In the anthology I found a range of genres and a multitude of perspectives.

With that program, the second volume of Women at Work took shape. The hardest part, to this editor's eye, was picking only twelve interviews. Eighty-four women have been interviewed in the Writers at Work series, and every woman warrants inclusion. Both the singular and the collective strength of these interviews come from the unique format for Writers at Work, established back in 1953 with the first Art of Fiction interview, featuring E. M. Forster: these would not be strictly journalism or criticism, but would take a third way. Following founding editor George Plimpton's editorial mandate to never think "of the interviews as inquisitions but rather as documentations of the authors-at-work," a more collaborative tone was struck than in your typical interview. After a *Paris Review* interview is transcribed, it is then heavily edited, with interviewer, subject, and editor all weighing in. As Joyce Carol Oates posited in her introduction to an earlier anthology of *Paris Review* interviews, "If the *PR* interviews are uniformly successful"—and I would argue they are!—"it is because they are highly stylized and collaborative." She saw no problem with that stylization, arguing that "the artifice of the form in no way interferes with the authenticity and consistently high worth of its contents."

Ultimately, I decided on the twelve highly worthy interviews presented here, which span from Marianne Moore's 1961 discussion of her poetry to Maxine Groffsky's 2017 conversation about her editorial career, which included several years as *The*

Paris Review's Paris editor.* This second volume represents writers working in the fields of fiction, poetry, theater, and editing—an art in and of itself. While the book may be bracketed by two New Yorkers and their talk of Paris (Moore visited with her mother in 1911, and Groffsky worked there from 1965 to 1974), the reader also travels to the quiet plains of Alice Munro's rural Ontario (she grew up on a fox and mink farm and, in later life, lives not far away) and the literary salons of Luisa Valenzuela's Buenos Aires childhood (she recalls Borges and Cortázar coming for visits with her mother). The reader voyages to Minnesota and Louise Erdrich's "small attic room pleasantly cluttered with photographs, artifacts, and many more Catholic and Ojibwe totems." Here the second half of the interview is conducted, and it is here that, "in a deeply slanted longhand, Erdrich still writes most of her books—sitting in the chair with a wooden board laid across its arms as a desk." However, not all writing spaces are so sacred: for a time, Wendy Wasserstein wrote her plays in a spare office at Comedy Central, until the availability of a telephone became a "problem."

Expanding Women at Work to a second anthology also made room for discovery, for surprises, and for a bit of strangeness. Discovery first: one of the joys of extending a series is to look for what was missed in the first pass through the archive. The novelist and poet May Sarton may not be a household

---

*Editor's note: Throughout the volume some very minor edits have been made to the original interviews. These were made with the intention of unifying style across the anthology, correcting errors, and amending instances of archaic language.

name today, but sixty years ago, she was a finalist for the National Book Award in two categories, fiction and poetry. Even more than that achievement, what resonated with me in reading her interview again in 2018 was her discussion of coming out as a lesbian in the sixties, with the publication of *Mrs. Stevens Hears the Mermaids Singing*. "At that time it was not done," she says. "At the time *Mrs. Stevens* was published, it was sneered at in reviews and I lost a couple of jobs. They weren't terribly important jobs, but I did lose them. Now I don't think that would happen." Reading this alongside Jeanette Winterson's account of writing *Oranges Are Not the Only Fruit*, published two decades later, showed the progress that has been made, progress that would not have happened without courageous writers such as Sarton.

As for the surprising moments, and the strange ones: Richard Nixon makes two *positive* appearances here (Moore and Erdrich both supported him at times). Marguerite Young, who spent eighteen years working on *Miss MacIntosh, My Darling*, also had a long relationship with an imagined Edgar Allan Poe. "I see him on misty nights on Sheridan Square, when the rain's falling. He's going into that little cigar store to get a cigar. I am on very close terms with Poe. Now rationally I don't believe all of this, but in an irrational way, I live it all, so what can we say?"

The Maya Angelou interview, while not inhabited by ghosts, is something of a surprise in its format, as compared with most Writers at Work interviews. It was conducted onstage at the 92nd Street Y. Many *Paris Review* interviews have started on that stage or another, but most continue to second and third sessions elsewhere, and the seams between conversations are subsequently erased by the rigorous editorial process (creating what has been informally called the "rewritten interview"). This jocular conversation—and George Plimpton's shorter, more descriptive introduction—speaks to that unique setting.

While I know the twelve women featured are the stars of this anthology, I want to point out the good company of the interviewers as well. Many are alumni of the magazine, from George Plimpton and the founding poetry editor, Donald Hall, to former editors—now board members—Mona Simpson and Jeanne McCulloch, who double-teamed Alice Munro (she requested not to have a tape recorder running; instead, one interviewer asked questions while the other scribbled down the replies). Each had a hand in making these conversations into compelling, incisive interviews. And of course the volume closes with the Art of Editing interview with Maxine Groffsky, a trailblazer for women literary editors everywhere. Over lunch a few weeks ago, Maxine admitted to me that the reason the magazine rarely hit its four-issues-a-year goal in those early days in Paris was because the interviews were slow to come together; she'd often have to wait for international mail from George, who would send along edits on the promised interview, before the issue could go to the printer. (As she explains in her interview, Pablo Neruda's interview was delayed by an abundance of California drapery.)

This volume is the antidote to that waiting, a hefty serving of women who have done remarkable work and who herein share their remarkable stories.

Emily Nemens

Women at Work

VOLUME II

Marianne Moore

THE ART OF POETRY NO. 4

Interviewed by Donald Hall

Amerian poetry is a great literature, and it has come to its maturity only in the last seventy years; Walt Whitman and Emily Dickinson in the last century were rare examples of genius in a hostile environment. One decade gave America the major figures of our modern poetry: Wallace Stevens was born in 1879, and T. S. Eliot in 1888. To the ten years that these dates enclose belong H. D., Robinson Jeffers, John Crowe Ransom, William Carlos Williams, Ezra Pound, and Marianne Moore.

Marianne Moore began to publish during the First World War. She was printed and praised in Europe by the expatriates T. S. Eliot and Ezra Pound. In Chicago, Harriet Monroe's magazine *Poetry*, which provided the enduring showcase for the new poetry, published her, too. But she was mainly a poet of New York, of the Greenwich Village group that created magazines called *Others* and *Broom*.

To visit Marianne Moore at her home in Brooklyn, you had to cross the Brooklyn Bridge, turn left at Myrtle Avenue, follow the elevated for a mile or two, and then turn right onto her street. It was pleasantly lined with a few trees, and Miss Moore's apartment was conveniently near a grocery store and the Presbyterian church that she attended.

The interview took place in November 1960, the day before the presidential election. The front door of Miss Moore's apartment opened onto a long narrow corridor. Rooms led off to the right, and at the end of the corridor was a large sitting room that overlooked the street. On top of a bookcase that ran the length of the corridor was a Nixon button.

Miss Moore and the interviewer sat in her sitting room, a microphone between them. Piles of books stood everywhere. On the walls hung a variety of paintings. One came from Mexico, a gift of Mabel Dodge; others were examples of the heavy, tea-colored oils that Americans hung in the years before 1914. The furniture was old-fashioned and dark.

Miss Moore spoke with an accustomed scrupulosity, and with a humor that her readers will recognize. When she ended a sentence with a phrase that was particularly telling, or even tart, she glanced quickly at the interviewer to see if he was amused, and then snickered gently. Later Miss Moore took the interviewer to an admirable lunch at a nearby restaurant. She decided not to wear her Nixon button because it clashed with her coat and hat.

INTERVIEWER

Miss Moore, I understand that you were born in Saint

Louis only about ten months before T. S. Eliot. Did your families know each other?

No, we did not know the Eliots. We lived in Kirkwood, Missouri, where my grandfather was pastor of the First Presbyterian Church. T. S. Eliot's grandfather—Dr. William Eliot—was a Unitarian. We left when I was about seven, my grandfather having died in 1894, on February 20. My grandfather, like Dr. Eliot, had attended ministerial meetings in Saint Louis. Also, at stated intervals, various ministers met for luncheon. After one of these luncheons my grandfather said, When Dr. William Eliot asks the blessing and says, And this we ask in the name of our Lord Jesus Christ, he is Trinitarian enough for me. The Mary Institute, for girls, was endowed by him as a memorial to his daughter Mary, who had died.

How old were you when you started to write poems?

Well, let me see, in Bryn Mawr. I think I was eighteen when I entered Bryn Mawr. I was born in 1887, I entered college in 1906. Now, how old would I have been? Can you deduce my probable age?

Eighteen or nineteen.

I had no literary plans, but I was interested in the undergraduate monthly magazine, and to my surprise—I wrote one or two little things for it—the editors elected me to the board. It was my sophomore year, I am sure it was, and I stayed on, I believe. And then when I had left college I offered contributions—we weren't paid—to the *Lantern*, the alumnae magazine. But I didn't feel that my product was anything to shake the world.

INTERVIEWER

At what point did poetry become world-shaking for you?

MOORE

Never! I believe I was interested in painting then. At least I said so. I remember Mrs. Otis Skinner asking at commencement time, the year I was graduated, "What would you like to be?"

"A painter," I said.

"Well, I'm not surprised," Mrs. Skinner answered. I had something on that she liked, some kind of summer dress. She commended it—said, "I'm not at all surprised."

I like stories. I like fiction. And—this sounds rather pathetic, bizarre as well—I think verse perhaps was for me the next best thing to it. Didn't I write something one time, "Part of a Poem, Part of a Novel, Part of a Play" (1932)? I think I was all too truthful. I could visualize scenes, and deplored the fact that Henry James had to do it unchallenged. Now, if I couldn't write fiction, I'd like to write plays. To me the theater is the most pleasant, in fact my favorite, form of recreation.

Do you go often?

No. Never. Unless someone invites me. Lillian Hellman invited me to *Toys in the Attic*, and I am very happy that she did. I would have had no notion of the vitality of the thing, have lost sight of her skill as a writer if I hadn't seen the play. I would like to go again. The accuracy of the vernacular! That's the kind of thing I am interested in, am always taking down little local expressions and accents. I think I should be in some philological operation or enterprise, am really much interested in dialect and intonations. I scarcely think of any that comes into my so-called poems at all.

I wonder what Bryn Mawr meant for you as a poet. You write that most of your time there was spent in the biological laboratory. Did you like biology better than literature as a subject for study? Did the training possibly affect your poetry?

I had hoped to make French and English my major studies, and took the required two-year English course—five hours a week—but was not able to elect a course until my junior year. I did not attain the requisite academic stand of eighty until that year. I then elected seventeenth-century imitative writing—Fuller, Hooker, Bacon, Bishop Andrewes, and others. Lectures in French were in French, and I had no spoken French.

Did laboratory studies affect my poetry? I am sure they did. I found the biology courses—minor, major, and histology—exhilarating. I thought, in fact, of studying medicine. Precision, economy of statement, logic employed to ends that are disinterested, drawing and identifying, liberate—at least have some bearing on—the imagination, it seems to me.

INTERVIEWER

Whom did you know in the literary world, before you came to New York? Did you know Bryher and H. D.?

MOORE

It's very hard to get these things seriatim. I met Bryher in 1921 in New York. H. D. was my classmate at Bryn Mawr. She was there, I think, only two years. She was a nonresident and I did not realize that she was interested in writing.

INTERVIEWER

Did you know Ezra Pound and William Carlos Williams through her? Didn't she know them at the University of Pennsylvania?

MOORE

Yes. She did. I didn't meet them. I had met no writers until 1916, when I visited New York, when a friend in Carlisle wanted me to accompany her.

INTERVIEWER

So you were isolated really from modern poetry until 1916?

MOORE

Yes.

INTERVIEWER

Was that your first trip to New York, when you went there for six days and decided that you wanted to live there?

MOORE

Oh, no. Several times my mother had taken my brother and me sightseeing and to shop, on the way to Boston, or Maine, and to Washington and Florida. My senior year in college in 1909, I visited Dr. Charles Sprague Smith's daughter, Hilda, at Christmastime in New York. And Louis Anspacher lectured in a very ornamental way at Cooper Union. There was plenty of music at Carnegie Hall, and I got a sense of what was going on in New York.

INTERVIEWER

And what was going on made you want to come back?

MOORE

It probably did, when Miss Cowdrey in Carlisle invited me to come with her for a week. It was the visit in 1916 that made me want to live there. I don't know what put it into her head to do it, or why she wasn't likely to have a better time without me. She was most skeptical of my venturing forth to bohemian parties. But I was fearless about that. In the first place, I didn't think anyone would try to harm me, but if they did I felt impervious. It never occurred to me that chaperones were important.

Do you suppose that moving to New York, and the stimulation of the writers whom you found there, led you to write more poems than you would otherwise have written?

MOORE

I'm sure it did—seeing what others wrote, liking this or that. With me it's always some fortuity that traps me. I certainly never intended to write poetry. That never came into my head. And now, too, I think each time I write that it may be the last time. Then I'm charmed by something and seem to have to say something. Everything I have written is the result of reading or of interest in people, I'm sure of that. I had no ambition to be a writer.

INTERVIEWER

Let me see. You taught at the Carlisle Indian School, after Bryn Mawr. Then after you moved to New York in 1918 you taught at a private school and worked in a library. Did these occupations have anything to do with you as a writer?

MOORE

I think they hardened my muscles considerably, my mental approach to things. Working as a librarian was a big help, a tremendous help. Miss Leonard of the Hudson Park branch of the New York Public Library opposite our house came to see me one day. I wasn't in, and she asked my mother did she think I would care to be on the staff, work in the library, because I was so fond of books and liked to talk about them to people. My mother said no, she thought not—the shoemaker's children never have shoes, I probably would feel if I joined the staff that I'd have no time to read. When I came home she told me, and I said, Why, certainly. Ideal. I'll tell her. Only I couldn't work more than half a day. If I had worked all day and maybe evenings or overtime, like the mechanics, why, it would *not* have been ideal.

As a free service we were assigned books to review and I did like that. We didn't get paid but we had the chance to diagnose. I reveled in it. Somewhere I believe I have carbon copies of those p-slip summaries. They were the kind of things that brought the worst/best out. I was always wondering why they didn't honor me with an art book or medical book or even a history, or criticism. But no, it was fiction, silent-movie fiction.

INTERVIEWER

Did you travel at this time? Did you go to Europe at all?

MOORE

In 1911. My mother and I went to England for about two months, July and August probably. We went to Paris and we stayed on the Left Bank, in a pension in the rue Valette, where Calvin wrote his *Institutes*, I believe. Not far from the Panthéon and the Luxembourg Gardens. I have been much interested in Sylvia Beach's book—reading about Ezra Pound and his Paris days. Where was I and what was I doing? I think, with the objective, an evening stroll—it was one of the hottest summers the world has ever known, 1911—we walked along to 12, rue de l'Odéon to see Sylvia Beach's shop. It wouldn't occur to me to say, Here I am, I'm a writer, would you talk to me awhile? I had no feeling at all like that. I wanted to observe things. And we went to every museum in Paris, I think, except two.

INTERVIEWER

Have you been back since?

MOORE

Not to Paris. Only to England in 1935 or 1936. I like England.

INTERVIEWER

You have mostly stayed put in Brooklyn, then, since you moved here in 1929?

MOORE

Except for four trips to the West to Los Angeles, San Francisco, Puget Sound, and British Columbia. My mother and I went through the canal previously, to San Francisco, and by rail to Seattle.

INTERVIEWER

Have you missed the Dodgers here, since *they* went West?

MOORE

Very much, and I am told that they miss us.

INTERVIEWER

I am still interested in those early years in New York. William Carlos Williams, in his *Autobiography*, says that you were "a rafter holding up the superstructure of our uncompleted building," when he talks about the Greenwich Village group of writers. I guess these were people who contributed to *Others*.

MOORE

I never was a rafter holding up anyone! I have his *Autobiography* and took him to task for his misinformed statements about Robert McAlmon and Bryher. In my indignation I missed some things I ought to have seen.

INTERVIEWER

To what extent did the *Others* contributors form a group?

MOORE

We did foregather a little. Alfred Kreymborg was editor, and was married to Gertrude Lord at the time,* one of the loveliest persons you could ever meet. And they had a little apartment somewhere in the Village. There was considerable unanimity about the group.

INTERVIEWER

Someone called Alfred Kreymborg your American discoverer. Do you suppose this is true?

MOORE

It could be said, perhaps. He did all he could to promote me. Miss Monroe and the Aldingtons had asked me simultaneously to contribute to *Poetry* and *The Egoist* in 1915. Alfred Kreymborg was not inhibited. I was a little different from the others. He thought I might pass as a novelty, I guess.

---

* Moore was likely referring to Dorothy Bloom.

What was your reaction when H.D. and Bryher brought out your first collection, which they called *Poems*, in 1921 without your knowledge? Why had you delayed to do it yourself?

MOORE

To issue my slight product—conspicuously tentative—seemed to me premature. I disliked the term *poetry* for any but Chaucer's or Shakespeare's or Dante's. I do not now feel quite my original hostility to the word, since it is a convenient, almost unavoidable term for the thing, although hardly for me—my observations, experiments in rhythm, or exercises in composition. What I write, as I have said before, could only be called poetry because there is no other category in which to put it. For the chivalry of the undertaking—issuing my verse for me in 1921, certainly in format choicer than the content—I am intensely grateful. Again, in 1935, it seemed to me not very self-interested of Faber and Faber, and simultaneously of the Macmillan Company, to propose a *Selected Poems* (1935) for me. Desultory occasional magazine publications seemed to me sufficient, conspicuous enough.

INTERVIEWER

Had you been sending poems to magazines before *The Egoist* printed your first poem?

MOORE

I must have. I have a little curio, a little wee book about two by three inches, or two and a half by three inches, in which I systematically entered everything sent out, when I got it back, if they took it, and how much I got for it. That lasted about a year, I think. I can't care as much as all that. I don't know that I submitted anything that wasn't extorted from me.

I have at present three onerous tasks, and each interferes with the others, and I don't know how I am going to write anything. If I get a promising idea I set it down, and it stays there. I don't make myself do anything with it. I've had several things in *The New Yorker*. And I said to them, I might never write again, and not to expect me to. I never knew anyone who had a passion for words who had as much difficulty in saying things as I do and I very seldom say them in a manner I like. If I do it's because I don't know I'm trying. I've written several things for *The New Yorker*—and I did want to write *them*.

INTERVIEWER
When did you last write a poem?

MOORE
It appeared in August. What was it about? Oh ... Carnegie Hall. You see, anything that really rouses me ...

INTERVIEWER
How does a poem start for you?

MOORE
A felicitous phrase springs to mind—a word or two, say—simultaneous usually with some thought or object of equal attraction: "Its leaps should be *set* / to the flageo*let*" or "katydid-wing / subdivided by *sun* / till the nettings are *legion*." I like light rhymes,

inconspicuous rhymes and unpompous conspicuous rhymes: Gilbert and Sullivan:

> Yet, when the danger's near,
> We manage to appear
> As insensible to fear
> As anybody here.

I have a passion for rhythm and accent, so blundered into versifying. Considering the stanza the unit, I came to hazard hyphens at the end of the line, but found that readers are distracted from the content by hyphens, so I try not to use them. My interest in La Fontaine originated entirely independent of content. I then fell prey to that surgical kind of courtesy of his:

> I fear that appearances are worshiped
>   throughout France
> Whereas pre-eminence perchance
> Merely means a pushing person.

I like the unaccented syllable and accented near rhyme: by Love and his blindness,

> Possibly a service was done,
> Let lovers say. A lonely man has no criterion.

INTERVIEWER

What in your reading or your background led you to write the way you do write? Was imagism a help to you?

MOORE

No. I wondered why anyone would adopt the term.

INTERVIEWER

The descriptiveness of your poems has nothing to do with them, you think?

MOORE

No, I really don't. I was rather sorry to be a pariah, or at least that I had no connection with anything. But I *did* feel gratitude to *Others*.

INTERVIEWER

Where do you think your style of writing came from? Was it a gradual accumulation, out of your character? Or does it have literary antecedents?

MOORE

Not so far as I know. Ezra Pound said, "Someone has been reading Laforgue, and French authors." Well, sad to say, I had not read any of them until fairly recently. Retroactively I see that Francis Jammes's titles and treatment are a good deal like my own. I seem almost a plagiarist.

INTERVIEWER

And the extensive use of quotations?

MOORE

I was just trying to be honorable and not to steal things. I've always felt that if a thing has been said in the *best* way, how can you say it better? If I wanted to say something and somebody had said it ideally, then

I'd take it but give the person credit for it. That's all there is to it. If you are charmed by an author, I think it's a very strange and invalid imagination that doesn't long to share it. Somebody else should read it, don't you think?

Did any prose stylists help you in finding your poetic style? Elizabeth Bishop mentions Poe's prose in connection with your writing, and you have always made people think of Henry James.

Prose stylists, very much. Dr. Johnson on Richard Savage: "He was in two months illegitimated by the Parliament, and disowned by his mother, doomed to poverty and obscurity, and launched upon the ocean of life only that he might be swallowed by its quicksands, or dashed upon its rocks... It was his peculiar happiness that he scarcely ever found a stranger whom he did not leave a friend; but it must likewise be added, that he had not often a friend long without obliging him to become a stranger." Or Edmund Burke on the colonies: "What! shear a wolf? Yes. But will he comply?" Or Sir Thomas Browne: "States are not governed by ergotisms." He calls a bee "that industrious flie," and his home his "hive." His manner is a kind of erudition-proof sweetness. Or Sir Francis Bacon: "A civil war, indeed, is like the heat of fever; a foreign war is like the heat of exercise." Or Cellini: "[I was] fuming with fury and swelling like an asp... I had a dog, black as mulberry." Or Caesar's *Commentaries*, and Xenophon's *Cynegeticus*: the gusto and interest in every detail! In Henry James it is the essays and letters especially that affect me. In Ezra Pound, *The Spirit of Romance*: his definiteness, his indigenously unmistakable accent. Charles Norman says in his biography of Ezra Pound that he said to a poet, "Nothing, *nothing*, that you couldn't in some circumstance, in the stress of some emotion, *actually say*." And Ezra said of Shakespeare and Dante, "Here we are with the masters; of neither can we say, 'He is the greater'; of each we must say, 'He is unexcelled.' "

INTERVIEWER
Do you have in your own work any favorites and unfavorites?

MOORE
Indeed, I do. I think the most difficult thing for me is to be satisfactorily lucid, yet have enough implication in it to suit myself. That's a problem. And I don't approve of my "enigmas," or as somebody said, "the not ungreen grass." I said to my mother one time, How did you ever permit me to let this be printed? And she said, You didn't ask my advice.

INTERVIEWER
One time I heard you give a reading, and I think you said that you didn't like "In Distrust of Merits" (1943), which is one of your most popular poems.

MOORE
I do like it. It is sincere but I wouldn't call it a poem. It's truthful. It is testimony to the fact that war is intolerable, and unjust.

How can you call it not a poem, on what basis?

Haphazard. As form, what has it? It is just a pro-
test—disjointed, exclamatory. Emotion overpow-
ered me. First this thought and then that.

Your mother said that you hadn't asked her advice.
Did you ever? Do you go for criticism to your family
or friends?

Well, not friends, but my brother if I get a chance.
When my mother said "you didn't ask my advice"
must have been years ago, because when I wrote "A
Face" (1947), I had written something first about
"the adder and the child with a bowl of porridge,"
and she said, "It won't do." "All right," I said, "but
I have to produce something." Cyril Connolly had
asked me for something for *Horizon*. So I wrote "A
Face." That is one of the few things I ever set down
that didn't give me any trouble. She said, "I like it."
I remember that.

   Then, much before that, I wrote "The Buffalo"
(1934). I thought it would probably outrage a number of persons because it had to me a kind of pleasing
jerky progress. I thought, Well, if it seems bad my
brother will tell me, and if it has a point he'll detect
it. And he said, with considerable gusto, "It takes my
fancy." I was happy as could be.

Did you ever suppress anything because of family objections?

MOORE

Yes, "the adder and the child with a bowl of porridge." I never even wanted to improve it. You know, Mr. Saintsbury said that Andrew Lang wanted him to contribute something on Poe, and he did, and Lang returned it. Mr. Saintsbury said, Once a thing has been rejected, I would not offer it to the most different of editors. That shocked me. I have offered a thing, submitted it thirty-five times. Not simultaneously, of course.

INTERVIEWER

A poem?

MOORE

Yes. I am very tenacious.

INTERVIEWER

Do people ever ask you to write poems for them?

MOORE

Continually. Everything from on the death of a dog to a little item for an album.

INTERVIEWER

Do you ever write them?

MOORE

Oh, perhaps—I usually quote something. Once when I was in the library we gave a party for Miss

Leonard, and I wrote a line or two of doggerel about a bouquet of violets we gave her. It has no life or point. It was meant well but didn't amount to anything. Then in college, I had a sonnet as an assignment. The epitome of weakness.

INTERVIEWER

I'm interested in asking about the principles, and the methods, of your way of writing. What is the rationale behind syllabic verse? How does it differ from free verse, in which the line length is controlled visually but not arithmetically?

MOORE

It never occurred to me that what I wrote was something to define. I am governed by the pull of the sentence as the pull of a fabric is governed by gravity. I like the end-stopped line and dislike the reversed order of words, like symmetry.

INTERVIEWER

How do you plan the shape of your stanzas? I am thinking of the poems, usually syllabic, which employ a repeated stanza form. Do you ever experiment with shapes before you write, by drawing lines on a page?

MOORE

Never, I never "plan" a stanza. Words cluster like chromosomes, determining the procedure. I may influence an arrangement or thin it, then try to have successive stanzas identical with the first. Spontaneous initial originality—say, impetus—seems difficult to reproduce consciously later. As Stravinsky said about pitch, "If I transpose it for some reason I am in danger of losing the freshness of first contact and I will have difficulty in recapturing its attractiveness."

No, I never "draw lines." I make a rhyme conspicuous, to me at a glance, by underlining with red, blue, or other pencil—as many colors as I have rhymes to differentiate. However, if the phrases recur in too incoherent an architecture—as print—I notice that the words as a tune do not sound right. I may start a piece, find it obstructive, lack a way out, and not complete the thing for a year, or years, am thrifty. I salvage anything promising and set it down in a small notebook.

I wonder if the act of translating La Fontaine's *Fables* (1954) helped you as a writer.

Indeed it did. It was the best help I've ever had. I suffered frustration. I'm so naive, so docile, I *tend* to take anybody's word for anything the person says, even in matters of art. The publisher who had commissioned the *Fables* died. I had no publisher. Well, I struggled on for a time and it didn't go very well. I thought, I'd better ask if they don't want to terminate the contract, then I could offer it elsewhere. I thought Macmillan, who took an interest in me, might like it. *Might.* The editor in charge of translations said, "Well, I studied French at Cornell, took a degree in French, I love French, and … well, I think you'd better put it away for a while." "How long?" I said. "About ten years. Besides, it will hurt your own work. You won't write so well afterward."

"Oh," I said, "that's one reason I was undertaking it. I thought it would train me and give me momentum." Much dejected, I asked, "What is wrong? Have I not a good ear? Are the meanings not sound?"

"Well, there are conflicts," the editor reiterated, as it seemed to me, countless times. I don't know yet what they are or were. A little editorial.

I said, "Don't write me an extenuating letter, please. Just send back the material in the envelope I put with it." I had submitted it in January and this was May. I had had a kind of uneasy hope that all would be well. Meanwhile, I had volumes, hours, and years of work yet to do and might as well go on and do it, I had thought. The ultimatum was devastating.

At the same time Monroe Engel of the Viking Press wrote to me and said that he had supposed I had a commitment for my *Fables*, but if I hadn't would I let the Viking Press see them? I feel an everlasting gratitude to him.

However, I said, "I can't offer you something which somebody else thinks isn't fit to print. I would have to have someone to stabilize it and guarantee that the meanings are sound."

Mr. Engel said, "Who do you think could do that? Whom would you like?"

I said, Harry Levin, because he had written a cogent, very shrewd review of Edna St. Vincent Millay and George Dillon's translation of Baudelaire. I admired its finesse.

Mr. Engel said, "I'll ask him. But you won't hear for a long time. He's very busy. And how much do you think we ought to offer him?"

"Well," I said, "not less than ten dollars a book. There would be no incentive in undertaking the bother of it, if it weren't twenty."

He said, "That would reduce your royalties too much on an advance."

I said, "I don't want an advance, wouldn't even consider one."

And then Harry Levin said, quite soon, that he would be glad to do it as a "refreshment against the chores of the term," but of course he would accept no remuneration. It was a very dubious refreshment, let me tell you. He is precise, and not abusive, and did not "resign."

INTERVIEWER

I've been asking you about your poems, which is of course what interests me most. But you were editor of *The Dial*, too, and I want to ask you a few things about that. You were editor from 1925 until it ended in 1929, I think. How did you first come to be associated with it?

MOORE

Let me see. I think I took the initiative. I sent the editors a couple of things and they sent them back. And Lola Ridge had a party—she had a large apartment on a ground floor somewhere—and John Reed and Marsden Hartley, who was very confident with the brush, and Scofield Thayer, editor of *The Dial*, were there. And much to my disgust, we were induced each to read something we had written. And Scofield Thayer said of my piece, "Would you send that to us at *The Dial*?"

"I did send it," I said.

And he said, "Well, send it again." That is how it began, I think. Then he said, one time, "I'd like you to meet my partner, Sibley Watson," and invited me to tea at 152 West Thirteenth Street. I was impressed. Dr. Watson is rare. He said nothing, but what he did say was striking and the significance would creep over you as being extremely unanticipated. And they asked me to join the staff at *The Dial*.

INTERVIEWER
I have just been looking at that magazine, the years when you edited it. It's an incredible magazine.

MOORE
The Dial? There *were* good things in it, weren't there?

INTERVIEWER
Yes. It combined George Saintsbury and Ezra Pound in the same issue. How do you account for it? What made it so good?

MOORE
Lack of fear, for one thing. We didn't care what other people said. I never knew a magazine that was so self-propulsive. Everybody liked what he was doing, and when we made grievous mistakes we were sorry but we laughed over them.

INTERVIEWER
Louise Bogan said that *The Dial* made clear "the obvious division between American avant-garde and American conventional writing." Do you think this kind of division continues or has continued? Was this in any way a deliberate policy?

I think that individuality was the great thing. We were not conforming to anything. We certainly didn't have a policy, except I remember hearing the word *intensity* very often. A thing must have *intensity*. That seemed to be the criterion.

The thing applied to it, I think, that should apply to your own writing. As George Grosz said, at that last meeting he attended at the National Institute, "How did I come to be an artist? Endless curiosity, observation, research—and a great amount of joy in the thing." It was a matter of taking a liking to things. Things that were in accordance with your taste. I think that was it. And we didn't care how unhomogeneous they might seem. Didn't Aristotle say that it is the mark of a poet to see resemblances between apparently incongruous things? There was any amount of attraction about it.

INTERVIEWER

Do you think there is anything in the change of literary life in America that would make *The Dial* different if it existed today under the same editors? Were there any special conditions in the twenties that made the literary life of America different?

MOORE

I think it is always about the same.

INTERVIEWER

I wonder, if it had survived into the thirties, if it might have made that rather dry literary decade a little better.

I think so. Because we weren't in captivity to anything.

Was it just finances that made it stop?

No, it wasn't the Depression. Conditions changed. Scofield Thayer had a nervous breakdown, and he didn't come to meetings. Dr. Watson was interested in photography—was studying medicine—is a doctor of medicine, and lived in Rochester. I was alone. I didn't know that Rochester was about a night's journey away, and I would say to Dr. Watson, Couldn't you come in for a makeup meeting, or send us these manuscripts and say what you think of them? I may, as usual, have exaggerated my enslavement and my preoccupation with tasks—writing letters and reading manuscripts. Originally I had said I would come if I didn't have to write letters and didn't have to see contributors. And presently I was doing both. I think it was largely chivalry—the decision to discontinue the magazine—because I didn't have time for work of my own.

I wonder how you worked as an editor. Hart Crane complains, in one of his letters, that you rearranged "The Wine Menagerie" and changed the title. Do you feel that you were justified? Did you ask for revisions from many poets?

No. We had an inflexible rule—do not ask changes

of so much as a comma. Accept it or reject it. But in that instance I felt that in compassion I should disregard the rule. Hart Crane complains of me? Well, I complain of *him*. He liked *The Dial* and we liked him—friends, and with certain tastes in common. He was in dire need of money. It seemed careless not to so much as ask if he might like to make some changes—"like" in quotations. His gratitude was ardent and later his repudiation of it commensurate—he perhaps being in both instances under a disability with which I was not familiar. Penalizing us for compassion? I say *us*, and should say *me*. Really I am not used to having people in that bemused state. He was so anxious to have us take that thing, and so delighted. "Well, if you would modify it a little," I said, "we would like it better." I never attended their wild parties, as Lachaise once said. It was lawless of me to suggest changes. I disobeyed.

INTERVIEWER

Have you had editors suggest changes to you? Changes in your own poems, I mean?

MOORE

No, but my ardor to be helped being sincere, I sometimes *induced* assistance. The *Times*, the *Herald Tribune*, *The New Yorker*, have a number of times had to patch and piece me out. If you have a genius of an editor, you are blessed. T. S. Eliot and Ezra Pound, Harry Levin and others—Irita Van Doren and Miss Belle Rosenbaum.

Have I found help helpful? I certainly have. And in three instances when I was at *The Dial*, I hazarded suggestions the results of which were to me drama.

Excoriated by Herman George Scheffauer for offering to suggest a verbal change or two in his translation of Thomas Mann's *Disorder and Early Sorrow*, I must have posted the suggestions before I was able to withdraw them. In any case, his joyous subsequent retraction of abuse, and his pleasure in the narrative, were not unwelcome. Gilbert Seldes strongly commended me for excisions proposed by me in his "Jonathan Edwards" for *The Dial*. I have not ceased to marvel at the overrating by Mark Van Doren of editorial conscience on my reverting, after an interval, to keeping some final lines I had wished he would omit. Verse! But not a sonnet.

We should try to judge the work of others by the most that it is, and our own, if not by the least that it is, take the least into consideration. I feel that I would not be worth a button if not grateful to be preserved from myself, and informed if what I have written is not to the point. I think we should feel free, like La Fontaine's captious critic, to say, if asked, "Your phrases are too long, and the content is not good. Break up the type and put it in the font." As Kenneth Burke says in *Counter-Statement*, "Great artists … feel partially as opportunity what others must feel solely as a menace. This ability does not, I believe, derive from exceptional strength; it probably arises purely from the 'professional interest' the artist may take in his difficulties."

Lew Sarett says, in the *Poetry Society Bulletin*, we ask of a poet, Does this mean something? Does the poet say what he has to say and in his own manner? Does it stir the reader?

Shouldn't we replace vanity with honesty, as Robert Frost recommends? Annoyances abound.

We should not find them lethal ... a baffled printer's emendations for instance—my "elephant with
frog-colored skin" instead of "fog-colored skin," and
"the power of the invisible is the invisible," instead of
"the power of the visible is the invisible"—sounding
like a parody on my meticulousness—a "glasshop-
per" instead of a "grasshopper."

Editing *The Dial* must have acquainted you with the
writers of the day whom you did not know already.
Had you known Hart Crane earlier?

MOORE

Yes, I did. You remember *Broom*? Toward the beginning of that magazine, in 1921, Lola Ridge was very
hospitable, and she invited to a party—previous to
my work on *The Dial*—Kay Boyle and her husband,
a French soldier, and Hart Crane, Elinor Wylie, and
some others. I took a great liking to Hart Crane. We
talked about French bindings, and he was diffident
and modest and seemed to have so much intuition,
such a feel for things, for books—really a biblio-
phile—that I took special interest in him. And Dr.
Watson and Scofield Thayer liked him—felt that he
was one of our talents, that he couldn't fit himself into
an IBM position to find a livelihood, that we ought
to, whenever we could, take anything he sent us.

I know a cousin of his, Joe Nowak, who is
rather proud of him. He lives here in Brooklyn, and
is* at the Dry Dock Savings Bank and used to work

---

* *Was*; killed; his car run into by a reckless driver in April 1961. —M.M.

in antiques. Joe was very convinced of Hart's sincerity and his innate love of all that I have specified. Anyhow, *The Bridge* is a grand theme. Here and there I think he could have firmed it up. A writer is unfair to himself when he is unable to be hard on himself.

Did Crane have anything to do with *Others*?

Others antedated *Broom*. *Others* was Alfred Kreymborg and Skipwith Cannéll, Wallace Stevens, William Carlos Williams. Wallace Stevens—odd. I nearly met him a dozen times before I did meet him in 1943 at Mount Holyoke, at the college's Entretiens de Pontigny, of which Professor Gustave Cohen was chairman. Wallace Stevens was Henry Church's favorite American poet. Mr. Church had published him and some others, and me, in *Mésure*, in Paris. Raymond Queneau translated us.

During the French program at Mount Holyoke one afternoon Wallace Stevens had a discourse, the one about Goethe dancing on a packet boat in black wool stockings. My mother and I were there, and I gave a reading with commentary. Henry Church had an astoundingly beautiful Panama hat—a sort of porkpie with a wide brim, a little like Bernard Berenson's hats. I have never seen as fine a weave, and he had a pepper-and-salt shawl that he draped about himself. This lecture was on the lawn.

Wallace Stevens was extremely friendly. We should have had a tape recorder on that occasion, for at lunch they seated us all at a kind of refectory table and a girl kept asking him questions such as, Mr. Stevens, have you read the *Four Quartets*?

"Of course, but I can't read much of Eliot or I wouldn't have any individuality of my own."

INTERVIEWER

Do you read new poetry now? Do you try to keep up?

MOORE

I am always seeing it—am sent some every day. Some, good. But it does interfere with my work. I can't get much done. Yet I would be a monster if I tossed everything away without looking at it. I write more notes, letters, cards in an hour than is sane.

Although everyone is penalized by being quoted inexactly, I wonder if there is anybody alive whose remarks are so often paraphrased as mine—printed as verbatim. It is really martyrdom. In his book *Ezra Pound*, Charles Norman was very scrupulous. He got several things exactly right. The first time I met Ezra Pound, when he came here to see my mother and me, I said that Henry Eliot seemed to me more nearly the artist than anyone I had ever met. "Now, now," said Ezra. "Be careful." Maybe that isn't exact, but he quotes it just the way I said it.

INTERVIEWER

Do you mean Henry Ware Eliot, T. S. Eliot's brother?

MOORE

Yes. After the Henry Eliots moved from Chicago to New York to—is it Sixty-Eighth Street? It's the street on which Hunter College is—to an apartment there, they invited me to dinner, I should think at T. S. Eliot's suggestion, and I took to them immediately. I felt as if I'd known them a great while. It was some time before I felt that way about T. S. Eliot.

About inaccuracies—when I went to see Ezra Pound at Saint Elizabeths, about the third time I went, the official who escorted me to the grounds said, "Good of you to come to see him," and I said, "Good? You have no idea how much he has done for me, and others." This pertains to an early rather than final visit.

I was not in the habit of asking experts or anybody else to help me with things that I was doing, unless it was a librarian or someone whose business it was to help applicants, or a teacher. But I was desperate when Macmillan declined my *Fables*. I had worked about four years on them and sent Ezra Pound several—although I hesitated. I didn't like to bother him. He had enough trouble without that. But finally I said, "Would you have time to tell me if the rhythms grate on you? Is my ear not good?"

INTERVIEWER

He replied?

MOORE

Yes, said, "The least touch of merit upsets these blighters."

INTERVIEWER

When you first read Pound in 1916, did you recognize him as one of the great ones?

MOORE

Surely did. *The Spirit of Romance*. I don't think anybody could read that book and feel that a flounderer was writing.

INTERVIEWER

What about the early poems?

MOORE

Yes. They seemed a little didactic, but I liked them.

INTERVIEWER

I wanted to ask you a few questions about poetry in general. Somewhere you have said that originality is a by-product of sincerity. You often use moral terms in your criticism. Is the necessary morality specifically literary, a moral use of words, or is it larger? In what way must a man be good if he is to write good poems?

MOORE

If emotion is strong enough, the words are unambiguous. Someone asked Robert Frost—is that right?—if he was selective. He said, "Call it passionate preference." Must a man be good to write good poems? The villains in Shakespeare are not illiterate, are they? But rectitude *has* a ring that is implicative, I would say. And with *no* integrity, a man is not likely to write the kind of book I read.

INTERVIEWER

Eliot, in his introduction to your *Selected Poems*, talks about your function as poet relative to the living language, as he calls it. Do you agree that this is a function of a poet? How does the poetry have the effect on the living language? What's the mechanics of it?

MOORE

You accept certain modes of saying a thing. Or strongly repudiate things. You do something of your own, you modify, invent a variant or revive a root meaning. Any doubt about that?

INTERVIEWER

I want to ask you a question about your correspondence with the Ford Motor Company, those letters that were printed in *The New Yorker*. They were looking for a name for the car they eventually called the Edsel, and they asked you to think of a name that would make people admire the car—

MOORE

Elegance and grace, they said it would have—

INTERVIEWER

"... some visceral feeling of elegance, fleetness, advanced features and design. A name, in short, that flashes a dramatically desirable picture in people's minds."

MOORE

Really?

INTERVIEWER

That's what they said, in their first letter to you. I was thinking about this in connection with my question about language. Do you remember Pound's talk about expression and meaning? He says that when expression and meaning are far apart, the culture is in a bad way. I was wondering if this request doesn't ask you to remove expression a bit further from meaning.

No, I don't think so. At least, to exposit the irresist-ibleness of the car. I got deep in motors and turbines and recessed wheels. No. That seemed to me a very worthy pursuit. I was more interested in the mechan-ics. I am interested in mechanisms, mechanics in gen-eral. And I enjoyed the assignment, for all that it was abortive. Dr. Pick at Marquette University procured a young demonstrator of the Edsel to call for me in a black one, to convey me to the auditorium. Nothing was wrong with that Edsel! I thought it was a very handsome car. It came out the wrong year.

INTERVIEWER

Another thing—in your criticism you make frequent analogies between the poet and the scientist. Do you think this analogy is helpful to the modern poet? Most people would consider the comparison a para-dox, and assume that the poet and the scientist are opposed.

MOORE

Do the poet and scientist not work analogously? Both are willing to waste effort. To be hard on himself is one of the main strengths of each. Each is attentive to clues, each must narrow the choice, must strive for precision. As George Grosz says, "In art there is no place for gossip and but a small place for the satirist." The objective is fertile proce-dure. Is it not? Jacob Bronowski says in *The Satur-day Evening Post* that science is not a mere collection of discoveries, but that science is the process of discovering. In any case it's not established once and for all. It's evolving.

One last question. I was intrigued when you wrote that "America has in Wallace Stevens at least one artist whom professionalism will not demolish." What sort of literary professionalism did you have in mind? And do you find this a feature of America still?

MOORE

Yes. I think that writers sometimes lose verve and pugnacity, and he never would say "frame of reference" or "I wouldn't know." A question I am often asked is, What work can I find that will enable me to spend my whole time writing? Charles Ives, the composer, says, "The fabric of existence weaves itself whole. You cannot set an art off in the corner and hope for it to have vitality, reality, and substance... My work in music helped my business and my work in business helped my music." I am like Charles Ives. I guess Lawrence Durrell and Henry Miller would not agree with me.

INTERVIEWER

But how does professionalism make a writer lose his verve and pugnacity?

MOORE

Money may have something to do with it, and being regarded as a pundit. Wallace Stevens was really very much annoyed at being catalogued, categorized, and compelled to be scientific about what he was doing—to give satisfaction, to answer the teachers. He wouldn't do that. I think the same of William Carlos Williams. I think he wouldn't make so much of the great American language if he were plausible and tractable. That's the beauty of it—he is willing to be reckless. If you can't be that, what's the point of the whole thing?

(1961)

Katherine Anne Porter

THE ART OF FICTION NO. 29

Interviewed by Barbara Thompson Davis

T he Victorian house in which Katherine Anne Porter lived was narrow and white, reached by an iron-railed stairway curving up from the shady brick-walked Georgetown street. The parlor to which a maid admitted the caller was an elegant mélange of several aspects of the past, both American and European. Dim and cool after the midsummer glare, the high-ceilinged room was dominated by a bottle-green settee from the period of Napoleon III. Outside the alcove of windows there was a rustle of wind through ginkgo trees, then a hush.

Finally, a voice in the upper hallway: its tone that of someone talking to a bird, or coquetting with an old beau—light and feathery, with a slight flutter. A few moments later, moving as lightly as her voice, Miss Porter hurried through the wide doorway, unexpectedly modern in a soft green suit of woven Italian silk. Small and elegant, she explained her tardiness, related an anecdote from the morning's mail,

41

offered a minted iced tea, and speculated aloud on where we might best conduct our conversation.

She decided on the dining room, a quiet, austere place overlooking the small enclosed garden. Here the aspect was a different one. "I want to live in a world capital or the howling wilderness," she said once, and did. The drawing room was filled with pieces that had once been part of the house on the rue Notre Dame des Champs; this one was bright with Mexican folk art—whistles and toy animals collected during a recent tour for the Department of State—against simpler, heavier pieces of furniture. The round table at which we sat was of Vermont marble, mottled and colored like milk glass, on a wrought-iron base of her own design. There was a sixteenth-century cupboard from Ávila, and a refectory table of the early Renaissance from a convent in Fiesole. Here we settled the tape recorder, under an image of the great god Horus.

We tried to make a beginning. She was an experienced lecturer, familiar with microphone and tape recorder, but now she was to talk about herself as well as her work, the link between, and the inexorable winding of the tape from one spool to the other acted almost as a hypnotic. Finally we turned it off and talked for a while of other things, more frivolous and more autobiographical, hoping to surprise an easier revelation.

INTERVIEWER

You were saying that you had never intended to make a career of writing.

I've never made a career of anything, you know, not even of writing. I started out with nothing in the world but a kind of passion, a driving desire. I don't know where it came from, and I don't know why—or why I have been so stubborn about it that nothing could deflect me. But this thing between me and my writing is the strongest bond I have ever had—stronger than any bond or any engagement with any human being or with any other work I've ever done. I really started writing when I was six or seven years old. But I had such a multiplicity of half talents, too. I wanted to dance, I wanted to play the piano, I sang, I drew. It wasn't really dabbling—I was investigating everything, experimenting in everything. And then, for one thing, there weren't very many amusements in those days. If you wanted music, you had to play the piano and sing yourself. Oh, we saw all the great things that came during the season, but after all, there would only be a dozen or so of those occasions a year. The rest of the time we depended upon our own resources, our own music and books. All the old houses that I knew when I was a child were full of books, bought generation after generation by members of the family. Everyone was literate as a matter of course. Nobody told you to read this or not to read that. It was there to read, and we read.

INTERVIEWER

Which books influenced you most?

PORTER

That's hard to say, because I grew up in a sort of mélange. I was reading Shakespeare's sonnets when I was thirteen years old, and I'm perfectly certain that they made the most profound impression upon me of anything I ever read. For a time I knew the whole sequence by heart. Now I can only remember two or three of them. That was the turning point of my life, when I read the Shakespeare sonnets, and then all at one blow, all of Dante—in that great big book illustrated by Gustave Doré. The plays I saw on the stage, but I don't remember reading them with any interest at all. Oh, and I read all kinds of poetry—Homer, Ronsard, all the old French poets in translation. We also had a very good library of—well, you might say secular philosophers. I was incredibly influenced by Montaigne when I was very young. And one day when I was about fourteen, my father led me up to a great big line of books and said, Why don't you read this? It'll knock some of the nonsense out of you! It happened to be the entire set of Voltaire's philosophical dictionary with notes by Smollett. And I plowed through it—it took me about five years.

And of course we read all the eighteenth-century novelists, though Jane Austen, like Turgenev, didn't really engage me until I was quite mature. I read them both when I was very young, but I was grown up before I really took them in. And I discovered for myself *Wuthering Heights*. I think I read that book every year of my life for fifteen years. I simply adored it. Henry James and Thomas Hardy were really my introduction to modern literature— Grandmother didn't much approve of it. She thought Dickens might do, but she was a little against Mr. Thackeray. She thought he was too trivial. So that was as far as I got into the modern world until I left home!

Don't you think this background—the comparative isolation of Southern rural life and the atmosphere of literary interest—helped to shape you as a writer?

PORTER

I think it's something in the blood. We've always had great letter writers, readers, great storytellers in our family. I've listened all my life to articulate people. They were all great storytellers, and every story had shape and meaning and point.

INTERVIEWER

Were any of them known as writers?

PORTER

Well, there was my sixth or seventh cousin once removed, poor William Sidney. O. Henry, you know. He was my father's second cousin—I don't know what that makes him to me. And he was more known in the family for being a bank robber. He worked in a bank, you know, and he just didn't seem to find a talent for making money. No Porter ever did. But he had a wife who was dying of TB and he couldn't keep up with the doctor's bills. So he took a pitiful little sum—oh, about three hundred and fifty dollars—and ran away when he was accused. But he came back, because his wife was dying, and went to prison. And there was Horace Porter, who spent his whole eight years as ambassador to France looking for the bones of John Paul Jones. And when he found them, and brought them back, he wrote a book about them.

It seems to me that your work is pervaded by a sense of history. Is that part of the family legacy?

PORTER

We were brought up with a sense of our own history, you know. My mother's family came to this country in 1648 and went to the John Randolph territory of Virginia. And one of my great-great-grandfathers was Jonathan Boone, the brother of Daniel. On my father's side I'm descended from Colonel Andrew Porter, whose father came to Montgomery County, Pennsylvania, in 1720. He was one of the circle of George Washington during the revolution, a friend of Lafayette, and one of the founders of the Society of the Cincinnati—oh, he really took it seriously!—and when he died in 1809—well, just a few years before that he was offered the post of secretary of war, but he declined. We were never very ambitious people. We never had a president, though we had two governors and some in the army and the navy. I suppose we did have a desire to excel but not to push our way to higher places. We thought we'd already arrived!

INTERVIEWER

The *we* of family is very strong, isn't it? I remember that you once wrote of the ties of blood as the "absolute point of all departure and return." And the central character in many of your stories is defined, is defining herself often, in relation to a family organization. Even the measure of time is human—expressed in terms of the very old and the very young, and how much of human experience they have absorbed.

Yes, but it wasn't a conscious made-up affair, you know. In those days you belonged together, you lived together, because you were a family. The head of our house was a grandmother, an old matriarch, you know, and a really lovely and beautiful woman, a good soul, and so she didn't do us any harm. But the point is that we did live like that, with Grandmother's friends, all reverend old gentlemen with frock coats, and old ladies with jet breastplates. Then there were the younger people, the beautiful girls and the handsome young boys, who were all ahead of me. When I was a little girl, eight or nine years old, they were eighteen to twenty-two, and they represented all glamour, all beauty, all joy and freedom to me. Then there was my own age, and then there were the babies. We simply lived that way—to have four generations in one house, under one roof, there was nothing unusual about that. That was just my experience, and this is just the way I've reacted to it. Many other people didn't react, who were brought up in very much the same way.

I remember when I was very young, my older sister wanted to buy some old furniture. It was in Louisiana, and she had just been married. And I went with her to a wonderful old house in the country where we'd been told there was a very old gentleman who probably had some things to sell. His wife had died, and he was living there alone. So we went to this lovely old house, and, sure enough, there was this lonely beautiful old man, eighty-seven or eighty-eight. But his wife was dead and his children were married and gone. He said yes, he had a few things he wanted to sell. So he showed us through the house. And finally he opened a door, and showed us a bedroom with a beautiful four-poster bed, with a wonderful satin coverlet—the most wonderful, classical-looking bed you ever saw. And my sister said, "Oh, that's what I want." And he said, "Oh, madame, that is my marriage bed. That is the bed that my wife brought with her as a bride. We slept together in that bed for nearly sixty years. All our children were born there. Oh," he said, "I shall die in that bed, and then they can dispose of it as they like."

I remember that I felt a little suffocated and frightened. I felt a little trapped. But why? Only because I understood that. I was brought up in that. And I was at the age of rebellion then, and it really scared me. But I look back on it now and think how perfectly wonderful, what a tremendously beautiful life it was. Everything in it had meaning.

INTERVIEWER

But it seems to me that your work suggests someone who was searching for new—perhaps broader—meanings ... that while you've retained the South of your childhood as a point of reference, you've ranged far from that environment itself. You seem to have felt little of the peculiarly Southern preoccupation with racial guilt and the death of the old agrarian life.

PORTER

I'm a Southerner by tradition and inheritance, and I have a very profound feeling for the South. And, of course, I belong to the guilt-ridden, white-pillar crowd myself, but it just didn't rub off on me. Maybe I'm just not Jewish enough, or Puritan enough, to feel that the sins of the father are visited on the third and fourth generations. Or maybe it's because of my European influences—in Texas and Louisiana. But, you know, I was always restless, always a roving spirit. When I was a little child I was always running away. I never got very far, but they were always having to come and fetch me. Once when I was about six, my father came to get me somewhere I'd gone, and he told me later he'd asked me, "Why are you so restless? Why can't you stay here with us?" and I said to him, "I want to go and see the world. I want to know the world like the palm of my hand."

INTERVIEWER

And at sixteen you made it final.

PORTER

At sixteen I ran away from New Orleans and got married. And at twenty-one I bolted again, went to Chicago, got a newspaper job, and went into the movies.

INTERVIEWER

The movies?

PORTER

The newspaper sent me over to the old Essanay movie studio to do a story. But I got into the wrong line, and then was too timid to get out. "Right over this way, Little Boy Blue," the man said, and I found myself in a courtroom scene with Francis X. Bushman. I was horrified by what had happened to me, but they paid me five dollars for that first day's work, so I stayed on. It was about a week before I remembered what I had been sent to do, and when I went back to the newspaper they gave me eighteen dollars for my week's nonwork and fired me!

I stayed on for six months—I finally got to nearly ten dollars a day—until one day they came in and said, "We're moving to the coast." "Well, I'm not," I said. "Don't you want to be a movie actress?" "Oh, no!" I said. "Well, be a fool!" they said, and they left. That was 1914 and world war had broken out, so in September I went home.

INTERVIEWER

And then?

PORTER

Oh, I sang old Scottish ballads in costume—I made it myself—all around Texas and Louisiana. And then I was supposed to have TB, and spent about six weeks in a sanatorium. It was just bronchitis, but I was in Denver, so I got a newspaper job.

INTERVIEWER

I remember that you once warned me to avoid that at all costs—to get a job "hashing" in a restaurant in preference.

PORTER

Anything, anything at all. I did it for a year and that is what confirmed for me that it wasn't doing me any good. After that I always took little dull jobs that didn't take my mind and wouldn't take all of my time, and that, on the other hand, paid me just enough to subsist. I think I've only spent about ten percent of my energies on writing. The other ninety percent went to keeping my head above water.

And I think that's all wrong. Even Saint Teresa said, "I can pray better when I'm comfortable," and she refused to wear her haircloth shirt or starve herself. I don't think living in cellars and starving is any better for an artist than it is for anybody else. The only thing is that sometimes the artist has to take it, because it is the only possible way of salvation, if you'll forgive that old-fashioned word. So I took it rather instinctively. I was inexperienced in the world, and likewise I hadn't been trained to do anything, you know, so I took all kinds of laborious jobs. But, you know, I think I could probably have written better if I'd been a little more comfortable.

INTERVIEWER
Then you were writing all this time?

PORTER
All this time I was writing, writing no matter what else I was doing—no matter what I thought I was doing, in fact. I was living almost as instinctively as a little animal, but I realize now that all that time a part of me was getting ready to be an artist. That my mind was working even when I didn't know it, and didn't care if it was working or not. It is my firm belief that all our lives we are preparing to be somebody or something, even if we don't do it consciously. And the time comes one morning when you wake up and find that you have become irrevocably what you were preparing all this time to be. Lord, that could be a sticky moment, if you had been doing the wrong things, something against your grain. And, mind you, I know that can happen. I have no patience with this dreadful idea that whatever you have in you has

to come out, that you can't suppress true talent. People can be destroyed. They can be bent, distorted, and completely crippled. To say that you can't destroy yourself is just as foolish as to say of a young man killed in war at twenty-one or twenty-two that that was his fate, that he wasn't going to have anything anyhow.

I have a very firm belief that the life of no man can be explained in terms of his experiences, of what has happened to him, because in spite of all the poetry, all the philosophy to the contrary, we are not really masters of our fate. We don't really direct our lives unaided and unobstructed. Our being is subject to all the chances of life. There are so many things we are capable of, that we could be or do. The potentialities are so great that we never, any of us, are more than one-fourth fulfilled. Except that there may be one powerful motivating force that simply carries you along, and I think that was true of me ... When I was a very little girl I wrote a letter to my sister saying I wanted glory. I don't know quite what I meant by that now, but it was something different from fame or success or wealth. I know that I wanted to be a good writer, a good artist.

INTERVIEWER

But weren't there certain specific events that crystallized that desire for you—something comparable to the experience of Miranda in "Pale Horse, Pale Rider" (1939)?

PORTER

Yes, that was the plague of influenza, at the end of the First World War, in which I almost died. It just simply divided my life, cut across it like that. So that everything before that was just getting ready, and after that I was in some strange way altered, ready. It took me a long time to go out and live in the world again. I was really alienated, in the pure sense. It was, I think, the fact that I really had participated in death, that I knew what death was, and had almost experienced it. I had what the Christians call the "beatific vision," and the Greeks call the "happy day," the happy vision just before death. Now if you have had that, and survived it, come back from it, you are no longer like other people, and there's no use deceiving yourself that you are. But you see, I did. I made the mistake of thinking I was quite like anybody else, of trying to live like other people. It took me a long time to realize that that simply wasn't true, that I had my own needs and that I had to live like me.

INTERVIEWER

And that freed you?

PORTER

I just got up and bolted. I went running off on that wild escapade to Mexico, where I attended, you might say, and assisted at, in my own modest way, a revolution.

INTERVIEWER

That was the Obregón revolution of 1921?

PORTER

Yes—though actually I went to Mexico to study the Aztec and Mayan art designs. I had been in New

York, and was getting ready to go to Europe. Now, New York was full of Mexican artists at that time, all talking about the renaissance, as they called it, in Mexico. And they said, Don't go to Europe, go to Mexico. That's where the exciting things are going to happen. And they were right! I ran smack into the Obregón revolution and had, in the midst of it, the most marvelous, natural, spontaneous experience of my life. It was a terribly exciting time. It was alive, but death was in it. But nobody seemed to think of that—life was in it, too.

INTERVIEWER

What do you think are the best conditions for a writer, then? Something like your Mexican experience, or—

PORTER

Oh, I can't say what they are. It would be such an individual matter. Everyone needs something different... But what I find most dreadful among the young artists is this tendency toward middle-classness—this idea that they have to get married and have lots of children and live just like everybody else, you know? Now, I am all for human life, and I am all for marriage and children and all that sort of thing, but quite often you can't have that and do what you were supposed to do, too. Art is a vocation, as much as anything in this world. For the real artist, it is the most natural thing in the world, not as necessary as air and water, perhaps, but as food and water. But we really do lead almost a monastic life, you know—to follow it you very often have to give up something.

But for the unproven artist that is a very great act of faith.

It *is* an act of faith. But one of the marks of a gift is to have the courage of it. If they haven't got the courage, it's just too bad. They'll fail, just as people with lack of courage in other vocations and walks of life fail. Courage is the first essential.

In choosing a pattern of life compatible with the vocation?

The thing is not to follow a pattern. Follow your own pattern of feeling and thought. The thing is to accept your own life and not try to live someone else's life. Look, the thumbprint is not like any other, and the thumbprint is what you must go by.

In the current vernacular, then, you think it's necessary for an artist to be a loner—not to belong to any literary movement?

I've never belonged to any group or huddle of any kind. You cannot be an artist and work collectively. Even the fact that I went to Mexico when everybody else was going to Europe—I went to Mexico because I felt I had business there. And there I found friends and ideas that were sympathetic to me. That was my entire milieu. I don't think anyone even knew I was a writer. I didn't show my work to anybody or talk about it, because—well, no one was particularly interested in that. It was a time of revolution, and I was running with almost pure revolutionaries!

INTERVIEWER

And you think that was a more wholesome environment for a writer than, say, the milieu of the expatriated artist in Europe at the same time?

PORTER

Well, I know it was good for me. I would have been completely smothered—completely disgusted and revolted—by the goings-on in Europe. Even now when I think of the twenties and the legend that has grown up about them, I think it was a horrible time, shallow and trivial and silly. The remarkable thing is that anybody survived in such an atmosphere—in a place where they could call F. Scott Fitzgerald a great writer!

INTERVIEWER

You don't agree?

PORTER

Of course I don't agree. I couldn't read him then and I can't read him now. There was just one passage in a book called *Tender Is the Night*—I read that and thought, Now I will read this again, because I couldn't be sure. Not only didn't I like his writing, but I didn't like the people he wrote about. I thought they weren't worth thinking about, and I still think so. It seems to me that your human beings have to have some kind of meaning. I just can't be interested in those perfectly stupid meaningless lives. And I don't like the same thing going on now—the way the artist simply will not face up to the final reckoning of things.

In a philosophical sense?

I'm thinking of it now in just the artistic sense—in the sense of an artist facing up to his own end meanings. I suppose I shouldn't be mentioning names, but I read a story some time ago, I think it was in *The Paris Review*, called "The McCabes." Now I think William Styron is an extremely gifted man. He's very ripe and lush and with a kind of Niagara Falls of energy, and a kind of power. But he depends so on violence and a kind of exaggerated heat—at least it looks like heat, but just turns out to be summer lightning. Because there is nothing in the world more meaningless than that whole escapade of this man going off and winding up in the gutter. You sit back and think, Well, let's see, where are we now? All right, it's possible that that's just what Styron meant—the whole wicked pointlessness of things. But I tell you, nothing is pointless, and nothing is meaningless if the artist will face it. And it's his business to face it. He hasn't got the right to sidestep it like that. Human life itself may be almost pure chaos, but the work of the artist—the only thing he's good for—is to take these handfuls of confusion and disparate things, things that seem to be irreconcilable, and put them together in a frame to give them some kind of shape and meaning. Even if it's only his view of a meaning. That's what he's for—to give his view of life. Surely, we understand very little of what is happening to us at any given moment. But by remembering, comparing, waiting to know the consequences, we can sometimes see what an event really meant, what it was trying to teach us.

INTERVIEWER

You once said that every story begins with an ending, that until the end is known there is no story.

PORTER

That is where the artist begins to work—with the consequences of acts, not the acts themselves. Or the events. The event is important only as it affects your life and the lives of those around you. The reverberations, you might say, the overtones—that is where the artist works. In that sense it has sometimes taken me ten years to understand even a little of some important event that had happened to me. Oh, I could have given a perfectly factual account of what had happened, but I didn't know what it meant until I knew the consequences. If I didn't know the ending of a story, I wouldn't begin. I always write my last lines, my last paragraph, my last page first, and then I go back and work toward it. I know where I'm going. I know what my goal is. And how I get there is God's grace.

INTERVIEWER

That's a very classical view of the work of art—that it must end in resolution.

Any true work of art has got to give you the feeling of reconciliation—what the Greeks would call catharsis, the purification of your mind and imagination—through an ending that is endurable because it is right and true. Oh, not in any pawky individual idea of morality or some parochial idea of right and wrong. Sometimes the end is very tragic, because it needs to be. One of the most perfect and marvelous endings in literature—it raises my hair now—is the little boy at the end of *Wuthering Heights*, crying that he's afraid to go across the moor because there's a man and woman walking there.

And there are three novels that I reread with pleasure and delight—three almost perfect novels, if we're talking about form, you know. One is *A High Wind in Jamaica* by Richard Hughes, one is *A Passage to India* by E. M. Forster, and the other is *To the Lighthouse* by Virginia Woolf. Every one of them begins with an apparently insoluble problem, and every one of them works out of confusion into order. The material is all used so that you are going toward a goal. And that goal is the clearing up of disorder and confusion and wrong, to a logical and human end. I don't mean a happy ending, because after all at the end of *A High Wind in Jamaica* the pirates are all hanged and the children are all marked for life by their experience, but it comes out to an orderly end. The threads are all drawn up. I have had people object to Mr. Thompson's suicide at the end of "Noon Wine" (1939) and I'd say, All right, where was he going? Given what he was, his own situation, what else could he do? Every once in a while when I see a character of mine just going toward perdition,

I think, Stop, stop, you can always stop and choose, you know. But no, being what he was, he already has chosen, and he can't go back on it now. I suppose the first idea that man had was the idea of fate, of the servile will, of a deity who destroyed as he would, without regard for the creature. But I think the idea of free will was the second idea.

INTERVIEWER

Has a story never surprised you in the writing? A character suddenly taken a different turn?

PORTER

Well, in the vision of death at the end of "Flowering Judas" (1930) I knew the real ending—that she was not going to be able to face her life, what she'd done. And I knew that the vengeful spirit was going to come in a dream to tow her away into death, but I didn't know until I'd written it that she was going to wake up saying, "No!" and be afraid to go to sleep again.

INTERVIEWER

That was, in a fairly literal sense, a true story, wasn't it?

PORTER

The truth is, I have never written a story in my life that didn't have a very firm foundation in actual human experience—somebody else's experience quite often, but an experience that became my own by hearing the story, by witnessing the thing, by hearing just a word perhaps. It doesn't matter, it just takes a little—a tiny seed. Then it takes root, and it grows. It's an organic thing. That story had been on my mind for years, growing out of this one little thing that happened in Mexico. It was forming and forming in my mind, until one night I was quite desperate. People are always so sociable, and I'm sociable, too, and if I live around friends... Well, they were insisting that I come and play bridge. But I was very firm, because I knew the time had come to write that story, and I had to write it.

INTERVIEWER
What was that little thing from which the story grew?

PORTER
Something I saw as I passed a window one evening. A girl I knew had asked me to come and sit with her, because a man was coming to see her, and she was a little afraid of him. And as I went through the courtyard, past the flowering Judas tree, I glanced in the window and there she was sitting with an open book on her lap, and there was this great big fat man sitting beside her. Now Mary and I were friends, both American girls living in this revolutionary situation. She was teaching at an Indian school, and I was teaching dancing at a girls' technical school in Mexico City. And we were having a very strange time of it. I was more skeptical, and so I had already begun to look with a skeptical eye on a great many of the revolutionary leaders. Oh, the idea was all right, but a lot of men were misapplying it.

And when I looked through that window that evening, I saw something in Mary's face, something in her pose, something in the whole situation, that set up a commotion in my mind. Because until that moment I hadn't really understood that she was not able to take care of herself, because she was not able to face her own nature and was afraid of everything. I don't know why I saw it. I don't believe in intuition. When you get sudden flashes of perception, it is just the brain working faster than usual. But you've been getting ready to know it for a long time, and when it comes, you feel you've known it always.

INTERVIEWER

You speak of a story forming in your mind. Does it begin as a visual impression, growing to a narrative? Or how?

PORTER

All my senses were very keen. Things came to me through my eyes, through all my pores. Everything hit me at once, you know. That makes it very difficult to describe just exactly what is happening. And then, I think the mind works in such a variety of ways. Sometimes an idea starts completely inarticulately. You're not thinking in images or words or—well, it's exactly like a dark cloud moving in your head. You keep wondering what will come out of this, and then it will dissolve itself into a set of—well, not images exactly, but really thoughts. You begin to think directly in words. Abstractly. Then the words transform themselves into images. By the time I write the story my people are up and alive and walking around and taking things into their own hands. They exist as independently inside my head as you do before me now. I have been criticized for not enough detail in describing my characters, and not enough furniture in the house. And the odd thing is that I see it all so clearly.

What about the technical problems a story presents—its formal structure? How deliberate are you in matters of technique? For example, the use of the historical present in "Flowering Judas"?

PORTER

The first time someone said to me, "Why did you write 'Flowering Judas' in the historical present?" I thought for a moment and said, "Did I?" I'd never noticed it. Because I didn't *plan* to write it any way. A story forms in my mind and forms and forms, and when it's ready to go, I strike it down—it takes just the time I sit at the typewriter. I never think about form at all. In fact, I would say that I've never been interested in anything about writing after having learned, I hope, to write. That is, I mastered my craft as well as I could. There is a technique, there is a craft, and you have to learn it. Well, I did as well as I could with that, but now all in the world I am interested in is telling a story. I have something to tell you that I, for some reason, think is worth telling, and so I want to tell it as clearly and purely and simply as I can. But I had spent fifteen years at least learning to write. I practiced writing in every possible way that I could. I wrote a pastiche of other people, imitating Dr. Johnson and Laurence Sterne, and Petrarch's and Shakespeare's sonnets, and then I tried writing my own way. I spent fifteen years learning to trust myself. That's what it comes to. Just as a pianist runs his scales for ten years before he gives his concert. Because when he gives that concert, he can't be thinking of his fingering or of his hands, he has to be thinking of his interpretation, of the music he's playing. He's thinking of what he's trying to communicate. And if he hasn't got his technique perfected by then, he needn't give the concert at all.

From whom would you say you learned most during this period of apprenticeship?

The person who influenced me most, the real revelation in my life as a writer—though I don't write in the least like him—was Laurence Sterne, in *Tristram Shandy*. Why? Because, you know, I loved the grand style, and he made it look easy. The others, the great ones, really frightened me. They were so grand and magnificent they overawed me completely. But Laurence Sterne—well, it was just exactly as if he said, Oh, come on, do it this way. It's so easy. So I tried to do it that way, and that taught me something, that taught me more than anybody else had. Because Laurence Sterne is a most complex and subtle man.

What about your contemporaries? Did any of them contribute significantly to your development as a writer?

I don't think I learned very much from my contemporaries. To begin with, we were all such individuals, and we were all so argumentative and so bent on our own courses that although I got a kind of support and personal friendship from my contemporaries, I didn't get very much help. I didn't show my work to anybody. I didn't hand it around among my friends for criticism, because, well, it just didn't occur to me to do it. Just as I didn't even try to publish anything until quite late because I didn't think I was ready. I published my first story in 1923. That was "María Concepción," the first story I ever finished. I rewrote "María Concepción" fifteen or sixteen times. That was a real battle, and I was thirty-three years old. I think it is the most curious lack of judgment to publish before you are ready. If there are echoes of other people in your work, you're not ready. If anybody has to help you rewrite your story, you're not ready. A story should be a finished work before it is shown. And after that, I will not allow anyone to change anything, and I will not change anything on anyone's advice. Here is my story. It's a finished story. Take it or leave it!

You are frequently spoken of as a stylist. Do you think a style can be cultivated, or at least refined?

PORTER

I've been called a stylist until I really could tear my hair out. And I simply don't believe in style. The style is you. Oh, you can cultivate a style, I suppose, if you like. But I should say it remains a cultivated style. It remains artificial and imposed, and I don't think it deceives anyone. A cultivated style would be like a mask. Everybody knows it's a mask, and sooner or later you must show yourself—or at least, you show yourself as someone who could not afford to show himself, and so created something to hide behind. Style is the man. Aristotle said it first, as far as I know, and everybody has said it since, because it is one of those unarguable truths. You do not create a style. You work, and develop yourself. Your style is an emanation from your own being. Symbolism is the same way. I never consciously took or adopted a symbol in my life. I certainly did not say, This blooming tree upon which Judas is supposed to have hanged himself is going to be the center of my story. I named "Flowering Judas" after it was written, because when reading back over it I suddenly saw the whole symbolic plan and pattern of which I was totally unconscious while I was writing. There's a pox of symbolist theory going the rounds these days in American colleges in the writing courses. Miss Mary McCarthy, who is one of the wittiest and most acute and in some ways the worst-tempered woman in American letters, tells about a little girl who came to her with a story. Now Miss McCarthy is an extremely good critic, and she found this to be a good story, and she told the girl that it was—that she considered it a finished work, and that she could with a clear conscience go on to something else. And the little girl said, But Miss McCarthy, my writing teacher said, Yes, it's a good piece of work, but now we must go back and put in the symbols! I think that's an amusing story, and it makes my blood run cold.

INTERVIEWER

But certainly one's command of the language can be developed and refined?

PORTER

I love the purity of language. I keep cautioning my students and anyone who will listen to me not to use the jargon of trades, not to use scientific language, because they're going to be out of date the day after tomorrow. The scientists change their vocabulary, their jargon, every day. So do the doctors, and the politicians, and the theologians—everybody, every profession, every trade changes its vocabulary all of the time. But there is a basic pure human speech that exists in every language. And that is the language of the poet and the writer. So many words that had good meanings once upon a time have come to have meanings almost evil—certainly shabby, certainly inaccurate. And *psychology* is one of them. It has been so abused. This awful way a whole segment, not a generation but too many of the young writers, have got so soaked in the Freudian and post-Freudian vocabulary that they can't speak—not only can't speak English, but they can't speak any human language anymore. You can't write about people out of textbooks, and you can't use a jargon. You have to speak clearly and simply and purely in a language that a six-year-old child can understand, and yet have the meanings and the overtones of language, and the implications, that appeal to the highest intelligence—that is, the highest intelligence that one is able to reach. I'm not sure that I'm able to appeal to the highest intelligence, but I'm willing to try.

INTERVIEWER

You speak of the necessity of writing out of your own understanding rather than out of textbooks, and I'm sure any writer would agree. But what about the creation of masculine characters, then? Most women writers, even the best of them like George Eliot, have run aground there. What about you? Was Mr.

Thompson, say, a more difficult imaginative problem than Miranda?

PORTER

I never did make a profession of understanding people, man or woman or child, and the only thing I know about people is exactly what I have learned from the people right next to me. I have always lived in my immediate circumstances, from day to day. And when men ask me how I know so much about men, I've got a simple answer—everything I know about men, I've learned from men. If there is such a thing as a man's mind and a woman's mind—and I'm sure there is—it isn't what most critics mean when they talk about the two. If I show wisdom, they say I have a masculine mind. If I am silly and irrelevant— and Edmund Wilson says I often am—why then, they say I have a typically feminine mind! That's one thing about reaching my age—you can always quote the authorities about what you are. But I haven't ever found it unnatural to be a woman.

INTERVIEWER

But haven't you found that being a woman presented to you, as an artist, certain special problems? It seems to me that a great deal of the upbringing of women encourages the dispersion of the self in many small bits, and that the practice of any kind of art demands a corralling and concentrating of that self and its always insufficient energies.

PORTER

I think that's very true and very right. You're brought up with the notion of feminine chastity and inaccessibility, yet with the curious idea of feminine avail-ability in all spiritual ways, and in giving service to anyone who demands it. And I suppose that's why it has taken me twenty years to write this novel. It's been interrupted by just anyone who could jimmy his way into my life.

INTERVIEWER

Hemingway said once that a writer writes best when he's in love.

PORTER

I don't know whether you write better, but you feel so good you think you're writing better! And certainly love does create a rising of the spirit that makes every-thing you do seem easier and happier. But there must come a time when you no longer depend upon it, when the mind—not the will, really, either—takes over.

INTERVIEWER

In judging that the story is ready? You said a moment ago that the actual writing of a story is always done in a single spurt of energy—

PORTER

I always write a story in one sitting. I started "Flow-ering Judas" at seven P.M. and at one thirty I was standing on a snowy windy corner putting it in the mailbox. And when I wrote my short novels, two of them, I just simply took the manuscript, packed a suit-case, and departed to an inn in Georgetown, Penn-sylvania, without leaving any forwarding address! Fourteen days later I had finished "Old Mortality" (1939) and "Noon Wine."

But the new novel, *Ship of Fools*, has been in the writing since 1942. The regime for writing this must have been a good deal different.

PORTER

Oh, it was. I went up and sat nearly three years in the country, and while I was writing it I worked every day, anywhere from three to five hours. Oh, it's true I used to do an awful lot of just sitting there thinking what comes next, because this is a great big unwieldy book with an enormous cast of characters—it's four hundred of my manuscript pages, and I can get four hundred and fifty words on a page. But all that time in Connecticut, I kept myself free for work. No telephone, no visitors—oh, I really lived like a hermit, everything but being fed through a grate! But it is, as Yeats said, a solitary, sedentary trade. And I did a lot of gardening, and cooked my own food, and listened to music, and of course I would read. I was really very happy. I can live a solitary life for months at a time, and it does me good, because I'm working. I just get up bright and early—sometimes at five o'clock—have my black coffee, and go to work.

INTERVIEWER

You work best in the morning, then?

PORTER

I work whenever I'm let. In the days when I was taken up with everything else, I used to do a day's work, or housework, or whatever I was doing, and then work at night. I worked when I could. But I prefer to get up very early in the morning and work. I don't want to speak to anybody or see anybody. Perfect silence. I work until the vein is out. There's something about the way you feel, you know when the well is dry, that you'll have to wait till tomorrow and it'll be full up again.

The important thing, then, is to avoid any breaks or distractions while you're writing?

To keep at a boiling point. So that I can get up in the morning with my mind still working where it was yesterday. Then I can stop in the middle of a paragraph and finish it the next day. I began writing *Ship of Fools* twenty years ago, and I've been away from it for several years at a time and stopped in the middle of a paragraph—but, you know, I can't tell where the crack is mended, and I hope nobody else can.

You find no change in style, or in attitudes, over the years?

It's astonishing how little I've changed. Nothing in my point of view or my way of feeling. I'm going back now to finish some of the great many short stories that I have begun and not been able to finish for one reason or another. I've found one that I think I can finish. I have three versions of it—I started it in 1923, and it's based on an episode in my life that took place when I was twenty. Now here I am, seventy, and it's astonishing how much it's like me now. Oh, there are certain things, certain turns of sentence, certain phrases that I think I can sharpen and make more clear, more simple and direct, but my point of view, my being, is strangely unchanged. We change, of course, every day. We are not the same people who sat down at this table, yet there is a basic and innate being that is unchanged.

INTERVIEWER

Ship of Fools, too, is based upon an event that took place ten years or more before the first writing, isn't it? A sea voyage just before the beginning of the European war.

PORTER

It is the story of my first voyage to Europe in 1931. We embarked on an old German ship at Veracruz and we landed in Bremen twenty-eight days later. It was a crowded ship, a great mixture of nationalities, religions, political beliefs—all that sort of thing. I don't think I spoke a half dozen words to anybody. I just sat there and watched—not deliberately, though. I kept a diary in the form of a letter to a friend, and after I got home the friend sent it back. And, you know, it is astonishing what happened on that boat, and what happened in my mind afterward. Because it is fiction now.

INTERVIEWER

The title—isn't it from a medieval emblem?— suggests that it might also be an allegory.

PORTER

It's just exactly what it seems to be. It's an allegory if

you like, though I don't think much of the allegorical as a standard. It's a parable, if you like, of the ship of this world on its voyage to eternity.

I remember your writing once—I think in the preface to "Flowering Judas"—of an effort to understand what you called the "majestic and terrible failure" of Western man. You were speaking then of the world war and what it signified of human folly. It seems to me that *Ship of Fools* properly belongs to that investigation of betrayal and self-delusion—

Betrayal and treachery, but also self-betrayal and self-deception—the way that all human beings deceive themselves about the way they operate... There seems to be a kind of order in the universe, in the movement of the stars and the turning of the earth and the changing of the seasons, and even in the cycle of human life. But human life itself is almost pure chaos. Everyone takes his stance, asserts his own rights and feelings, mistaking the motives of others, and his own... Now, nobody knows the end of the life he's living, and neither do I. Don't forget I am a passenger on that ship. It's not the other people altogether who are the fools! We don't really know what is going to happen to us, and we don't know why. Quite often the best we can do is to keep our heads, and try to keep at least one line unbroken and unobstructed. Misunderstanding and separation are the natural conditions of man. We come together only at these prearranged meeting grounds. We were all passengers on that ship, yet at his destination, each one was alone.

Did you find that the writing of *Ship of Fools* differed from the writing of shorter fiction?

It's just a longer voyage, that's all. It was the question of keeping everything moving at once. There are about forty-five main characters, all taking part in each other's lives, and then there was a steerage of sugar workers, deportees. It was all a matter of deciding which should come first, in order to keep the harmonious moving forward. A novel is really like a symphony, you know, where instrument after instrument has to come in at its own time, and no other. I tried to write it as a short novel, you know, but it just wouldn't confine itself. I wrote notes and sketches. And finally I gave in. Oh, no, this is simply going to have to be a novel, I thought. That was a real horror. But it needed a book to contain its full movement—of the sea, and the ship on the sea, and the people going around the deck, and into the ship, and up from it. That whole movement felt as one forward motion. I can feel it while I'm reading it. I didn't intend it, but it took hold of me.

INTERVIEWER
As writing itself, perhaps, took hold of you—we began by your saying that you had never intended to be a professional anything, even a professional writer.

PORTER
I look upon literature as an art, and I practice it as an art. Of course, it is also a vocation, and a trade, and a

profession, and all kinds of things, but first it's an art, and you should practice it as that, I think. I know a great many people disagree, and they are welcome to it. I think probably the important thing is to get your work done, in the way you can—and we all have our different and separate ways. But I look upon literature as an art, and I believe that if you misuse it or abuse it, it will leave you. It is not a thing that you can nail down and use as you want. You have to let it use you, too.

(1963)

Marguerite Young

THE ART OF FICTION NO. 66

Interviewed by Charles E. Ruas

arguerite Young published her first collec-
tion of verse, *Prismatic Ground*, in 1939.
In 1945 came the double appearance of
Moderate Fable, her last volume of verse, and *Angel
in the Forest*, a history of two utopian communities in
New Harmony, Indiana, in the nineteenth century.
Subsequently, portions of the novel to which she
was to devote eighteen years, *Miss MacIntosh, My
Darling*, began to appear in excerpt. The novel
appeared in its entirety in 1965. In the late sixties she
abandoned a near completed life of James Whitcomb
Riley to write a brief biography of her friend Eugene
Debs, the first socialist candidate for the presidency,
which resulted in a large-scale study of utopian and
anti-utopian trends.

She lives on a quiet tree-lined street in Greenwich
Village. The walls of her apartment are painted red
and lined with bookcases. On one shelf, the room is
replicated in miniature sofas and miniature chairs set

on easy rugs and lit by tiny lamps and chandeliers. The room in which we sat was dominated by a merry-go-round horse with ribbons streaming free from the pole, which reached the ceiling. A life-size antique doll was seated in a Victorian chair, exquisitely dressed in lace. Miss Young placed an ashtray within easy reach. She smoked continuously. Her voice has a Midwestern flavor, sometimes drawling, sometimes rapid.

MARGUERITE YOUNG

I was born in Indianapolis, Indiana, "the Athens of the West," as it had been called in an earlier day. That was when Booth Tarkington, Meredith Nicholson, James Whitcomb Riley, various writers of the old Hoosier group lived there. We were brought up to believe that to be born in Indiana was to be born a poet—a myth that I can't accept now, but I did then. I remember telling my grandmother, when I was about seven years old, that I intended to be a poet.

INTERVIEWER

She had a literary sensibility, didn't she?

YOUNG

She was a very beautiful, gifted, artistic personality. She painted, she wrote poems. She would never think of publishing. I don't think that she even thought of herself as frustrated. She was a woman who could have been a surgeon, a poet, anything. She was a genius personality.

INTERVIEWER

I know when you were an adolescent your grandmother became ill and that was when you yourself had to assume responsibility.

She had a series of strokes the last year or two of her life. She would speak in a semihallucinated way to me and my little sister. We were left to hear these wild hallucinatory statements, and yet maintain a sense of equilibrium, with no one's help. As I remember her now, there were many beautiful speeches—it was like Lear on the heath. She was not mad, she was just in a state between dream and reality, knowing that she was going to die, and speaking and dancing at the edge of her grave.

INTERVIEWER

You mentioned Lear—was it rage?

YOUNG

No! Never! It was always poetic and cosmic. It had a great deal to do with angels and unearthly creatures. I know there were angels in the house. Of course, I had always been taught there were angels, and if you did anything wrong, you were to say, Get thee behind me, Satan ... and I was always whirling around to try to catch Satan as he was getting behind me. When she died, I imagined she would call on Anatole France in heaven. She had introduced me to him along with Dickens, Eliot, *Adam Bede*, and Victor Hugo, but it was Anatole France I truly loved, I read all of him, his work in French, and when my grandmother died my first thought was, Oh well, now she can tell Anatole France that she has a little granddaughter on Earth who adores him. I really believed that she would tell him this. I missed her so much. It was the first death I ever knew. If I had been sure I could find her and Anatole France, I would have joined them.

INTERVIEWER

Anaïs Nin tells the story of your attempting to commit suicide.

YOUNG

Which time? I never really attempted to commit suicide. I used to think about committing suicide when I was about eighteen. I had it worked out that I would do it in multiple ways, all at once. It would take place in a tree house overlooking the river. I would put a rope around my neck, take poison, shoot myself, and fall into the river all at once. I think I worked this out because of Dorothy Parker's poem, "nooses give ..."—all these reasons suicide was so difficult. Also I had heard about Cowper's various attempts to commit suicide and how he was frustrated in everyone. So I figured out a way to do it. It was not surprising. At the age of eighteen all young poets are sure they will be dead at twenty-one—of old age.

INTERVIEWER

Did your grandmother make you write as a game, or an exercise? Did she direct you?

YOUNG

She praised my writing, and knew from when I began to pick up a pencil that I would be a writer. She said I would be either a writer, or the first woman president of the United States, or that I would become a lawyer who would work to restore the lost family fortune. There were so many lost family fortunes that my little sister and I used to be afraid of kidnappers who would kidnap us for our golden crowns—although, of course, we were not rich, but we didn't know that.

INTERVIEWER

If your grandmother was the great personal influence, the geographical impact was Indiana, wasn't it? Indiana is the center of all your subsequent writing. But you are more interested in the psychology of character than you are in landscape, aren't you? You do not have that love of the prairie grasses and the low horizon line of Willa Cather, for example?

YOUNG

No. It was my fate to be born in Indiana. I probably would have chosen Edinburgh if you had asked me, or perhaps Rome. But I believe we start with what we are, as writers, and Indiana is a land rich in legend. I tried to transmute this legend into a universal and cosmic statement of some kind, and not be strictly a regionalist. If you are asking me if I love nature, I could not really say that I do. I love the sea and the sand, but I am not a person who just loves nature. Yet, I write about it continually because I am interested in the birds and the beasts for their symbolic value—their value as icons, as ways of saying things about people. As a poet, I have been an expert in that realm, studying birds and beasts from Heraclitus onward, and I love the old bestiaries. I wrote my master's thesis at the University of Chicago on the

birds and beasts of Eupheus—his England—and
for that, I had to study the history of every bird and
beast there ever was.

Do you like the work of Cather and the regionalist
writers?

No, not particularly. I like Willa Cather, I don't love
her. I love Mark Twain because he had this cosmic,
dark, brooding pessimism. I love Theodore Dreiser.

For what reasons? Their portrayal of characters?
Their study of psychology?

Mainly because they were great thinkers, great
dreamers, who happened to come from the Midwest.

So, you make a distinction between regionalist writers and those who adopted an international style?

I have always said that Southern writers seem to be
born to sing. They live in small towns where they
hear the most beautiful balladry every day. I have
lived in Southern towns in the very heart of Kentucky and Tennessee. I have always envied Southern
writers because experience is so accessible to them.
But the Midwest is more prosperous and more middle class. If you are going to be a writer from the

Midwest, you have to become highly sophisticated, highly educated, in order to interpret that land. You cannot be just a natural-born singer—I could not imagine anything less possible. I think the Midwest begets bizarre, beautiful writers who have been dipped and dyed in education.

Did you feel the urge to go abroad to develop your talent, like other writers of your generation, such as Henry Miller, Anaïs Nin, Malcolm Lowry, Gertrude Stein, Fitzgerald, and Hemingway? They went to Paris, to Mexico, even to Hollywood.

No. I felt the urge to go by mule's back to the mountains of Tennessee, collecting ballads, old Scottish ballads. I was very much an admirer of Stiff Thompson, the great ballad authority who was a professor at Indiana University. Those people you mention were so far away. I never thought of them. They were like people of another planet. I was never a person who ever, then or now, watched what other writers do. During the depressed thirties, I was at the University of Chicago studying the Elizabethans and the Jacobeans, and then I became involved with *Angel in the Forest*. I had lived in and out of many Kentucky and Tennessee towns and had become very much fascinated by the individual history of each, such as Horse Cave, Kentucky, and the graveyards in those towns. So, you might say that I was a graveyard poetess at that time.

Did you go to New Harmony specifically to research the town for *Angel in the Forest*?

YOUNG

I never did any research whatever on New Harmony. My mother and stepfather moved there and they called me. They said, You'll love this new town. It is the scene of two lost utopias and it has in it the footprints of the angel Gabriel. It has cruciform shapes on the doors and a maze.

So I went there, and lived there for seven years, and gradually I began to write about it. But there was no artificial research, except for the experience of living there, and talking to the old-timers in that town. Some were in the party of Father Rapp, who was the founder of the first utopia. They loved him because he left visible evidence of his place, the cruciform, and the maze. The sundial was the way people told time. There were no watches in evidence until the railroad came to the land.

INTERVIEWER

You were going to write a series of poems?

YOUNG

I started with a series of sixty ballads, in a Robert Browning manner, since I was a poet and interested in balladry. I was unique in my interest. I hardly ever saw another writer. In Indiana, you are one thousand miles away from the next writer. I still do not watch what other writers do. Knowing the most recent vogue in literature is not the source of my creative strength. In fact, if I knew there was a vogue, I would avoid it.

INTERVIEWER
But isn't it tempting to follow the fashion of the day, to become involved in the literary movements?

YOUNG
In the Midwest we didn't know flocks of writers. Each writer was isolated, and thus he developed an inner vision. One read on a vast scale. It was not as if we were sitting around in cafés talking about literary movements. That would have been beyond imagination.

INTERVIEWER
How much influence, or instruction, can one expect from one's peers?

YOUNG
I once visited Thornton Wilder's writing class at the University of Chicago. He had a habit of smoking in class, which one was not supposed to do, and when somebody approached he would put his cigarettes in the desk drawer ... and I remember one time the desk catching fire. I recall only one thing he said in that class ... to remember above all things, "the patient loves his malady."

I remembered that when I began *Miss MacIntosh* ... I fully thought it would take two years. If I had known it would take eighteen years I would have dropped in holy horror. Who could conceive spending eighteen years obsessed by one book and working from nine to five? I was pleased that when the book came out, a reviewer said, "When Miss Young finished her *Miss MacIntosh, My Darling*, she must have been as happy as when Sir Philip Sidney took the manuscript of 'Arcadia' and threw it at his sister's feet and said, There it is, it's finished."

INTERVIEWER

You are interested in psychology, but you are not interested in personality. You have often said that.

YOUNG

Peculiarly enough, as a person, I am not interested much in individuals, even my closest friends. They could have deep secrets, and I would never ask them to tell me. As a writer, I would never spend pages analyzing the love life of a character. I have a muralist imagination. I like to see the epic swing of the thing, the many as opposed to the one. I am a pluralist in that sense.

INTERVIEWER

That is very much William James's concept of the imagination.

YOUNG

Yes, and it is also my temperament. It was true of *Angel in the Forest* when I was writing of the utopian society, true of *Miss MacIntosh* when I had surrounded her with every kind of individual pathology of which I had ever heard or known, and true in my present biographies, where the central figures are surrounded by vast numbers of characters. Through them, you see the neurosis unfolding, everything unfolding, in relation to society as a whole. I could not, like Gide, sit and think about the troubles of one person—it would bore me to death. It would bore me to death in real life, too.

INTERVIEWER

Do you have a concept of how to portray character?

YOUNG

Yes. According to the logic of a pathology working itself out in strange, unusual, and ultimate ways, which are recognizable, true to life, and which are always based on people whom either I have known or, more likely, have read about in the daily newspapers.

INTERVIEWER

You get your concepts from newspapers?

YOUNG

I get my characters from the newspapers, and from biographies and medical histories, and a thousand sources. I believe, like Browning, that the poet is a reporter. I can understand his writing, for instance, that beautiful long poem "The Ring and the Book," which was based on a real murder in Rome. I do not believe in inventing characters.

INTERVIEWER

Is the opium lady a real person?

YOUNG

I knew an opium lady while I was a student at the University of Chicago, and with whom I spent much time, reading aloud the works of Shakespeare. That is how I worked my way through school.

INTERVIEWER

Who was she?

YOUNG

She had been under opium for about fifteen or twenty years and had not walked for at least ten years. She was one of the original patronesses of *Poetry: A Magazine of Verse*, and of Jane Addams's Hull-House. She was also a friend of Thornton Wilder, Harriet Monroe, and many of the other intellectuals of that day. I was with her during her opium dreams. I was with her when the golden bird, who was the spirit of Heraclitus, perched upon the bedpost. I was literally with her when she had a long conversation with the head of John the Baptist.

INTERVIEWER

After decapitation?

YOUNG

After decapitation. I was also there when she spoke with a little rabbit. I was with her when she entertained an imaginary elephant, and when blue fish would be floating over her bed. I began to write my novel quite unexpectedly. I had planned to write a biography of Toussaint-Louverture, the Haitian rebel, but my publisher wanted me to write a novel ... she was the most fabulous single person I had ever known. I was interested in her for her dreams and her beautiful personality and surroundings.

And the problems of opium addiction?

No. The doctors in her household were always rushing about with Elizabeth Barrett Browning letters to try to explain this beautiful opium lady who was their patient. She was like an Elizabeth Barrett Browning, whom, of course, I had read, along with De Quincey's *Confessions of an English Opium Eater.* I had read Coleridge, too.

So that you would understand her?

No. All this was in my background before I ever arrived. Her house was just right for a young poet. There couldn't have been a better place. I was offered opium every evening. But I always said, No, thanks, and for that reason, she used to call me the prosaic sprite, because I didn't need drugs to dream. I stayed with her most of the time. I was offered the bed in which Edna St. Vincent Millay had slept, when she was a visitor in Chicago, and the idea of sleeping in Millay's bed—it would mean nothing to me now, but at that age ... it seemed to be the most marvelous thing that could ever happen to any young person. On the opium lady's bedside was a silver drinking cup that had belonged to John Keats, a little mosaic Persian letter set, and a beautiful bird with a seashell. I have these things at my bedside now. Her daughter gave them to me when she died.

INTERVIEWER

You did not enter the opium lady's dreams?

YOUNG

I do not think she dreamed about people. She dreamed about mandarins and human-size black-birds standing in the hallways, or invisible elephants. Adlai Stevenson—he may have known her, by the way—talked about the invisible elephant when he was running for office. I don't know if he ever got a letter I wrote him, telling him about the invisible elephant in the opium lady's dreams. He had the same idea—that the thing you think is not there may be there.

INTERVIEWER

But now you are talking about an individual, and yet you say you are not interested in individuals.

YOUNG

I met Thornton Wilder several years later at a Gotham Book Mart party, and he asked me what I had been doing. I said that I was writing a novel in which the opium lady was one of the leading characters. He said, "Oh! As a way of revealing the unconscious." He knew exactly what the theme would be. It was the unconscious that interested me. I say that I am not interested in people, but I am interested in the bizarre and in people at an edge. I am interested in extreme statements about people because that is where drama is most apparent. Being a Scot and economical about my working so hard, I begin with what I know is easy—with something strange and beautiful that then starts to activate itself. When you start with the normal or the neutral or the average, it becomes difficult. I imagine it does, anyway—I have never tried it and I never will.

INTERVIEWER

Did you have to do research for such characters as the nursemaid?

YOUNG

No. Not for *Miss MacIntosh*, because I knew all these things, or had observed them.

INTERVIEWER

What about the love story with the deaf man?

YOUNG

Well, I knew this stone-deaf man in Greenwich Village who was, in fact, a close friend of mine. He was most interesting because of his brilliant mind and missing sense. He was a painter. I put him in my novel because he was a sensual contrast to some of the other characters. He was a perfect lover for Vera Cartwheel in the end because I figured she could not marry a man who was absolutely normal—she would be bored to death after what she had been through. So, she ends up by marrying a man whose hearing was missing. So often I get stimulating ideas for my characters from what is actually happening in the world. I always read the newspapers. Sometimes events happen after I write about them. You'll remember that I had Miss MacIntosh walk into the sea, stark naked except for a pair of black gloves, which she had carefully darned the night before, as if she were going to her wedding, all of her clothes left along the beach, including her red wig on the back of a horseshoe crab, and her Admiral Dewey corset, and her sea boots, and her plaid mackintosh ... walking into the sea at dawn, when both sun and moon were in the sky, carrying her black umbrella, until her bald head reached sea level. Later I read about a boy in northern Long Island, who was stark naked except for a pair of black gloves, and who walked into the black sea. The fact that such a bizarre thing happened after I wrote about it made me feel that I was psychologically correct in the kind of death I had imagined for Miss MacIntosh. Of course, that death was originally based, in part, upon the death of Virginia Woolf, who had walked into the river Ouse in England.

INTERVIEWER

What is the psychological significance of that gloved death?

YOUNG

Well, I wondered about that myself. I used to distrust my imagination for fear that I was simply fantasizing. But I thought I knew what I meant, and when I consulted with my friend Dr. Hammerschlag, the psychiatrist, he explained the entire case—the meanings of the word *black*, and the gloves, in relation to psychology and guilt and why it was the correct image. Similarly, when I had the detective in the novel who would not handle a case in which anything black appears—a black rooster or the ace of spades—I thought, Well, I must have gone mad to imagine such a character. I asked Dr. Hammerschlag again and he said, Well, that is a classic case of schizophrenia, and he gave me a long series of similar case histories.

Scribner's commissioned *Miss MacIntosh* but it took you eighteen years to finish it. Did you get sidetracked in the writing of the book?

No. They commissioned me in 1944 to write it. I submitted about fifteen pages of it, that is all. Mainly, they gave me the contract on the basis of *Angel in the Forest* and my poetry book, *Moderate Fable*. I did not know when I began it that it would be such a long novel. I had all the major characters in my head the first day, and I knew the theme of the book would be an inquest into the illusions individuals suffer from. I had already written a book about the illusions society suffers from in utopian states, and I wanted to shift from the society to the individual. I thought it would take two years and perhaps the book would be about two hundred pages long. But the book started expanding because my characters became increasingly lively, and more interesting to me on so many levels. I had chosen very rich characters to begin with, who were capable of development, and I had the patience to allow them to develop. I was enchanted by the whole project. I hear music when I am writing, and I worked from nine to five, for what was to be eighteen years of breathless writing. I never stopped. I was never bored. If I was bored, I would have stopped. I realized somewhere along the line, early, that it would take a long time. I wanted it to be a book of books, a song of songs. I knew for sure that nothing else in life was going to interfere—I would not easily marry, I would not easily travel. I wanted to write this book—and I don't regret it.

INTERVIEWER
How do you get started in the morning?

YOUNG
I always leave off the day before, as Thomas Mann advised, "When the going is good …," when you know exactly where you are, and you are in a moment of exuberance, you stop. When I hook on the next morning, if the going was good, I just go. I feel it emotionally, almost in the blood, the pulse, the excitement. I always hear inner music when I write. I hear strange music. I have all my life, which is very odd, because I am not at all musical.

INTERVIEWER
Dreams are also a strong influence, aren't they?

YOUNG
Once I dreamed that I was in Iowa City at a party in my house. Henry James was there and he was sitting in a corner, pouring whiskey into his high silk hat. Two weeks later, I came to New York, and on Seventh Avenue I found a book, *Memories, by a Publisher's Wife*, in which I read, "Henry James was here the other evening, and was so drunk that he sat

in a corner, pouring whiskey into his high silk hat."
It was a very obscure little memoir, and I had never
read it, or heard of it, or even dreamed that Henry
James would take a drink. But I do believe that
there are visitations in dreams. He would come to
me in my dreams, night after night, during the writing of *Miss MacIntosh*, and read what I had done.
Sometimes I was typing, and sometimes writing in
longhand, beautiful pages—which of course faded
from my mind—and he used to say, That's beautiful ... go right ahead ... go right ahead ... you're
the late twentieth-century development of what I
was doing, and things like that. Which I don't think
I am, of course, but in my dreams I thought so.

INTERVIEWER

You've often said that you feel the presence of other
writers.

YOUNG

When I'm teaching, I often say, Come in, Mr.
James... My students love this. I will stop... Oh,
how do you do Henry James, won't you be seated.
Oh, they all look, they think he's really there.
Boswell will come, and Cervantes, I spend a great
deal of time with him. I entertain. I see Emily Dickinson, quite often, Virginia Woolf, and Dickens.
Poe, oh ... all the time. I see him on misty nights on
Sheridan Square, when the rain's falling. He's going
into that little cigar store to get a cigar. I am on very
close terms with Poe. Now rationally I don't believe
all of this, but in an irrational way, I live it all, so
what can we say?

INTERVIEWER

I know you have this theory that individuals speak through many voices. Do you see most people as possible writers?

YOUNG

No. Most people are not, though I think talent is fairly common. I see innumerable talents in my teaching of fiction writing at Fordham University and the New School of Social Research and Seton Hall. I see much talent. But so many of them will be lawyers, or bridge builders. Many of them will think they are going to write, but will be turned aside by fate.

INTERVIEWER

One must have incredible desire in addition to the talent.

YOUNG

I met Norman Mailer at a cocktail party after *Miss MacIntosh* was published. I had never seen him before. He came up to me and said, "Were there any fighters in your family?" I answered, "Why yes. My half brother was a champion in the ring." "I knew it," he said, "I knew you had a fighter in the family." "Well, what made you think that?" I asked. He said, "Because it took a lot of strength hanging out in the sawdust ring like that, punching away for eighteen years the way you did." Then he wrote to my publisher to say I was a "gentle Hercules in high heels." My publisher's publicity department gave that letter to a cartoonist at the *Herald Tribune* who did it up and showed it to me—a cartoon of me punching it out with Mailer with that caption, "a gentle Hercules in high heels." So Mailer was congratulating me for the stamina of spending so many years on a novel. I suppose it took stamina in a way, but it takes stamina to write anything for eighteen minutes.

(1977)

May Sarton

THE ART OF POETRY NO. 32

Interviewed by Karen Saum

The author of a remarkably varied body of
work, May Sarton lives by herself in York,
Maine, in a former "summer cottage," quite
isolated, at the end of a long dirt road. The road
curves through a well-kept wood ending at "The
House by the Sea" (the title of one of her journals).
The house, formal in design, is of pale yellow clapboard fronted by a flagstone terrace. It faces, across
a rolling meadow, the deep blue of the ocean marked
here and there by a line of white foam. It is a late
November afternoon and growing cold. The flower
beds around the house, running along the fence and
at the edge of the terraces, are all banked for winter.
Her little sheltie, Tamas, alerts her to the arrival of a
guest, and she comes to greet me at the gate.

Possessed of that profound attentiveness charac-
teristic of true charm, May Sarton has, at the same
time, an exuberant nature. Her voice, full of inflec-
tion and humor, expresses the range of her person-

ality. It has been called a "burnished" voice and it makes for spellbinding poetry readings, which she gives frequently—at places from small New England churches to the Library of Congress, and at colleges everywhere.

In the library, a fire is blazing, and Bramble, the once wild cat, is asleep on the couch. Sarton brings in a tea tray, complete with cinnamon toast and cookies. In this room, with the shelves of her work—novels, books of poems, memoirs, and journals—and the shelves of her father's works (George Sarton was the noted Harvard historian of science), under the benign gaze of Duvet de La Tour, "The Ancestor" ("always referred to as if he were the only one"), the interview begins.

INTERVIEWER

Would you say a word about your work as a whole?

MAY SARTON

My first book was a book of poems, *Encounter in April* (1937), followed by my first novel, *The Single Hound* (1938). There was quite an interval before the second novel, *The Bridge of Years* (1946). And then *Shadow of a Man* (1950). Then it goes on and on for a long time with a book of poems between every novel. That was my wish, that the poems should be equal in number, that the novels should not be more important than the poems because the poems were what I cared about most. Much later, when I was forty-five or so, I began to do nonfiction—first the memoirs and finally the journals, which came as the last of the forms that I have been using. All together now I think it amounts to seventeen novels, I don't know, five or six memoirs and journals, and then twelve books of poems, which are mostly in the *Collected Poems* (1973) now.

INTERVIEWER

Has it been easy to shift amongst all these different forms?

SARTON

Sometimes the demon of self-doubt comes to tell me that I've been fatally divided between two crafts, that of the novel and that of poetry, but I've always believed that in the end it was the total work that would communicate a vision of life, and it really needs different modes to do that. The novels have been written in order to find something out about what I was thinking, questions I was asking myself that I needed to answer. Take a very simple example, *A Shower of Summer Days* (1952). The great house that dominates the novel was Bowen's Court. What interested me was the collision between a rich nature, a young girl in revolt against everything at home in America, and ceremony, tradition, and beauty as represented by the house in Ireland.

INTERVIEWER

Is it safe to assume that the rebellious young woman is based partly on you?

SARTON

Not at all. It's a complete invention. The only person who is not invented in that book is the husband of Violet, and he is based on Elizabeth Bowen's husband. The house is, as I said, Bowen's Court. I stayed there.

And you knew Elizabeth Bowen.

SARTON

Oh, yes. I was in love with her. I've said what I really want to say about her in the portrait [*A World of Light*]. She was a marvelous friend. A very warm and giving person.

INTERVIEWER

What intrigues me in your portrait of her is that although she had a tremendous effect on you emotionally, she had no influence on you artistically. You never emulated her work.

SARTON

No. Very little influence. None. Her style is too mannered. At her best, in *The Death of the Heart*, it's marvelous, but in the later books her style became too literary in a not very attractive way to me. For instance, a sentence is very rarely a straight sentence.

INTERVIEWER

It's convoluted?

SARTON

It's convoluted and put upside down. "Very strange was the house" instead of "The house was very strange." Incidentally, Elizabeth Bowen appears in my novel *The Single Hound*, as the lover of Mark. I made her into a painter.

We were talking, before this digression, about why you write novels. You say you write them to find out what you are thinking, to answer a question. Could you give another example?

In the case of *Faithful Are the Wounds* (1955), the question was, How can a man be wrong and right at the same time? This book was based on the suicide of F. O. Matthiessen during the McCarthy era. At that time, people outside his intimate circle, and I was never an intimate of Mattie's, did not know that he was a homosexual, so that is only suggested in the novel. But what interested me was that Mattie believed that socialists and communists could work together in Czechoslovakia and had gone way out on a limb to say this was possible and was going to happen and might be the answer to world peace. Then the communists took over and the socialists were done in. It was a terrible blow to Mattie and some people thought the suicide came from that. I wrote the novel partly because I was very angry at the way people I knew at Harvard reacted after his suicide. At first, as always happens with a suicide, people close to him thought, What could we have done? There was guilt. Then very soon I heard, Poor Mattie, he couldn't take it. That was what enraged me, because these people didn't care that much, were not involved. And Mattie did care. I'm sure the suicide was personal as well as political, and perhaps everything was all wound up together at that point ... but he was right in the deepest sense, you see, only he had bet on the wrong horse. His belief that people could work together, and that the Left must join, not divide, was correct. It proved to be unrealistic. But he wasn't nearly as wrong as the people who didn't care. That's what I wrote the novel out of.

INTERVIEWER

You've spoken of the novel. Earlier, you spoke of the body of your work as a whole. Would you talk about how the different parts fit together?

SARTON

The thing about poetry—one of the things about poetry—is that in general one does not follow growth and change through a poem. The poem is an essence. It captures perhaps a moment of violent change but it captures a moment, whereas the novel concerns itself with growth and change. As for the journals, you actually see the writer living out a life, which you don't in any of the other forms, not even the memoirs. In memoirs you are looking back. The memoir is an essence, like poetry. The challenge of the journal is that it is written on the pulse, and I don't allow myself to go back and change things afterward, except for style. I don't expand later on. It's whatever I am able to write on the day about whatever is happening to me on that day. In the case of a memoir like *Plant Dreaming Deep* (1968), I'm getting at the essence of five years of living alone in a house in a tiny village in New Hampshire, trying to pin down for myself what those five years had meant, what they had done to me, how I had changed. And that's very different from the journals. I must say, I'm not as crazy about the journals as some of my readers are. I get quite irritated when people say the journals are the best thing. God knows, I've struggled with certain things in the journals, especially about being a woman and about being a lesbian. The militant lesbians want me to be a militant and I'm just not.

But as for the vision of life in the whole of my work, I would like to feel that my work is universal and human on the deepest level. I think of myself as a maker of bridges—between the heterosexual and the homosexual world, between the old and the young. *As We Are Now* (1973), the novel about a nursing home, has been read, curiously enough, by far more young people than old people. It terrifies old people to read about other old people in nursing homes. But the young have been moved by it. Many young people write me to say that they now visit elderly relatives in these places. This is the kind of bridge I want to make. Also, the bridge between men and women in their marriages, which I've dealt with in quite a few of the novels, especially in the last one, *Anger* (1982).

So what one hopes, or what I hope, is that the whole work will represent the landscape of a nature that is not primarily intellectual but rather a sensibility quite rich and diverse and large in its capacities to understand and communicate.

INTERVIEWER

How do you see your novels fitting into the tradition of the novel form?

SARTON

Well, they are quite traditional. I certainly haven't broken the forms. This is true in the poetry too. I think this may be one reason I have not had a great deal of critical attention, because the critics, I mean the real critics, not just the reviewers, are interested in the innovators. I suppose that *Mrs. Stevens Hears the Mermaids Singing* (1965) is innovative in that the material had not been dealt with as openly before, or at least not quite in the same way. But the technique isn't extraordinarily radical.

I have done all kinds of things with points of view in my novels, but I prefer the omniscient view, which I used in *Kinds of Love* (1970). I think it's better for me, and perhaps for a poet, because you are able to describe things. In a novel like *Crucial Conversations* (1975), the point of view is that of a friend of the marriage, an observer, and there is so much you simply cannot describe. You can't describe the atmosphere, the landscape, the interior of a house, say, without being quite awkward in the way you do it. "He walked in and noticed the roses were faded on the little eighteenth-century table." It's a little self-conscious. Ever since Henry James, there has been this big quibble about the point of view. As I say, I prefer the omniscient view, although it's very unfashionable and is constantly pounced upon by the critics.

And the dialogue, of course. Elizabeth Bowen has said the great thing about dialogue, "Speech is what characters do to each other." *Anger* is a perfect example. The war between these two characters is a war of dialogue. To some extent also in *Crucial Conversations* and even in an old novel of mine, *Shadow of a Man*, which I dipped into the other day because people are reading it now that it's in paperback, a great deal happens in the dialogue.

For which of the novels do you have the greatest affinity?

Mrs. Stevens, I think, *Faithful Are the Wounds*, and *As We Are Now* would be my three ... and *A Reckoning* (1978). Those four. Of course, they are all very different. *Faithful Are the Wounds* is a passionate political book, and I haven't done that any other time. In *As We Are Now* I think I did succeed in making the reader absolutely identify with Caro, the old woman who is stuffed into a ghastly rural nursing home and who is trying to stay alive emotionally. I look at *As We Are Now* as a descent into hell in which there are different steps down. The first is the person being captured, so to speak, and put in jail. The final step is when genuine love is made dirty. Caro had come alive again because a gentle nurse came into this terrible place and she sort of fell in love with her. Then that love is made dirty by the people who own the home. She tries to run away at that point. That's the final step—after that she begins to go mad and suffers despair. That's when she decides to burn the place down. She has a long conversation about God with her minister. One thing I like about this book is that there is a good minister in it. Ministers are almost always treated ironically in fiction, or made into monsters of some kind. This minister really listens. He isn't trying to tell her something. He's interested in what she has to say.

So the end represents madness, not in any way a cleansing.

Well, it's partly a cleansing action for her. The end
has been questioned, and I myself question it because
she burns up innocent people in the fire. But I felt it
had to end that way. The innocent people were just
vegetables, and so ill-treated that one felt death was
better, really. And Caro probably does feel this way,
only it isn't quite sane. She has all the inventiveness
of the mad person who has an idée fixe of how she is
going to proceed.

INTERVIEWER

At what point does the end become inevitable?

SARTON

When genuine love is defiled. That's when everything goes. There is nothing left. Then she is in hell.

INTERVIEWER

And the reason for your particular affinity with the
novel *A Reckoning*?

SARTON

The origin of the book is rather interesting. I wrote
it before I myself had cancer, and a mastectomy. But
at an earlier date I thought I had cancer, and for a
few days while the biopsy was being done I had an
immense feeling of relief that I could lay the burden of
my life down, get rid of all the clutter, and for the last
six months of it, simply live and look at the world ...
look at the sun rise and not do anything that I ought
to do. And then when I heard that I was all right and
had to pick up the burden again of answering letters
and living my life, which is a very good one but very

demanding, I cried. I went out to Raymond, the gardener, and said, "I'm all right, Raymond," and burst into tears.

That was the clue to the novel, you see. Then I thought, Ah! I'm going to write it. What would it have been like if I had had cancer, and six months to live my own death? Really, the book is about how to live as much as it is about how to die. From much that I hear about it, I know it has been a helpful book. It's used in the hospices, and in nursing homes, and often read by nurses and people who are dealing with the dying. It has been useful, there is no doubt, and that is a wonderful feeling.

INTERVIEWER

Have any particular novelists been mentors?

SARTON

Yes. Certainly Virginia Woolf. She was the novelist who meant the most to me when I was learning. But she is a dangerous mentor from the technical point of view because she can't be imitated. It's too much her own genius. My first novel is written in a very Woolfian way. There's a description of a woman walking down some steps and it's summer and it's like a pastiche of Woolf. I never did that again.

INTERVIEWER

You've written in your journals about your meetings with Virginia Woolf, but can you cast your mind back and describe the very first moment you met her?

SARTON

I had left my first book of poems at her door, with

some flowers, and the darling maid opened the door just then and said, Oh, won't you come up? I said, Oh, no, I wouldn't think of it. I just left the book. Elizabeth Bowen knew that I wanted to meet Virginia Woolf desperately, so she invited the two of us and a couple of other people to dinner. That was when I first met her. She walked in, in a robe de style, a lovely, rather eighteenth-century-looking, long dress with a wide collar, and she came into the room like a dazzled deer and walked right across—this was a beautiful house on Regent's Park—to the long windows and stood there looking out. My memory is that she was not even introduced at that point, that she just walked across, very shyly, and stood there looking absolutely beautiful. She was much more beautiful than any of the photographs show. And then she discovered that I was the person who had left the poems.

She was very canny ... she answered my gift of that book with a lovely note, which is now in the Berg Collection, just saying, "Thank you so much, and the flowers came just as someone had given me a vase, and were perfect, and I shall look forward to reading the poems." In other words, never put yourself in a position of having to judge. So she never said a word about the poems. But she was delighted to find out that I was the person who had left them.

Then, later, we talked—Elizabeth and Virginia Woolf and I. The gentlemen were having their brandy and cigars in the other room. We talked about hairdressers. It was all like something in *The Waves*! We all talked like characters in a Virginia Woolf novel. She had a great sense of humor. Very malicious. She liked to tease people, in a charming way, but she was a great tease.

INTERVIEWER
Did you feel shy?

SARTON
Of course! But she put me at ease and I saw her quite often after that. Every time I was in England I would have tea with her, which was a two-hour talk. She would absolutely ply me with questions. That was the novelist. I always felt the novelist at work. Where did I buy my clothes? Whom was I seeing? Whom was I in love with? Everything. So it was enrapturing to a young woman to be that interesting to Virginia Woolf. But I think it was her way of living, in a sense. Vicariously. Through people.

INTERVIEWER
But you've written that you felt a certain coldness, in spite of ...

SARTON
Yes. She was never warm. That's true. There was no warmth. It was partly physical, I think. She was a physically unwarm person. I can't imagine kissing her, for instance, I mean on the cheek. But she was delightful, and zany, full of humor and laughter. Never did you feel a person on the brink of madness. That has distorted the image, because she was so in control.

You were speaking of influences. Whom else would you add?

The person who influenced me the most has been François Mauriac. I greatly admired the economy and thrust of his books. He was able to create so much between the lines. I was aiming for that. I was aiming to eliminate what at first I was praised for, a so-called poetic style. I wanted to get rid of that and to make the poetry less obvious, to make it sharper and purer and simpler. I've worked to get a more and more clarified style, but I think this has been misunderstood in my case. Somebody said of *As We Are Now*, "A ninth grader could have written it"—meaning the style. I mean, this person simply didn't get it! Other people did get it, fortunately. Of course, the thing that is so tremendous with Mauriac, and isn't possible for me because I don't belong to the Church, is the Catholic in him, which gives this extra dimension to everything that he wrote. I envy him that.

How was it that you began to write the journals?

I wrote the first one, *Journal of a Solitude* (1973), as an exercise to handle a serious depression and it worked quite well. I did have publication in mind. It wasn't written just for me. I think it's part of the discipline. It keeps you on your toes stylistically and prevents too much self-pity, knowing that it's going to be read and that it will provide a certain standard for other people who are living isolated lives and who are depressed. If you just indulge in nothing but moaning, it wouldn't be a good journal for others to read. I also found that by keeping a journal I was looking at things in a new way because I would think, That—good! That will be great in the journal. So it took me out of myself, out of the depression to some extent. This happened again with *Recovering* (1980).

INTERVIEWER

You write for publication. Do you have an imagined audience?

SARTON

It's really one imaginary person.

INTERVIEWER

Would you talk a little about this imaginary person?

SARTON

Well, I don't mean that when I sit down I think, Oh, there is that imaginary person over there I'm writing for, but ... yes! Somebody who sees things the way I do, who will be able to read with heart and intelligence. I suppose somebody about my age. It used to be somebody about forty-five, now it's somebody about seventy. But then *Journal of a Solitude* brought me a whole new audience, a college-age audience. That was very exciting because until then my work had appealed mostly to older people.

INTERVIEWER

Isn't it true that lately you have been embraced by the spiritual establishment?

Yes, this has happened only recently and has been extremely moving to me. I have come out as a lesbian. And although I have no shame about this at all, I still feel it's quite extraordinary that religious groups would be so receptive to me, as the Methodists were, for instance. They asked me to be one of the speakers at their yearly retreat for pastors. The other speakers were religious in a way that I am not. Then, the Unitarians gave me their Ministry to Women Award last year and I was touched by what they said ... that I'd helped women by my honesty. The Methodists also talked about honesty.

I must say it was quite brave of me to come out as I did in *Mrs. Stevens*, in 1965. At that time it was not done. When I spoke at colleges I would never have stated, I'm a lesbian. But this all changed in the seventies. It's marvelous now that one can be honest and open. At the time *Mrs. Stevens* was published, it was sneered at in reviews and I lost a couple of jobs. They weren't terribly important jobs, but I did lose them. Now I don't think that would happen. It might if you were a professor in a college, but coming as a visiting speaker you can be absolutely open. Women's studies have helped me enormously, there's no doubt about it. This is one way my work is now getting through.

I know of no other writer who has had such a strange career as I've had. When I started writing, the first novels were received with ovations. In 1958, I was a finalist for the National Book Award in two categories, fiction and poetry. But after my fifth novel, *Faithful Are the Wounds*, the one that was nominated, this never happened again and I began to have bad reviews. I was no longer in fashion. I can't think of another writer who has had as hard a time with reviewers over a period of twenty years as I have but whose work has been so consistently read. It's word of mouth. It's people ... every day I get letters saying things like, I loved such and such a book and I'm buying five copies to give to people. That's how books get around. And then the public libraries. Without the public libraries, serious writers, unfashionable serious writers like me, really wouldn't have a chance. Again, I hear from people, I was wandering around the library and saw the title *Plant Dreaming Deep*. It caught my attention ... now I'm reading everything you've written. It's wonderful to have this happen at the age of seventy.

INTERVIEWER

Will you talk about the relationship between the poet and the muse?

SARTON

Many of my poems are love poems. I'm only able to write poetry, for the most part, when I have a muse, a woman who focuses the world for me. She may be a lover, may not. In one case it was a person I saw only once, at lunch in a room with a lot of other people, and I wrote a whole book of poems. Many of these poems have not been published. But this is the mystery. Something happens that touches the source of poetry and ignites it. Sometimes it is the result of a long love affair, as the "A Divorce of Lovers" (1960) poems, the sonnet sequence. But not always. So who is the audience for my poetry? The audience is the loved one for me. But usually the loved one isn't really interested in the poems.

You, and Robert Graves with his White Goddess, are perhaps the only modern poets to be so strongly and personally inspired by the muse as a mythological figure. A literal figure. Do your muses, diverse as they must be, possess any one thing in common?

Maybe so. The word that popped into my mind when you asked the question was *distance*. Maybe there is something about the Distant Admired Person. I had a curious experience in Berkeley recently, where I stayed with a friend I went to school with, the Shady Hill School, in Cambridge, Massachusetts. She had saved a book of poems that a group of us had written. We used to meet, four of us, and read our poems to each other and savagely criticize them. These poems were passionate love poems to our teacher, Anne Thorp, the person I'm now trying to write a novel about. I was absolutely floored by the intensity of these poems! We were completely inexperienced. In that generation there was no sex, I mean nothing like what goes on now. We were asexual because we just didn't know anything yet. But we felt so intensely. And I saw that I haven't changed that much. I'm not innocent in the way I was then, but my feelings have remained very much as they were.

If Anne Thorp had possessed all those qualities you worshipped, but had been a man ... could you have been writing those love poems to a man?

Yes, it's possible. I just don't know. The three other people did not become homosexual. Only I among the four.

You have spoken of poems as coming from the subconscious.

It's not the poem that comes from the subconscious so much as the image. Also the single line, *la ligne donnée*. If I'm truly inspired, the line comes in meter and sets the form. But what comes from the subconscious is only the beginning. Then you work with it.

In the case of metaphor, it has everything to teach you about what you have felt, experienced. I write in order to find out what has happened to me in the area of feeling, and the metaphor helps. A poem, when it is finished, is always a little ahead of where I am. "My poem shows me where I have to go." That's from Roethke. His line actually reads, "I learn by going where I have to go."

So you write novels to find out what you think, and poems to find out what you feel?

Yes, it works out that way. In the novel or the journal you get the journey. In a poem you get the arrival. The advantage of free verse, for instance in "Gestalt at Sixty" (1965), is that you do get the journey. Form is so absolute, as if it had always been there, as if there had been no struggle. The person who sees the lyric poem on the page doesn't realize there may have been sixty drafts to get it to the point where you cannot change a single word. It has been worked for. But something has been given, and that's the difference between the inspired poem and what Louise Bogan calls the imitation poem. In the inspired poem, something is given. In the imitation poem you do it alone on will and intelligence. I mean, you say something like, It might be a good idea to write a poem about a storm down here at the end of the field when the fountains of spray come up. And so you go ahead and do it. But the difference is simply immense, as far as the poet goes. He knows, or she knows, what is inspired and what is imitation.

INTERVIEWER

Would the reader know?

SARTON

I think so.

INTERVIEWER

What about the advantages and disadvantages of form?

SARTON

Form is not fashionable these days. What's being thrown out, of course, is music, which reaches the reader through his senses. In meter, the whole force is in the beat and reaches the reader, or the listener, below the rational level. If you don't use meter, you are throwing away one of the biggest weapons to get at the reader's subconscious and move him.

The advantage of form, far from being formal and sort of off-putting and intellectual, is that through form you reach the reader on this subliminal level. I love form. It makes you cut down. Many free verse poems seem to me too wordy. They sound prose-y, let's face it. When you read a poem in form, it's pared down, it's musical, and it haunts. Very few free-verse poems are memorable. You don't learn them by heart unless they are very short. But a lyric poem is easy to remember.

INTERVIEWER

You have written poems in free verse.

SARTON

Oh, yes, a lot. I find it exhilarating.

INTERVIEWER

How do you know when you're finished?

SARTON

That's the problem. I can go on revising almost forever. But with form, at a certain point it's all there. Another problem, or danger, with free verse is that it depends almost entirely on the image, so you get people using what I call hysterical images, images that are too powerful because you've got to hit the reader over the head with something big ... like talking about love in terms of the Crucifixion. Or the Holocaust. A tremendously strong image to say something that doesn't deserve that intensity and only shocks the reader, but in a rather superficial way.

INTERVIEWER

What poets have had the most influence on you?

SARTON

H.D., when I was young. It was the age of Millay. Millay was the great ... well, everybody adored her. And I did, too. I loved those lyrics. But I was fascinated by H.D. because of the freshness she managed to get into free verse. Then the other women lyric poets. Elinor Wylie certainly influenced me, and later on Louise Bogan, who I think was probably the most distinguished pure lyric poet of our time. There you get that marvelous economy and music and depth and also the archetypal images. And then Valéry, whom I translated with Louise Bogan.

INTERVIEWER

Because your parents were European, and you yourself were born in Belgium, has that made a difference to you as a poet?

SARTON

I think an enormous difference. Because the things that touched me most, the literary things, were mostly in French, and later on, at fourteen, I came under the influence of Jean Dominique.*

INTERVIEWER

What about those very early years?

---

* Nom de plume of Marie Closset of the Institut Belge de Culture Française.

120

During the first two years of my life we lived in a small heaven of a house in Wondelgem, Belgium. Then we were driven out by the war and went to England. In 1916, when I was four, we settled for good in Cambridge, Massachusetts. Even so, every seven years, when my father had a sabbatical, we all went to Europe. It took me until I was forty-five to become an American at heart. It was in 1958, after my parents were both dead, that I bought a house in Nelson, a small village in New Hampshire, and settled in for fifteen years and made roots. I describe that in *Plant Dreaming Deep*. I planted the dreams then and became an American.

But for very long, all my youth, from nineteen on anyway, I went to Europe every year. Although we never had much money, my father gave me a hundred dollars a month allowance, and an extra three hundred dollars, which at the time covered a boat round-trip, tourist class. I either stayed with friends or, in London, in one of those dreary one-room flats which cost £2 a week with an English breakfast thrown in. I felt European partly because—I still believe this—the emotional loam is deeper in Europe. People are less afraid of feeling. The lesbian part of me came into this because in the Bloomsbury society of the thirties there was no trouble about that. I didn't feel like a pariah. I didn't feel that I had to explain myself. And among my mother's generation there were passionate friendships between women that were probably not sexually played out, but it was common for women to be a little in love with each other. It was taken for granted. It wasn't a big issue.

One of the themes in all I have written is the fear of feeling. It comes into the last novel where Anna asks, "Must it go on from generation to generation, this fear of feeling?" I want feelings to be expressed, to be open, to be natural, not to be looked on as strange. It's not weird, I mean, if you feel deeply. And, really, most Americans think it is. Sex is all right, but feeling is not. You can have five people in your bed and no one will worry much, but if you say, I've fallen in love at seventy, people's hair is going to stand on end. They'll think, The poor thing, there's something awfully wrong with her.

INTERVIEWER

Young people read *Halfway to Silence* (1980) and quote the poems ... it goes so much against our cultural norms, the idea of a woman of sixty-five writing a passionate love poem to another woman.

SARTON

Yes, I know. And I have done it more than once. The poem "Old Lovers at the Ballet" (1980) is really about this. How is the sexuality different for an older couple, old lovers watching these magnificent bodies that they don't have and the grace that they no longer have? I suggest that what they do have is something else, an ability to communicate spiritually through sex. I believe that at its deepest, sex is a communication of souls through the body. That can go on forever.

INTERVIEWER

Did you ever write poems in French?

I wrote poems for Jean Dominique in French, but I didn't know the language well enough, the prosody, and so they have a certain charm but nothing more. I'd never publish them.

So the European influence is in the emotional climate more than anything.

Yes. But as I said, the seminal influences in my writing were French—Mauriac for the novels, Valéry for the poetry, and also Gide at a certain time, particularly in the journals.

Would you talk about the poems you're writing now?

I'm writing new poems now called "Letters from Maine." It's a new form for me. I've written so many poems in sonnet form, or in other forms, and I wish I could find something a little freer that is not free verse. These are a sort of loose iambic pentameter. They don't rhyme, and they flow. It's impossible for me to tell whether they're any good. In six months I'll look back and say, That was a bad idea, it didn't work, or I'll say, These are really quite good. Then I can begin to revise.

The poems come from a new muse. A very distant one whom I probably won't see very much of. But it's opened up that mysterious door again. It's amazing, so mysterious, so extremely hard to talk about. Why should it happen that among all the people, the great many women whom I see and am fond of, suddenly somebody I meet for half an hour opens the door into poetry? Something is released. The deepest source is reached. Some of my best poems have been written for occasions that did not materialize, if you will. "In Time Like Air" (1956) is an example. "In time like air is essence stated" is the final line. Here is an example of an image that haunts for years, an archetypal image, *salt*, which I got from the French philosopher Gaston Bachelard. Bachelard has written a whole series of books analyzing images. In one of them he talks about the image of salt, and says it is a Janus material because it dissolves in water, crystallizes in air. I put that in a notebook and carried it around for years. Then I met somebody who started poetry for me again. I realized that salt was the image I needed. A metaphysical poem about love. And time. Love and time. There's only that one poem.

INTERVIEWER

You've discussed the different forms, or modes, you use to express your vision of life—poetry, novels, journals, memoirs. Were you ever tempted to write short stories?

SARTON

I did at one time write a number of stories when I was living in Cambridge and making very little money. I sold some to the then slicks, a lot of which don't exist anymore, and also to places like *Redbook* and *Ladies' Home Journal*. There are about thirty stories. I broke some taboos. For instance, I wrote about a woman dying of cancer and you weren't supposed to do that—write about it, I mean. *Ladies' Home Journal* published that. But they were not wonderful and I wouldn't like to see them reprinted. They were just ... well, I sold one little piece for $600, which to me was a fortune, so that sort of set me off. I thought—Well! This is great! I'll write lots! And I did write quite a few but I finally had to stop because when I sat at the typewriter dollar signs were floating around in my eyes. It was the money. I somehow couldn't handle it.

INTERVIEWER

Could you write stories now?

SARTON

The form doesn't appeal to me very much. The short story is too much like a lyric, so that side goes into poetry.

INTERVIEWER

You have spoken with great admiration of Yeats, who changed his style and grew in poetic power even when he was an old man. Earlier, you mentioned the new form of your latest poems. Using that sort of comparison, how does it feel to be seventy?

SARTON

For the first time in my life I have a sense of achievement. I've written all these books and they're there! Nobody can take that from me. And the work is getting through at last. For so long I felt there were people who would like to read me but didn't know I existed. So I'm more relaxed inside now, less compulsive ... somewhat less compulsive.

You don't find that your past achievement acts as a brake on further achievement?

Not at all. I feel much more creative now that I'm not carrying around that load of bitterness and despair because I was getting so little critical attention and therefore the readers weren't finding my work. Now they are finding it.

You once wrote that to be worthy of the task, the poet moves toward a purer innocence where "the familiar is wonderful and the wonderful is familiar ..."

That's a quote from Coleridge, of course. Where did I say that? In *Writings on Writing* (1980), maybe. One of the good things about old age is that one often feels like a child. There is a childlike innocence, often, that has nothing to do with the childishness of senility. The moments become precious.

Ideally, one would live as if one were going to die the next day. I mean, if you were going to die the next day it would be well worth sitting and watching the sun set, or rise. It might not be worth doing a huge laundry.

Your aspirations for yourself when you were young were quite lofty ...

Where did you read that?

You told me.

What do you mean? Of course my ambitions were lofty. I knew that I was a poet. This, like mathematical or musical gifts, you know when you are very young. My first poems were published in *Poetry* magazine when I was seventeen—five sonnets that open the first book, *Encounter in April*. Of course, I did think for a long time that I was going to be in the theater because I had fallen in love with a theater, the Civic Repertory Theatre founded by Eva Le Gallienne in New York. She accepted me as an apprentice. I could have gone to Vassar, but I chose the theater. It was a difficult decision for my parents to accept, but in the end they backed the whole precarious plan.

If you could be the seventeen-year-old looking at the woman of seventy, what would you think?

I think I would be proud of myself. I've done what I set out to do and without a great deal of help. I never took permanent jobs in the academic world, which most poets have to do, not that they want to, and this has cost me something because the critical acclaim comes from the academic world, which launches a poet. But yes, I think that if at seventeen I'd known there'd be twelve books of poems—at that time I never imagined novels at all—I would feel pretty good. I'd say, You did what was in you to do.

But I don't sit here and think, Oh, how wonderful you are, Sarton. I think, on the contrary, Oh, how much there is still to do!

INTERVIEWER
You often see other poets and writers at conferences. Are you stimulated by this mixing with your peers, so to speak?

SARTON
I don't like writers. I don't like seeing writers. I'm not good at it. It upsets me. It's been too hard a struggle. I'm very competitive, and that side comes out. I'm uncomfortable with writers. I love painters and sculptors.

In relation to writers, the people whom I did love to see were the people who I felt were way ahead of me, like Louise Bogan and Elizabeth Bowen and Virginia Woolf. People from whom I had everything to learn and where my position was that of a neophyte. That I enjoyed. I have one very good new friend, a poet, Bill Heyen. He's a marvelously good poet, I think. But I really like to see what I call real people—who are not writers!

INTERVIEWER
One theme I wanted to ask you about is the phoenix.

SARTON
The phoenix, yes. The mythical bird that is consumed by fire and rises again from its ashes. That

was D.H. Lawrence's symbol. I've appropriated it. I think I have died and been reborn quite a few times. One renewal from the ashes, to stick to the symbol, is recorded in my latest journal, *Recovering*, which describes a combination of the end of a love affair, a mastectomy, and a third very hard blow, an attack on my novel *A Reckoning*. I knew this novel was going to have value for people who were dying, and for their children and friends and so on, and it was more or less damned in the *New York Times* as a lesbian novel. This hurt. So I was getting over a lot of things. Again, as with *Journal of a Solitude*, I used the journal as a way of coming to terms with depression, and that journal is helping a lot of people. I get many letters about it.

INTERVIEWER

Have you been reborn recently?

SARTON

Yes. Yes, I have. I had gotten to a very sterile place because I was seeing so many people this summer and making so many public appearances, and yet at the center there was a kind of emptiness. I began to feel like a well that had gone dry. And then I did meet a woman who started the poems again, and has centered everything again for me. It's quite miraculous.

INTERVIEWER

Would you talk about the theme of the creative woman as a monster?

SARTON

Ruth Pitter, the poet, said in a letter to me once, "We

are all monsters," meaning women poets. *Le monstre sacré.* As I say in the poem "My Sisters, Oh My Sisters" (1946), I think that was to some extent true. It isn't now. Now it's possible for women to have much more complete lives, and that's what we're working toward, really.

But let me go back for a minute to the phoenix. You see, at twenty-six I had been in the theater for six or seven years, first as an apprentice to Le Gallienne and then, when her theater failed, I kept the apprentices together and founded something called the Apprentice Theater. We did a season at the New School for Social Research in New York—rehearsal performances of modern European plays in translation that had never been seen on Broadway. We got quite a lot of notice. It was a kind of first off-Broadway theater. But then we had to go into production in order to be a theater. I was offered a small theater in Hartford and we did a season there that was not a great success. I was looking all the time for new American plays and didn't find one. Finally we opened in Boston the following year and failed immediately, having spent $5,000 that I had managed to raise. So at twenty-six I faced failure, the complete failure of my dream of making a studio theater a little bit like the Moscow Art Theatre Studio. This was one of the times when the phoenix died and had to be reborn again, and I was reborn as a writer. I was very ill after the theater failed. I guess I had what used to be called a nervous breakdown. My mother announced, "May has to rest," and took over. I rested for three months, just lay out on a chaise lounge. I was exhausted. Emptied out. But one has extraordinary powers of remaking oneself.

I learned it physically with the mastectomy. I was amazed at the power of the body to come back after such a shock. For that reason, the mastectomy was a thrilling experience, odd as it sounds. The body has this power, and so does the mind and the soul, to remake itself. That is the phoenix.

INTERVIEWER

Given your experience in the theater, might you not have been reborn as a playwright? Especially since you have such a strong sense of dialogue.

SARTON

I've written two full-length plays.

INTERVIEWER

Should I know that?

SARTON

No, you shouldn't. They were never produced, although Archibald MacLeish thought one of them had real possibilities and tried to get Robert Brustein at Yale to do it. The other one won a prize but I can't even remember what sort of contest it was. I wrote them quite fast, in about three weeks each, which is probably why they weren't better! But I wrote them long after the theater failed. Ten years, at least. Maybe twenty years.

It was like a fever, the theater, for me, but it was so closely connected with the Civic Repertory and Eva Le Gallienne and that marvelous theater, which was so pure. The theater is heartbreak. I admire people who have the guts to take it.

Apart from the informal teaching arrangements, you've earned your living entirely by your writing, isn't that true?

SARTON

Yes. I've never had a bonanza, but my books have been consistently read and now many of them are in paperback. It's been tough at times, but my writing has kept me afloat financially.

INTERVIEWER

Everyone wants to know about a writer's work habits . . .

SARTON

I do all my work before eleven in the morning. That's why I get up so early. Around five.

INTERVIEWER

Have you pretty much stuck to the same kind of discipline over the years?

SARTON

Yes, I have. That I got from my father. I think the great thing he gave me was an example of what steady work, disciplined work, can finally produce. In not waiting for the moment, you know, but saying, I'm going to write every day for two or three hours. The trouble, for me, is the letters. They interrupt, and I give much too much energy to that. It's an insoluble problem.

INTERVIEWER

Would it be helpful, say, if you were stuck in your work, to switch over to the letters?

SARTON

I sometimes start the day with the letters. Just to get the oil into the machine.

INTERVIEWER

Do you have other ways of getting oil into the machine?

SARTON

Music. I play records, mostly eighteenth-century music. I find that the Romantics—Beethoven— don't work for me. I love them to listen to, but not to work with, alongside of, whereas Mozart, Bach, Albinoni... Haydn, I love. I feel the tremendous masculine joy of Haydn. That gets me going.

INTERVIEWER

It gets you going, but do you keep it going?

SARTON

Yes. It's probably a terrible thing to do to the music but it does a lot for me.

INTERVIEWER

You have mentioned that you are writing a journal, and there are the new poems ...

SARTON

And a novel. I'm hoping now to get back to a novel that went dead on me before I wrote *Anger*, called

The Magnificent Spinster (1985). I'm looking forward to doing it because it will be rather rich and poetic in a way that *Anger* was not. *Anger* was a novel like a blow, trying to get at things almost brutally.

This brings up an interesting point, I think. Here I have this novel, which I set aside for a long time and which I am going back to. In other words, you can plan for a novel. You can say, I'm going to write a novel next year, and then go ahead and do it. Except that it might not work out, but still you can plan for it. You simply cannot do this with poems, they come out of a seizure of feeling. You can't plan for a seizure of feeling, and for this reason I put everything else aside when I'm inspired, because, as I've said, you can't summon a poem. You can try, but it won't be much good if it's written on command.

You've written movingly about your parents in *A World of Light.*

That is a memoir recapturing twelve different people, a celebration of great friendships. All of the people were dead, or "gone into the world of light"—the Henry Vaughan quote—at the time I wrote it, except one. I included my parents because their friendship has weighed on me all my life. Their influence was the most difficult to deal with, and the most inspiring. I've spoken about the value of memoirs as the past considered, as essences. In "The Fervent Years," the chapter in *I Knew a Phoenix* (1954), I talk about my parents' youth. It taught me an awful lot about them, and about a whole period. They were tremendously idealistic people. They had the nineteenth-century vision of life, the perfectibility of man. Ever since the Holocaust, something has happened to people, to all of us. We've had to face certain things that make it impossible for us to foresee a much better future. We're faced with a whole lot of choices that are pretty depressing. Whereas my parents still had that well of idealism and faith in humanity that runs through all of my father's work.

INTERVIEWER
What about your phrase "usable truth"?

SARTON
This is the function of poetry. To make people experience. That's where it's completely different from philosophy, where you think something out but don't have to experience it in your whole being so that you are changed. It's perfectly stated by Rilke in the sonnet "Archaic Torso of Apollo." One must visualize this ideally beautiful sculpture with no head and no eyes. The poem ends, "Here there is no place / that does not see you. You must change your life." That is what art is all about.

(1983)

Doris Lessing

THE ART OF FICTION NO. 102

Interviewed by Thomas Frick

Doris Lessing was interviewed at the home of Robert Gottlieb, in Manhattan's east forties. Her editor for many years at Knopf, Mr. Gottlieb was then the editor of *The New Yorker*. Ms. Lessing was briefly in town to attend some casting sessions for the opera Philip Glass has based on her novel *The Making of the Representative for Planet 8* (1982), for which she had written the libretto. Plans for the opera had been in more or less constant flux, and it was only after a minor flurry of postcards— Ms. Lessing communicates most information on postcards, usually ones from the British Museum— that the appointment was finally arranged.

While the tape recorder was being prepared, she said, "This is a noisy place here, when you think we're in a garden behind a row of houses." She points across the way at the townhouse where Katharine Hepburn lives; the talk is about cities for a while. She has lived in London for almost forty years, and still finds that "everything all the time in a city is extraordinary!" More speculatively, as she has remarked elsewhere, "I would not be at all surprised to find out ... that the dimensions of buildings affect us in ways we don't guess." She spoke about spending six months in England before the age of five, saying, "I think kids ought to travel. I think it's very good to carry kids around. It's good for them. Of course it's tough on the parents."

The interview was conducted on the garden patio. Silvery-streaked dark hair parted in the middle and pulled back in a bun, a shortish skirt, stockings, blouse, and jacket, she looked much like her book-jacket photos. If she seemed tired, it was hardly surprising considering the extent of her recent travels. She has a strong, melodious voice, which can be both amused and acerbic, solicitous and sarcastic.

INTERVIEWER

You were born in Persia, now Iran. How did your parents come to be there?

DORIS LESSING

My father was in the First World War. He couldn't stand England afterward. He found it extremely narrow. The soldiers had these vast experiences in the trenches and found they couldn't tolerate it at home. So he asked his bank to send him somewhere else. And they sent him to Persia, where we were given a very big house, large rooms and space, and horses to ride on. Very outdoors, very beautiful. I've just been told this town is now rubble. It's a sign of the times, because it was a very ancient market town with beautiful buildings. No one's noticed. So much is destroyed, we can't be bothered. And then they sent him to Tehran, which is a very ugly city, where my mother was very happy, because she became a part of what was called the legation set. My mother adored every second of that. There were dinner parties every night. My father hated it. He was back again with convention. Then in 1924, we came back to England, where something called the Empire Exhibition, which turns up from time to time in literature, was going on and which must have had an enormous influence. The Southern Rhodesian stand had enormous maize-cobs, corncobs, slogans saying "Make your fortune in five years" and that sort of nonsense. So my father, typically for his romantic temperament, packed up everything. He had this pension because of his leg, his war wounds—minuscule, about five thousand pounds—and he set off into unknown country to be a farmer. His childhood had been spent near Colchester, which was then a rather small town, and he had actually lived the life of a farmer's child and had a country childhood. And that's how he found himself in the veld of Rhodesia. His story is not unusual for that time. It took me some time, but it struck me quite forcibly when I was writing *Shikasta* how many wounded ex-servicemen there were out there, both English and German. All of them had been wounded, all of them were extremely lucky not to be dead, as their mates were.

INTERVIEWER

Perhaps a minor version of the same thing would be our Vietnam veterans coming back here and being unable to adjust, completely out of society.

I don't see how people can go through that kind of experience and fit in at once. It's asking too much.

INTERVIEWER
You recently published a memoir in the magazine *Granta*, which, according to its title, was about your mother. In some ways it really seemed to be more about your father.

LESSING
Well, how can one write about them separately? Her life was, as they used to say, devoted to his life.

INTERVIEWER
It's astonishing to read about his gold divining, his grand plans, his adventures ...

LESSING
Well, he was a remarkable bloke, my father. He was a totally impractical man. Partly because of the war, all that. He just drifted off, he couldn't cope. My mother was the organizer, and kept everything together.

INTERVIEWER
I get the feeling that he thought of this gold divining in a very progressive and scientific way.

LESSING
His idea was—and there's probably something true about it somewhere—that you could divine gold and other metal if you only knew how to do it. So he was always experimenting. I wrote about him actually, in a manner of speaking, in a story I called "Eldorado"

(1953). We were living in gold country. Gold mines, little ones, were all around.

So it wasn't out of place.

No! Farmers would always keep a hammer or a pan in the car, just in case. They'd always be coming back with bits of gold-bearing rock.

Were you around a lot of storytelling as a child?

No ... the Africans told stories, but we weren't allowed to mix with them. It would have been inconceivable for a white child. Now I belong to something called a Storytellers' College in England. About three years ago a group of people tried to revive storytelling as an art. It's doing rather well. The hurdles were—I'm just a patron, I've been to some meetings—first that people turn up thinking that storytelling is telling jokes. So they have to be discouraged! Then others think that storytelling is like an encounter group. There's always somebody who wants to tell about their personal experience, you know. But enormous numbers of real storytellers have been attracted. Some from Africa—from all over the place—people who are still traditional hereditary storytellers or people who are trying to revive it. And so, it's going on. It's alive and well. When you have storytelling sessions in London or anywhere, you get a pretty good audience. Which is quite astonishing when you think of what they could be doing instead—watching *Dallas* or something.

What was it like coming back to England? I remember J. G. Ballard, coming there for the first time from Shanghai, felt very constrained. He felt that everything was very small and backward.

Oh yes! I felt terribly constricted, very pale and damp—everything was shut in, and too domestic. I still find it so. I find it very pretty, but too organized. I don't imagine that there's an inch of the English landscape that hasn't been dealt with in some way or another. I don't think there is any wild grass anywhere.

Do you have any deep urges or longings to go back to some kind of mythical African landscape?

Well, I wouldn't be living in that landscape, would I? It wouldn't be the past. When I went back to Zimbabwe three years ago, which was two years after independence, it was very clear that if I went I would be from the past. My only function in the present would be as a kind of token. Inevitably! Because I'm the local girl made good. Under the white regime I was very much a baddie. No one had a good word to say for me. You've got no idea how wicked I was supposed to be. But now I'm okay.

INTERVIEWER

Were you bad because of your attitude to blacks?

LESSING

I was against the white regime.

INTERVIEWER

In the *Granta* memoir there's the image of you as a child, toting guns around, shooting game ...

LESSING

Well, there was a great deal of game around then. There's very little these days, partly because the whites shot it out.

INTERVIEWER

Did you have a desire to be a writer in those early days? You mention hiding your writings from your mother, who tried to make too much of them.

LESSING

My mother was a woman who was very frustrated. She had a great deal of ability, and all this energy went into me and my brother. She was always wanting us to be something. For a long time she wanted me to be a musician, because she had been a rather good musician. I didn't have much talent for it. But everybody had to have music lessons then. She was always pushing us. And, of course, in one way it was very good, because children need to be pushed. But she would then take possession of whatever it was. So you had to protect yourself. But I think probably every child has to find out the way to possess their own productions.

I just wondered if you thought of yourself as becoming a writer at an early age.

Among other things. I certainly could have been a doctor. I would have made a good farmer, and so on. I became a writer because of frustration, the way I think many writers do.

Because you've written novels in so many different modes, do people feel betrayed when you don't stick in one camp or another? I was thinking of the science-fiction fans, quite narrow-minded, who resent people who write science fiction who don't stick within their little club.

Well, it is narrow-minded, of course it is. Actually, the people who regard themselves as representatives of that community seem now to want to make things less compartmentalized. I've been invited to be guest of honor at the World Science Fiction Convention, in Brighton. They've invited two Soviet science-fiction writers, too. In the past there's always been trouble. Now they're hoping that glasnost might allow their writers to actually come. Actually, it never crossed my mind with these later books that I was writing science fiction or anything of the kind! It was only when I was criticized for writing science fiction that I realized I was treading on sacred ground. Of course, I don't really write science fiction. I've just read a book by the *Solaris* bloke, Stanisław Lem. Now that's real classic science fiction ... full of scientific ideas. Half of it, of course, is wasted on me because I don't understand it. But what I do understand is fascinating. I've met quite a lot of young people—some not so young either, if it comes to that—who say, I'm very sorry, but I've got no time for realism, and I say, My God! But look at what you're missing! This is prejudice. But they don't want to know about it. And I'm always meeting usually middle-aged people who say, I'm very sorry. I can't read your nonrealistic writing. I think it's a great pity. This is why I'm pleased about being guest of honor at this convention, because it does show a breaking down.

INTERVIEWER

What I most enjoyed about *Shikasta* was that it took all the spiritual themes that are submerged or repressed or coded in science fiction and brought them up into the foreground.

LESSING

I didn't think of that as science fiction at all when I was doing it, not really. It certainly wasn't a book beginning with, I don't know, say, At three o'clock on a certain afternoon in Tomsk, in 1883 ... which is, as opposed to the cosmic view, probably my second most favorite kind of opening, this kind of beginning!

INTERVIEWER

You've written introductions for many collections of Sufi stories and prose. How did your interest and involvement with Sufism come about?

Well, you know, I hate talking about this. Because really, what you say gets so clichéd, and it sounds gimmicky. All I really want to say is that I was looking for some discipline along those lines. Everyone agrees that you need a teacher. I was looking around for one, but I didn't like any of them because they were all gurus of one kind or another. Then I heard about this man Shah, who is a Sufi, who really impressed me. So I've been involved since the early sixties. It's pretty hard to summarize it all, because it's all about what you experience. I want to make a point of that because a lot of people walk around saying, I am a Sufi, probably because they've read a book and it sort of sounds attractive. Which is absolutely against anything that real Sufis would say or do. Some of the great Sufis have actually said, I would never call myself a Sufi—it's too large a name. But I get letters from people, letters like this, Hi, Doris! I hear you're a Sufi, too! Well, I don't know what to say, really. I tend to ignore them.

I imagine that people try to set you up as some sort of guru, whether political or metaphysical.

I think people are always looking for gurus. It's the easiest thing in the world to become a guru. It's quite terrifying. I once saw something fascinating here in New York. It must have been in the early seventies—guru time. A man used to go and sit in Central Park, wearing elaborate golden robes. He never once opened his mouth, he just sat. He'd appear at lunch-time. People appeared from everywhere, because he was obviously a holy man, and this went on for months. They just sat around him in reverent silence. Eventually he got fed up with it and left. Yes. It's as easy as that.

INTERVIEWER

Let me ask you one more question along these lines. Do you think that reincarnation is a plausible view?

LESSING

Well, I think it's an attractive idea. I don't believe in it myself. I think it's more likely that we dip into this realm on our way on a long journey.

INTERVIEWER

That this planet is merely one single stop?

LESSING

We're not encouraged—I'm talking about people studying with Shah—to spend a great deal of time brooding about this, because the idea is that there are more pressing things to do. It's attractive to brood about all this, of course, even to write books about it! But as far as I was concerned, in *Shikasta* the reincarnation stuff was an attractive metaphor, really, or a literary idea, though I understand that there are people who take *Shikasta* as some kind of a textbook.

INTERVIEWER

Prophecy, perhaps?

It was a way of telling a story—incorporating ideas that are in our great religions. I said in the preface to *Shikasta* that if you read the Old Testament and the New Testament and the Apocrypha and the Koran you find a continuing story. These religions have certain ideas in common, and one idea is, of course, this final war or apocalypse, or whatever. So I was trying to develop this idea. I called it space fiction because there was nothing else to call it.

I have the feeling that you are an extremely intuitive kind of fiction writer, and that you probably don't plan or plot out things extensively, but sort of discover them. Is that the case, or not?

Well, I have a general plan, yes, but it doesn't mean to say that there's not room for an odd character or two to emerge as I go along. I knew what I was going to do with *The Good Terrorist* (1985). The bombing of Harrods department store was the start of it. I thought it would be interesting to write a story about a group who drifted into bombing, who were incompetent and amateur. I had the central character, because I know several people like Alice—this mixture of very maternal caring, worrying about whales and seals and the environment, but at the same time saying, You can't make an omelet without breaking eggs, and who can contemplate killing large numbers of people without a moment's bother. The more I think about that, the more interesting it becomes. So I knew about her. I knew about the boyfriend, and I had a rough idea of the kinds of people I wanted. I wanted people of different kinds and types, so I created this lesbian couple. But then what interested me were the characters who emerged that I hadn't planned for, like Faye. And then Faye turned into this destroyed person, which was surprising to me. The little bloke Phillip turned up like this— right about then I was hearing about an extremely fragile young man, twenty-one or twenty-two, who was out of work, but was always being offered work by the authorities. I mean, loading very heavy rolls of paper onto lorries, in fact! You'd think they were lunatics! So he always got the sack at the end of about three days. I think it's quite a funny book.

INTERVIEWER

Really?

LESSING

Well, it is comic, in a certain way. We always talk about things as if they are happening in the way they're supposed to happen, and everything is very efficient. In actual fact, one's experience about anything at all is that it's a complete balls-up. I mean everything! So why should this be any different? I don't believe in these extremely efficient terrorists, and all that.

INTERVIEWER

Conspiracies, and so on?

LESSING

There's bound to be messes and muddles going on.

INTERVIEWER

Do you work on more than one fictional thing at a time?

LESSING

No, it's fairly straight. I do sometimes tidy up a draft of a previous thing while I'm working on something else. But on the whole I like to do one thing after another.

INTERVIEWER

I'd imagine then that you work from beginning to end, rather than mixing around ...

LESSING

Yes, I do. I've never done it any other way. If you write in bits, you lose some kind of very valuable continuity of form. It is an invisible inner continuity. Sometimes you only discover it is there if you are trying to reshape.

INTERVIEWER

Do you have a feeling of yourself as having evolved within each genre that you employ? For instance, I thought the realistic perspective in *The Good Terrorist*, and even sometimes in the Jane Somers books, was more detached than in your earlier realism.

LESSING

It was probably due to my advanced age. We do get detached. I see every book as a problem that you have to solve. That is what dictates the form you use. It's not that you say, I want to write a science-fiction book. You start from the other end, and what you have to say dictates the form of it.

Are you producing fairly continuously? Do you take a break between books?

Yes! I haven't written in quite a while. Sometimes there are quite long gaps. There's always something you have to do, an article you have to write, whether you want to or not. I'm writing short stories at the moment. It's interesting, because they're very short. My editor, Bob Gottlieb, said, quite by chance, that no one ever sends him very short stories, and he found this interesting. I thought, My God, I haven't written a very short story for years. So I'm writing them around fifteen hundred words, and it's good discipline. I'm enjoying that. I've done several, and I think I'm going to call them "London Sketches," because they're all about London.

So they're not parables, or exotic in any way?

No, not at all. They're absolutely realistic. I wander about London quite a lot. And any city, of course, is a theater, isn't it?

Do you have regular working habits?

It doesn't matter, because it's just habits. When I was bringing up a child I taught myself to write in very short concentrated bursts. If I had a weekend, or a week, I'd do unbelievable amounts of work. Now those habits tend to be ingrained. In fact, I'd do much better if I could go more slowly. But it's a habit. I've noticed that most women write like that, whereas Graham Greene, I understand, writes two hundred perfect words every day! So I'm told! Actually, I think I write much better if I'm flowing. You start something off, and at first it's a bit jagged, awkward, but then there's a point where there's a click and you suddenly become quite fluent. That's when I think I'm writing well. I don't write well when I'm sitting there sweating about every single phrase.

INTERVIEWER

What kind of a reader are you these days? Do you read contemporary fiction?

LESSING

I read a great deal. I'm very fast, thank God, because I could never cope with it otherwise. Writers get sent enormous amounts of books from publishers. I get eight or nine or ten books a week, which is a burden, because I'm always very conscientious. You do get a pretty good idea of what a book's like in the first chapter or two. And if I like it at all, I'll go on. That's unfair, because you could be in a bad mood, or terribly absorbed in your own work. Then there are the writers I admire, and I'll always read their latest books. And, of course, there's a good deal of what people tell me I should read. So I'm always reading.

INTERVIEWER

Could you tell us more about how you put the Jane Somers hoax over on the critical establishment? It strikes me as an incredibly generous thing to do, first of all, to put a pseudonym on two long novels to try to show the way young novelists are treated.

LESSING

Well, it wasn't going to be two to begin with! It was meant to be one. What happened was, I wrote the first book and I told the agent that I wanted to sell it as a first novel ... written by a woman journalist in London. I wanted an identity that was parallel to mine, not too different. So my agent knew, and he sent it off. My two English publishers turned it down. I saw the readers' reports, which were very patronizing. Really astonishingly patronizing! The third publisher, Michael Joseph, the publisher of my first book, was then run by a very clever woman called Philippa Harrison, who said to my agent, This reminds me of the early Doris Lessing. We got into a panic because we didn't want her going around saying that! So we took her to lunch and I said, This is me, can you go along with it? She was upset to begin with, but then she really enjoyed it all. Bob Gottlieb, who was then my editor at Knopf in the States, guessed, and so that was three people. Then the French publisher rang me up and said, I've just bought a book by an English writer, but I wonder if you haven't been helping her a bit! So I told him. So in all, four or five people knew. We all expected that when the book came out, everyone would guess. Well, before publication it was sent to all the experts on my work, and none of them guessed. All writers feel terribly caged by these experts—writers become their property. So, it was bloody marvelous! It was the best thing that happened! Four publishers in Europe bought it not knowing it was me, and that was nice. Then the book came out, and I got the reviews a first novel gets, small reviews, mostly by women journalists, who thought that I was one of their number. Then Jane Somers got a lot of fan letters, mostly nonliterary, from people looking after old people and going crazy. And a lot of social workers, either disagreeing or agreeing, but all saying they were pleased I'd written it. So then I thought, Okay, I shall write another one. By then I was quite fascinated with Jane Somers. When you're writing in the first person, you can't stray too far out of what is appropriate for that person. Jane Somers is middle class, English, from a very limited background. There are very few things more narrow than the English middle class. She didn't go to university. She started working very young, went straight to the office. Her life was in the office. She had a marriage that was no marriage. She didn't have children. She didn't really like going abroad. When she went abroad with her husband, or on trips for her firm and her office, she was pleased to get home. She was just about as narrow in her experience as you can get. So in the writing, I had to cut out all kinds of things that came to my pen, as it were. Out! Out! She's a very ordinary woman. She's very definite in her views about what is right and what is wrong.

INTERVIEWER

What to wear . . .

LESSING

Everything! I have a friend who is desperately concerned with her dress. The agonies she goes through to achieve this perfection I wouldn't wish on anyone! Jane Somers was put together from various people. Another was my mother. I wondered what she would be like if she were young now, in London. A third one was a woman I knew who used to say, I had a perfectly happy childhood. I adored my parents. I liked my brother. We had plenty of money. I loved going to school. I was married young, I adored my husband—she goes on like this. But then, her husband dies suddenly. And from becoming a rather charming child-woman, she became a person. So I used all these things to make one person. It's amazing what you find out about yourself when you write in the first person about someone very different from you.

INTERVIEWER

Your original idea with the Jane Somers books was to probe the literary establishment?

LESSING

Yes. I've been close to the literary machine now for a long time. I know what's good about it and what's bad about it. It's not the publishers I've had it in for so much as the reviewers and the critics, whom I find extraordinarily predictable. I knew everything that was going to happen with that book! Just before I came clean I had an interview with Canadian television. They asked, Well, what do you think's going to happen? and I said, The English critics are going to say that the book is no good. Exactly! I had these sour nasty little reviews. In the meantime the book did very well in every other country.

In your preface to *Shikasta* you wrote that people really didn't know how extraordinary a time this was in terms of the availability of all kinds of books. Do you feel that in fact we're going to be leaving the culture of the book? How precarious a situation do you see it?

LESSING

Well, don't forget, I remember World War II when there were very few books, very little paper available. For me to walk into a shop or look at a list and see anything that I want, or almost anything, is like a kind of miracle. In hard times, who knows if we're going to have that luxury or not?

INTERVIEWER

Do you feel any sense of responsibility in presenting these prophesies aside from telling a good story?

LESSING

I know people say things like, I regard you as rather a prophet. But there's nothing I've said that hasn't been, for example, in the *New Scientist* for the last twenty years. Nothing! So why am I called a prophet, and they are not?

INTERVIEWER

You write better.

LESSING

Well, I was going to say, I present it in a more interesting way. I do think that sometimes I hit a kind of wavelength—though I think a lot of writers do this—where I anticipate events. But I don't think it's very much, really. I think a writer's job is to provoke questions. I like to think that if someone's read a book of mine, they've had—I don't know what—the literary equivalent of a shower. Something that would start them thinking in a slightly different way perhaps. That's what I think writers are for. This is what our function is. We spend all our time thinking about how things work, why things happen, which means that we are more sensitive to what's going on.

INTERVIEWER

Did you ever do any of those sixties experiments with hallucinogens, that sort of thing?

LESSING

I did take mescaline once. I'm glad I did, but I'll never do it again. I did it under very bad auspices. The two people who got me the mescaline were much too responsible! They sat there the whole time, and that meant, for one thing, that I only discovered the hostess aspect of my personality, because what I was doing was presenting the damn experience to them the whole time! Partly in order to protect what I was really feeling. What should have happened was for them to let me alone. I suppose they were afraid I was going to jump out of a window. I am not the kind of person who would do such a thing! And then I wept most of the time. Which was of no importance, and they were terribly upset by this, which irritated me. So the whole thing could have been better. I wouldn't do it again. Chiefly because I've known people who had such bad trips. I have a friend who took mescaline once. The whole experience was a nightmare that kept on being a nightmare—people's heads came rolling off their shoulders for months. Awful! I don't want that.

Do you travel a great deal?

Too much. I mean to stop.

Mostly for obligations?

Just business, promoting, you know. Writers are supposed to sell their books! Astonishing development! I'll tell you where I've been this year, for my publishers. I was in Spain ... Barcelona and Madrid, which is enjoyable, of course. Then I went to Brazil, where I discovered—I didn't know this—that I sell rather well there. Particularly, of course, space fiction. They're very much into all that. Then I went to San Francisco. They said, While you're here, you might as well—that phrase, *you might as well*—pop up the coast to Portland. You've been there?

No, never.

Now there is an experience! In San Francisco, they're hedonistic, cynical, good-natured, amiable, easygoing, and well-dressed—in a casual way. Half an hour in the plane and you're in a rather straitlaced formal city that doesn't go in for casual behavior at all. It's amazing, just up the coast there. This is what America's like. Then I went to Finland for the second time. They've got some of the best bookstores in the world! Marvelous, wonderful! They say it's because of those long, dark nights! Now I'm here. Next I'm going to be in Brighton, for the science-fiction convention. Then I won a prize in Italy called the Mondello Prize, which they give in Sicily. I said, Why Sicily? and they said, deadpan, Well, you see, Sicily's got a bad image because of the Mafia... So I'll go to Sicily, and then I shall work for all the winter.

INTERVIEWER

I hear you've been working on a space opera with Philip Glass.

LESSING

What happens to books is so astonishing to me! Who would have thought *The Making of the Representative for Planet 8* would turn into an opera? I mean it's so surprising!

INTERVIEWER

How did that come about?

LESSING

Well, Philip Glass wrote to me, and said he'd like to make an opera, and we met.

INTERVIEWER

Had you known much of his music before?

Well, no, I hadn't! He sent some of his music. It took quite a bit of time for my ears to come to terms with it. My ear was always expecting something else to happen. You know what I mean? Then we met and we talked about it, and it went very well, which is astonishing because we couldn't be more different. We just get on. We've never had one sentence worth of difficulty over anything, ever. He said the book appealed to him, and I thought he was right, because it's suitable for his music. We met, usually not for enormous sessions, a day here and a day there, and decided what we would do, or not do. I wrote the libretto.

INTERVIEWER

Have you ever done anything like that before?

LESSING

No, never with music.

INTERVIEWER

Did you have music to work from?

LESSING

No, we started with the libretto. We've done six versions of the story so far, because it is a story, unlike most of the things he does. As something was done, he would do the music, saying he'd like six more lines here or three out there. That was a great challenge.

INTERVIEWER

Can you say anything about your next project?

Yes, my next book is a little book. It's a short story that grew. The joke is that a short novel in England is very much liked. They're not terribly popular here in the U.S. They like big books here. Getting your money's worth. It's about a very ordinary family that gives birth to a goblin. And this is realism. I got the idea from two sources. One was this fantastic writer called Loren Eiseley. He wrote a piece—I can't remember what it was actually about—where he's walking up the seashore in the dusk, and on a country road he sees a girl that he says is a Neanderthal girl, a country girl in a country district, nothing very much to be asked of her, hardly noticed except as a stumpy girl with a clumsy skull. It's just the most immensely touching, sad piece. It stuck in my mind, and I said, If Neanderthals, why not Cro-Magnons, why not dwarves, goblins, because all cultures talk about these creatures? The other source was the saddest piece in a magazine, from a woman who wrote in and said, I just want to write about this or I shall go crazy. She'd had three children, I think. Her last child, who was now seven or eight, had been born, she said, a devil. She put it in those terms. She said that this child had never done anything but hate everyone around. She's never done anything normal, like laugh or be happy. She destroyed the family, who couldn't stand her. The mother said, I go in at night and I look at this child asleep. I kiss her while she's asleep because I don't dare kiss her while she's awake. So, anyway, all this went into the story. The main point about this goblin is, he's perfectly viable in himself. He's a normal goblin. But we just cannot cope with him.

Is the space series going to continue?

Yes. I haven't forgotten it. If you read the last one, *The Sentimental Agents* (1983)—which is really satire, not science fiction—you'll see that I've ended it so that I've pointed it all to the next volume. The book ends in the middle of a sentence. In the next book, I send this extremely naive agent off to … What's the name of my bad planet?

Shammat?

Yes, to Shammat, in order to reform everything. It's going to be difficult to write about Shammat because I don't want to make it much like Earth! That's too easy! I have a plot, but it's the tone I need. You know what I mean?

Do you do many public readings of your own work?

Not very many. I do when I'm asked. They didn't ask me to in Finland. I don't remember when was the last. Oh, Germany last year, my God! That was the most disastrous trip. It was some academic institution in Germany. I said to them, Look, I want to do what I always do. I'll read the story and then I'll take questions. They said, the way academics always do, Oh, you can't expect our students to ask questions. I said,

Look, just let me handle this, because I know how. Anyway, what happened was typical in Germany. We met at four o'clock in order to discuss the meeting that was going to take place at eight. They cannot stand any ambiguity or disorder—no, no! Can't bear it. I said, Look, just leave it. The auditorium was very large and I read a story in English and it went down very well, perfectly okay. I said, I will now take questions. Then this bank of four bloody professors started to answer questions from the audience and debate among themselves, these immensely long academic questions of such tedium that finally the audience started to get up and drift out. A young man, a student sprawled on the gangway—as a professor finished something immensely long—called out, "BLAH, BLAH, BLAH, BLAH, BLAH." So with total lack of concern for the professors' feelings I said, Look, I will take questions in English from the audience. So they all came back and sat down, and it went well ... perfectly lively questions! The professors were absolutely furious. So that was Germany. The end.

INTERVIEWER

Recently, you've turned to writing nonfiction.

LESSING

Well, I've just written a book, a short book, about the situation in Afghanistan. I was there looking at the refugee camps, because what happens is that men usually go for the newspapers, and men can't speak to the women because of the Islamic attitudes. So we concentrated on the women. The book's called *The Wind Blows Away Our Words* (1987), which is a quote from one of their fighters, who said, "We cry to you for help, but the wind blows away our words."

INTERVIEWER

Did you ever worry about what sort of authority you could bring to such an enormous story, being an outsider visiting only for a short time?

LESSING

Do journalists worry about the authority they bring, visiting countries for such a short time? As for me, rather more than most journalists, I was well briefed for the trip, having been studying this question for some years knowing Afghans and Pakistanis—as I made clear in the book—and being with people who knew Farsi—this last benefit not being shared by most journalists.

INTERVIEWER

Your methods of reportage in that book have been the target of some criticism by American journalists, who charge that your trip to Afghanistan was sponsored by a particular pro-Afghan organization. How do you respond to that?

LESSING

This is the stereotypical push-button criticism from the Left, from people who I do not think can expect to be taken seriously, for I made it clear in the book that the trip was not organized by a political organization. I went for something called Afghan Relief, set up by some friends, among them myself, which has helped several people to visit Pakistan, but not with money. I paid my own expenses, as did the others I went with. The point about Afghan Relief is that it has close links with Afghans, both in exile and fighting inside Afghanistan, and includes Afghans living in London, as advisers. These Afghans are personal friends of mine, not political. Afghan Relief has so far not spent one penny on administration. All the fund-raising work, here and in Pakistan, is done voluntarily. To spell it out, no one has made anything out of Afghan Relief except the Afghans.

INTERVIEWER

From the tag that you used for the Jane Somers book, "If the young knew / If the old could ..." Do you have any things you would have done differently, or any advice to give?

LESSING

Advice I don't go in for. The thing is, you do not believe ... I know everything in this field is a cliché, everything's already been said ... but you just do not believe that you're going to be old. People don't realize how quickly they're going to be old, either. Time goes very fast.

(1988)

Maya Angelou

THE ART OF FICTION NO. 119

Interviewed by George Plimpton

This interview was conducted on the stage of the YMHA on Manhattan's Upper East Side. A large audience, predominantly women, was on hand, filling indeed every seat, with standees in the back ... a testament to Maya Angelou's drawing power. Close to the stage was a small contingent of black women dressed in the white robes of the Black Muslim order. Angelou's presence dominated the proceedings. Many of her remarks drew fervid applause, especially those that reflected her views on racial problems, the need to persevere, and "courage." She is an extraordinary performer and has a powerful stage presence. Many of the answers seemed as much directed to the audience as to the interviewer so that when Maya Angelou concluded the evening by reading aloud from her work—again to a rapt audience—it seemed a logical extension of a planned entertainment.

You once told me that you write lying on a made-up bed with a bottle of sherry, a dictionary, *Roget's Thesaurus*, yellow pads, an ashtray, and a Bible. What's the function of the Bible?

MAYA ANGELOU

The language of all the interpretations, the translations, of the Judaic Bible and the Christian Bible, is musical, just wonderful. I read the Bible to myself. I'll take any translation, any edition, and read it aloud, just to hear the language, hear the rhythm, and remind myself how beautiful English is. Though I do manage to mumble around in about seven or eight languages, English remains the most beautiful of languages. It will do anything.

INTERVIEWER

Do you read it to get inspired to pick up your own pen?

ANGELOU

For melody. For content also. I'm working at trying to be a Christian and that's serious business. It's like trying to be a good Jew, a good Muslim, a good Buddhist, a good Shintoist, a good Zoroastrian, a good friend, a good lover, a good mother, a good buddy—it's serious business. It's not something where you think, Oh, I've got it done. I did it all day, hotdiggety. The truth is, all day long you try to do it, try to be it, and then in the evening if you're honest and have a little courage you look at yourself and say, Hmm. I only blew it eighty-six times. Not bad. I'm trying to be a Christian and the Bible helps me to remind myself what I'm about.

INTERVIEWER

Do you transfer that melody to your own prose? Do you think your prose has that particular ring that one associates with the King James Version?

ANGELOU

I want to hear how English sounds. How Edna St. Vincent Millay heard English. I want to hear it, so I read it aloud. It is not so that I can then imitate it. It is to remind me what a glorious language it is. Then, I try to be particular and even original. It's a little like reading Gerard Manley Hopkins or Paul Laurence Dunbar or James Weldon Johnson.

INTERVIEWER

And is the bottle of sherry for the end of the day or to fuel the imagination?

ANGELOU

I might have it at six fifteen A.M. just as soon as I get in, but usually it's about eleven o'clock when I'll have a glass of sherry.

INTERVIEWER

When you are refreshed by the Bible and the sherry, how do you start a day's work?

ANGELOU

I have kept a hotel room in every town I've ever lived in. I rent a hotel room for a few months, leave my home at six, and try to be at work by six thirty. To write, I lie across the bed, so that this elbow is absolutely encrusted at the end, just so rough with calluses. I never allow the hotel people to change the bed, because I never sleep there. I stay until twelve thirty or one thirty in the afternoon, and then I go home and try to breathe. I look at the work around five. I have an orderly dinner—proper, quiet, lovely dinner. And then I go back to work the next morning. Sometimes in hotels I'll go into the room and there'll be a note on the floor that says, Dear Miss Angelou, let us change the sheets. We think they are moldy. But I only allow them to come in and empty waste-baskets. I insist that all things are taken off the walls. I don't want anything in there. I go into the room and I feel as if all my beliefs are suspended. Nothing holds me to anything. No milkmaids, no flowers, nothing. I just want to feel and then when I start to work I'll remember. I'll read something, maybe the Psalms, maybe, again, something from Mr. Dunbar, James Weldon Johnson. And I'll remember how beautiful, how pliable the language is, how it will lend itself. If you pull it, it says, okay. I remember that and I start to write. Nathaniel Hawthorne says, "Easy reading is damn hard writing." I try to pull the language in to such a sharpness that it jumps off the page. It must look easy, but it takes me forever to get it to look so easy. Of course, there are those critics—New York critics as a rule—who say, Well, Maya Angelou has a new book out and of course it's good but then she's a natural writer. Those are the ones I want to grab by the throat and wrestle to the floor because it takes me forever to get it to sing. I work at the language. On an evening like this, looking out at the auditorium, if I had to write this evening from my point of view, I'd see the rust-red, used, worn velvet seats and the lightness where people's backs have rubbed against the back of the seat so that it's a light orange, then the beautiful colors of the people's faces, the white, pink-white, beige-white, light beige and brown and tan—I would have to look at all that, at all those faces and the way they sit on top of their necks. When I would end up writing after four hours or five hours in my room, it might sound like, It was a rat that sat on a mat. That's that. Not a cat. But I would continue to play with it and pull at it and say, I love you. Come to me. I love you. It might take me two or three weeks just to describe what I'm seeing now.

INTERVIEWER

How do you know when it's what you want?

ANGELOU

I know when it's the best I can do. It may not be the best there is. Another writer may do it much better. But I know when it's the best I can do. I know that one of the great arts that the writer develops is the art of saying, No. No, I'm finished. Bye. And leaving it alone. I will not write it into the ground. I will not write the life out of it. I won't do that.

INTERVIEWER

How much revising is involved?

ANGELOU

I write in the morning and then go home about midday and take a shower, because writing, as you know, is very hard work, so you have to do a double ablution. Then I go out and shop—I'm a serious cook—and pretend to be normal. I play sane—Good morning! Fine, thank you. And you? And I go home. I prepare dinner for myself and if I have houseguests, I do the candles and the pretty music and all that. Then after all the dishes are moved away I read what I wrote that morning. And more often than not if I've done nine pages I may be able to save two and a half or three. That's the cruelest time, you know, to really admit that it doesn't work. And to blue-pencil it. When I finish maybe fifty pages and read them—fifty acceptable pages—it's not too bad. I've had the same editor since 1967. Many times he has said to me over the years or asked me, Why would you use a semicolon instead of a colon? And many times over the years I have said to him things like, I will never speak to you again. Forever. Goodbye. That is it. Thank you very much. And I leave. Then I read the piece and I think of his suggestions. I send him a telegram that says, Okay, so you're right. So what? Don't ever mention this to me again. If you do, I will never speak to you again. About two years ago I was visiting him and his wife in the Hamptons. I was at the end of a dining room table with a sit-down dinner of about fourteen people. Way at the end I said to someone, I sent him telegrams over the years. From the other end of the table he said, And I've kept every one! Brute! But the editing, one's own editing, before the editor sees it, is the most important.

The five autobiographical books follow each other in chronological order. When you started writing *I Know Why the Caged Bird Sings* (1969), did you know that you would move on from that? It almost works line by line into the second volume.

I know, but I didn't really mean to. I thought I was going to write *Caged Bird* and that would be it and I would go back to playwriting and writing scripts for television. Autobiography is awfully seductive. It's wonderful. Once I got into it I realized I was following a tradition established by Frederick Douglass—the slave narrative—speaking in the first-person singular talking about the first-person plural, always saying *I* meaning *we*. And what a responsibility! Trying to work with that form, the autobiographical mode, to change it, to make it bigger, richer, finer, and more inclusive in the twentieth century has been a great challenge for me. I've written five now and I really hope—the works are required reading in many universities and colleges in the United States—that people read my work. The greatest compliment I receive is when people walk up to me on the street or in airports and say, Miss Angelou, I wrote your books last year and I really—I mean I read . . . That is it—that the person has come into the books so seriously, so completely, that he or she, black or white, male or female, feels, That's my story. I told it. I'm making it up on the spot. That's the great compliment. I didn't expect, originally, that I was going to continue with the form. I thought I was going to write a little book and it would be fine and I would go on back to poetry, write a little music.

INTERVIEWER

What about the genesis of the first book? Who were the people who helped you shape those sentences that leap off the page?

Oh, well, they started years and years before I ever wrote, when I was very young. I loved the black American minister. I loved the melody of the voice and the imagery, so rich and almost impossible. The minister in my church in Arkansas, when I was very young, would use phrases such as "God stepped out, the sun over his right shoulder, the moon nestling in the palm of his hand." I mean, I just loved it, and I loved the black poets, and I loved Shakespeare, and Edgar Allan Poe, and I liked Matthew Arnold a lot—still do. Being mute for a number of years, I read and memorized, and all those people have had tremendous influence . . . in the first book and even in the most recent book.

Mute?

I was raped when I was very young. I told my brother the name of the person who had done it. Within a few days the man was killed. In my child's mind—seven and a half years old—I thought my voice had killed him. So I stopped talking for five years. Of course I've written about this in *Caged Bird*.

When did you decide you were going to be a writer? Was there a moment when you suddenly said, This is what I wish to do for the rest of my life?

Well, I had written a television series for PBS, and I

was going out to California. I thought I was a poet and playwright. That was what I was going to do the rest of my life. Or become famous as a real-estate broker. This sounds like name-dropping, and it really is, but James Baldwin took me over to dinner with Jules and Judy Feiffer one evening. All three of them are great talkers. They went on with their stories and I had to fight for the right to play it good. I had to insert myself to tell some stories, too. Well, the next day Judy Feiffer called Bob Loomis, an editor at Random House, and suggested that if he could get me to write an autobiography, he'd have something. So he phoned me and I said, No, under no circumstances. I certainly will not do such a thing. So I went out to California to produce this series on African and black American culture. Loomis called me out there about three times. Each time I said no. Then he talked to James Baldwin. Jimmy gave him a ploy that always works with me—though I'm not proud to say that. The next time he called, he said, Well, Miss Angelou. I won't bother you again. It's just as well that you don't attempt to write this book, because to write autobiography as literature is almost impossible. I said, What are you talking about? I'll do it. I'm not proud about this button that can be pushed and I will immediately jump.

INTERVIEWER

Do you select a dominant theme for each book?

ANGELOU

I try to remember times in my life, incidents in which there was the dominating theme of cruelty, or kindness, or generosity, or envy, or happiness, glee ...

perhaps four incidents in the period I'm going to write about. Then I select the one that lends itself best to my device and that I can write as drama without falling into melodrama.

INTERVIEWER

Did you write for a particular audience?

ANGELOU

I thought early on if I could write a book for black girls it would be good because there were so few books for a black girl to read that said, This is how it is to grow up. Then, I thought, I'd better, you know, enlarge that group, the market group that I'm trying to reach. I decided to write for black boys and then white girls and then white boys.

But what I try to keep in mind mostly is my craft. That's what I really try for. I try to allow myself to be impelled by my art—if that doesn't sound too pompous and weird—accept the impulse and then try my best to have a command of the craft. If I'm feeling depressed and losing my control then I think about the reader. But that is very rare—to think about the reader when the work is going on.

INTERVIEWER

So you don't keep a particular reader in mind when you sit down in that hotel room and begin to compose or write. It's yourself.

ANGELOU

It's myself ... and my reader. I would be a liar, a hypocrite, or a fool—and I'm not any of those—to say that I don't write for the reader. I do. But for the reader who hears, who really will work at it, going behind what I seem to say. So I write for myself and that reader who will pay the dues. There's a phrase in West Africa, in Ghana, it's called deep talk. For instance, there's a saying, "The trouble for the thief is not how to steal the chief's bugle but where to blow it." Now, on the face of it, one understands that. But when you really think about it, it takes you deeper. In West Africa they call that deep talk. I'd like to think I write deep talk. When you read me, you should be able to say, Gosh, that's pretty. That's lovely. That's nice. Maybe there's something else? Better read it again. Years ago I read a man named Machado de Assis who wrote a book called *Dom Casmurro*. Machado de Assis is a South American writer—black father, Portuguese mother— writing in 1865, say. I thought the book was very nice. Then I went back and read the book and said, Hmm. I didn't realize all that was in that book. Then I read it again, and again, and I came to the conclusion that what Machado de Assis had done for me was almost a trick: he had beckoned me onto the beach to watch a sunset. And I had watched the sunset with pleasure. When I turned around to come back in I found that the tide had come in over my head. That's when I decided to write. I would write so that the reader says, That's so nice. Oh boy, that's pretty. Let me read that again. I think that's why *Caged Bird* is in its twenty-first printing in hardcover and its twenty-ninth in paper. All my books are still in print, in hardback as well as paper, because people go back and say, Let me read that. Did she really say that?

The books are episodic, aren't they? Almost as if you had put together a string of short stories. I wondered if as an autobiographer you ever fiddled with the truth to make the story better.

ANGELOU

Well, sometimes. I love the phrase *fiddle with*. It's so English. Sometimes I make a character from a composite of three or four people, because the essence in any one person is not sufficiently strong to be written about. Essentially, though, the work is true, though sometimes I fiddle with the facts. Many of the people I've written about are alive today and I have them to face. I wrote about an ex-husband—he's an African—in *The Heart of a Woman* (1981). Before I did, I called him in Dar es Salaam and said, I'm going to write about some of our years together. He said, Now before you ask, I want you to know that I shall sign my release, because I know you will not lie. However, I am sure I shall argue with you about your interpretation of the truth.

INTERVIEWER

Did he enjoy his portrait finally or did you argue about it?

ANGELOU

Well, he didn't argue, but I was kind, too.

INTERVIEWER

I would guess this would make it very easy for you to move from autobiography into novel, where you can do anything you want with your characters.

Yes, but for me, fiction is not the sweetest form. I really am trying to do something with autobiography now. It has caught me. I'm using the first-person singular and trying to make that the first-person plural, so that anybody can read the work and say, Hmm, that's the truth, yes, uh-huh, and live in the work. It's a large, ambitious dream. But I love the form.

INTERVIEWER

Aren't the extraordinary events of your life very hard for the rest of us to identify with?

ANGELOU

Oh my God, I've lived a very simple life! You can say, Oh yes, at thirteen this happened to me and at fourteen ... But those are facts. But the facts can obscure the truth, what it really felt like. Every human being has paid the earth to grow up. Most people don't grow up. It's too damn difficult. What happens is most people get older. That's the truth of it. They honor their credit cards, they find parking spaces, they marry, they have the nerve to have children, but they don't grow up. Not really. They get older. But to grow up costs the earth, the *earth*. It means you take responsibility for the time you take up, for the space you occupy. It's serious business. And you find out what it costs us to love and to lose, to dare and to fail. And, maybe even more, to succeed. What it costs, in truth. Not superficial costs—anybody can have that—I mean in truth. That's what I write. What it really is like. I'm just telling a very simple story.

Aren't you tempted to lie? Novelists lie, don't they?

ANGELOU

I don't know about lying for novelists. I look at some of the great novelists, and I think the reason they are great is that they're telling the truth. The fact is they're using made-up names, made-up people, made-up places, and made-up times, but they're telling the truth about the human being—what we are capable of, what makes us lose, laugh, weep, fall down, and gnash our teeth and wring our hands and kill each other and love each other.

INTERVIEWER

James Baldwin, along with a lot of writers in this series, said that "when you're writing, you're trying to find out something which you don't know." When you write do you search for something that you didn't know about yourself or about us?

ANGELOU

Yes. When I'm writing, I am trying to find out who I am, who we are, what we're capable of, how we feel, how we lose and stand up, and go on from darkness into darkness. I'm trying for that. But I'm also trying for the language. I'm trying to see how it can really sound. I really love language. I love it for what it does for us, how it allows us to explain the pain and the glory, the nuances and the delicacies of our existence. And then it allows us to laugh, allows us to show wit. Real wit is shown in language. We need language.

Baldwin also said that his family urged him not to become a writer. His father felt that there was a white monopoly in publishing. Did you ever have any of those feelings—that you were going up against something that was really immensely difficult for a black writer?

ANGELOU

Yes, but I didn't find it so just in writing. I've found it so in all the things I've attempted. In the shape of American society, the white male is on top, then the white female, and then the black male, and at the bottom is the black woman. So that's been always so. That is nothing new. It doesn't mean that it doesn't shock me, shake me up ...

INTERVIEWER

I can understand that in various social stratifications, but why in art?

ANGELOU

Well, unfortunately, racism is pervasive. It doesn't stop at the university gate, or at the ballet stage. I knew great black dancers, male and female, who were told early on that they were not shaped, physically, for ballet. Today, we see very few black ballet dancers. Unfortunately, in the theater and in film, racism and sexism stand at the door. I'm the first black female director in Hollywood. In order to direct, I went to Sweden and took a course in cinematography so I would understand what the camera would do. Though I had written a screenplay, and even composed the score, I wasn't allowed to direct it. They brought in a young Swedish director who hadn't even shaken a black person's hand before. The film was *Georgia, Georgia* (1972) with Diana Sands. People either loathed it or complimented me. Both were wrong, because it was not what I wanted, not what I would have done if I had been allowed to direct it. So I thought, Well, what I guess I'd better do is be ten times as prepared. That is not new. I wish it was. In every case I know I have to be ten times more prepared than my white counterpart.

INTERVIEWER

Even as a writer, where ...

ANGELOU

Absolutely.

INTERVIEWER

Yet a manuscript is what arrives at the editor's desk, not a person, not a body.

ANGELOU

Yes. I must have such control of my tools, of words, that I can make this sentence leap off the page. I have to have my writing so polished that it doesn't look polished at all. I want a reader, especially an editor, to be a half hour into my book before he realizes it's reading he's doing.

INTERVIEWER

But isn't that the goal of every person who sits down at a typewriter?

Absolutely. Yes. It's possible to be overly sensitive, to carry a bit of paranoia along with you. But I don't think that's a bad thing. It keeps you sharp, keeps you on your toes.

INTERVIEWER

Is there a thread one can see through the five autobiographies? It seems to me that one prevailing theme is the love of your child.

ANGELOU

Yes, well, that's true. I think that that's a particular. I suppose, if I'm lucky, the particular is seen in the general. There is, I hope, a thesis in my work—we may encounter many defeats, but we must not be defeated. That sounds goody-two-shoes, I know, but I believe that a diamond is the result of extreme pressure and time. Less time is crystal. Less than that is coal. Less than that is fossilized leaves. Less than that it's just plain dirt. In all my work, in the movies I write, the lyrics, the poetry, the prose, the essays, I am saying that we may encounter many defeats—maybe it's imperative that we encounter the defeats—but we are much stronger than we appear to be and maybe much better than we allow ourselves to be. Human beings are more alike than unalike. There's no real mystique. Every human being, every Jew, Christian, backslider, Muslim, Shintoist, Zen Buddhist, atheist, agnostic, every human being wants a nice place to live, a good place for the children to go to school, healthy children, somebody to love, the courage, the unmitigated gall to accept love in return, someplace to party on Saturday or Sunday night, and someplace to perpetuate that God. There's no mystique. None. And if I'm right in my work, that's what my work says.

Have you been back to Stamps, Arkansas?

About 1970, Bill Moyers, Willie Morris, and I were at some affair. Judith Moyers as well—I think she was the instigator. We may have had two or three scotches, or seven or eight. Willie Morris was then with *Harper's* magazine. The suggestion came up, Why don't we all go back South? Willie Morris was from Yazoo, Mississippi. Bill Moyers is from Marshall, Texas, which is just a hop, skip, and a jump—about as far as you can throw a chitterling—from Stamps, my hometown. Sometime in the middle of the night there was this idea—why don't Bill Moyers and Maya Angelou go to Yazoo, Mississippi, to visit Willie Morris? Then why don't Willie Morris and Maya Angelou go to Marshall, Texas, to visit Bill Moyers? I said, Great. I was agreeing with both. Then they said Willie Morris and Bill Moyers would go to Stamps, Arkansas, to visit Maya Angelou, and I said, No way, José. I'm not going back to that little town with two white men! I will not do it! Well, after a while Bill Moyers called me—he was doing a series on creativity—and he said, Maya, come on, let's go to Stamps. I said, No way. He continued, I want to talk about creativity. I said, You know, I don't want to know where it resides. I really don't, and I still don't. One of the problems in the West is that people are too busy putting things under microscopes and so forth. Creativity is greater than the sum of its parts.

All I want to know is that creativity is there. I want to know that I can put my hand behind my back like Tom Thumb and pull out a plum. Anyway, Moyers went on and on and so did Judith and before I knew it, I found myself in Stamps, Arkansas. Stamps, Arkansas! With Bill Moyers, in front of my grandmother's door. My God! We drove out of town—me with Bill and Judith. Back of us was the crew, a New York crew, you know, very "Right, dig where I'm comin' from, like, get it on," and so forth. We got about three miles outside of Stamps and I said, Stop the car. Let the car behind us pull up. Get those people in with you and I'll take their car. I suddenly was taken back to being twelve years old in a Southern, tiny town where my grandmother told me, Sistah, never be on a country road with any white boys. I was two hundred years older than black pepper, but I said, Stop the car. I did. I got out of the car. And I knew these guys—certainly Bill. Bill Moyers is a friend and brother-friend to me—we care for each other. But dragons, fears, the grotesques of childhood always must be confronted at childhood's door. Any other place is esoteric and has nothing to do with the great fear that is laid upon one as a child. So anyway, we did Bill Moyers's show. And it seems to be a very popular program, and it's the first of the creativity programs . . .

INTERVIEWER
Did going back assuage those childhood fears?

ANGELOU
They are there like griffins hanging off the sides of old and tired European buildings.

It hadn't changed?

No, worse if anything.

But it was forty years before you went back to the South, to North Carolina. Was that because of a fear of finding griffins everywhere, Stamps being a typical community of the South?

Well, I've never felt the need to prove anything to an audience. I'm always concerned about who I am to me first—to myself and God. I really am. I didn't go South because I didn't want to pull up whatever clout I had, because that's boring, that's not real, not true. That doesn't tell me anything. If I had known I was afraid, I would have gone earlier. I just thought I'd find the South really unpleasant. I have moved South now. I live there.

Perhaps writing the autobiographies, finding out about yourself, would have made it much easier to go back.

I know many think that writing sort of clears the air. It doesn't do that at all. If you are going to write autobiography, don't expect that it will clear anything up. It makes it more clear to you, but it doesn't alleviate anything. You simply know it better, you have names for people.

There's a part in *Caged Bird* where you and your brother want to do a scene from *The Merchant of Venice*, and you don't dare do it because your grandmother would find out that Shakespeare was not only deceased but white.

ANGELOU

I don't think she'd have minded if she'd known he was deceased. I tried to pacify her—my mother knew Shakespeare but my grandmother was raising us. When I told her I wanted to recite—it was actually Portia's speech—Mama said to me, Now, sistah, what are you goin' to render? The phrase was so fetching. The phrase was "Now, little mistress Marguerite will render her rendition." Mama said, "Now, sistah, what are you goin' to render?" I said, "Mama, I'm going to render a piece written by William Shakespeare." My grandmother asked me, "Now, sistah, who is this very William Shakespeare?" I had to tell her that he was white, it was going to come out. Somebody would let it out. So I told Mama, "Mama, he's white but he's dead." Then I said, "He's been dead for centuries," thinking she'd forgive him because of this little idiosyncrasy. She said, "No Ma'am, little mistress you will not. No Ma'am, little mistress you will not." So I rendered James Weldon Johnson, Paul Laurence Dunbar, Countee Cullen, Langston Hughes.

INTERVIEWER

Were books allowed in the house?

ANGELOU

None of those books were in the house. They were in the school. I'd bring them home from school, and my brother gave me Edgar Allan Poe because he knew I loved him. I loved him so much I called him EAP. But as I said, I had a problem when I was young— from the time I was seven and a half to the time I was twelve and a half I was a mute. I could speak but I didn't speak for five years and I was what was called a volunteer mute. But I read and I memorized just masses—I don't know if one is born with photographic memory but I think you can develop it. I just have that.

INTERVIEWER

What is the significance of the title *All God's Children Need Traveling Shoes* (1986)?

ANGELOU

I never agreed, even as a young person, with the Thomas Wolfe title *You Can't Go Home Again.* Instinctively I didn't. But the truth is, you can never leave home. You take it with you. It's under your fingernails, it's in the hair follicles, it's in the way you smile, it's in the ride of your hips, in the passage of your breasts. It's all there, no matter where you go. You can take on the affectations and the postures of other places and even learn to speak their ways. But the truth is, home is between your teeth. Everybody's always looking for it. Jews go to Israel, black Americans and Africans in the diaspora go to Africa, Europeans, Anglo-Saxons go to England and Ireland, people of Germanic background go to Germany. It's a very queer quest. We can kid ourselves—we can tell ourselves, Oh yes, honey, I live in Tel Aviv, actually ... The truth is a stubborn fact. So this book is about trying to go home.

INTERVIEWER

If you had to endow a writer with the most necessary pieces of equipment, other than, of course, yellow legal pads, what would these be?

ANGELOU

Ears. Ears. To hear the language. But there's no one piece of equipment that is most necessary. Courage, first.

INTERVIEWER

Did you ever feel that you could not get your work published? Would you have continued to write if Random House had returned your manuscript?

ANGELOU

I didn't think it was going to be very easy, but I knew I was going to do something. The real reason black people exist at all today is because there's a resistance to a larger society that says you can't do it—you can't survive. And if you survive, you certainly can't thrive. And if you thrive, you can't thrive with any passion or compassion or humor or style. There's a saying, a song that says, "Don't you let nobody turn you 'round, turn you 'round. Don't you let nobody turn you 'round." Well, I've always believed that. So knowing that, knowing that nobody could turn me 'round, if I didn't publish, well, I would design this theater we're sitting in. Yes. Why not? Some human being did it. I agree with Terence. Terence said, "*Homo sum: humani nihil a me alienum puto.*" I am a human being. Nothing human can be alien to me. When you look up Terence in the encyclopedia, you see beside his name, in italics, "Sold to a Roman senator, freed by that senator." He became the most popular playwright in Rome. Six of his plays and that statement have come down to us from 154 B.C. This man, not born white, not born free, without any chance of ever receiving citizenship, said, I am a human being. Nothing human can be alien to me. Well, I believe that. I ingested that, internalized that at about thirteen or twelve. I believed if I set my mind to it, maybe I wouldn't be published but I would write a great piece of music or do something about becoming a real friend. Yes, I would do something wonderful. It might be with my next-door neighbor, my gentleman friend, with my lover, but it would be wonderful as far as I could do it. So I never have been very concerned about the world telling me how successful I am. I don't need that.

INTERVIEWER

You mentioned courage ...

ANGELOU

... the most important of all the virtues. Without that virtue you can't practice any other virtue with consistency.

What do you think of white writers who have written of the black experience—Faulkner's *The Sound and the Fury* or William Styron's *Confessions of Nat Turner?*

ANGELOU

Well, sometimes I am disappointed—more often than not. That's unfair, because I'm not suggesting the writer is lying about what he or she sees. It's my disappointment, really, in that he or she doesn't see more deeply, more carefully. I enjoy seeing Peter O'Toole or Michael Caine enact the role of an upper-class person in England. There the working class has had to study the upper class, has been obliged to do so, to lift themselves out of their positions. Well, black Americans have had to study white Americans. For centuries under slavery, the smile or the grimace on a white man's face or the flow of a hand on a white woman could inform a black person that you're about to be sold or flogged. So we have studied the white American, where the white American has not been obliged to study us. So often it is as if the writer is looking through a glass darkly. And I'm always a little—not a little—saddened by that poor vision.

INTERVIEWER

And you can pick it up in an instant if you ...

ANGELOU

Yes, yes. There are some who delight and inform. It's so much better, you see, for me, when a writer like

Edna St. Vincent Millay speaks so deeply about her concern for herself and does not offer us any altruisms. Then when I look through her eyes at how she sees a black or an Asian my heart is lightened. But many of the other writers disappoint me.

INTERVIEWER

What is the best part of writing for you?

ANGELOU

Well, I could say the end. But when the language lends itself to me, when it comes and submits, when it surrenders and says, I am yours, darling—that's the best part.

INTERVIEWER

You don't skip around when you write?

ANGELOU

No, I may skip around in revision, just to see what connections I can find.

INTERVIEWER

Is most of the effort made in putting the words down onto the paper or is it in revision?

ANGELOU

Some work flows and, you know, you can catch three days. It's like ... I think the word in sailing is *scudding*—you know, three days of just scudding. Other days it's just awful—plodding and backing up, trying to take out all the *and*s, *if*s, *to*s, *for*s, *but*s, *wherefore*s, *therefore*s, *however* ... you know, all those.

And then, finally, you write "The End" and there it is—you have a little bit of sherry.

A lot of sherry then.

(1990)

Alice Munro

THE ART OF FICTION NO. 137

Interviewed by Jeanne McCulloch and Mona Simpson

There is no direct flight from New York City to Clinton, Ontario, the Canadian town of three thousand where Alice Munro lives most of the year. We left LaGuardia early on a June morning, rented a car in Toronto, and drove for three hours on roads that grew smaller and more rural. Around dusk, we pulled up to the house where Munro lives with her second husband, Gerry Fremlin. It has a deep backyard and an eccentric flower garden and is, as she explained, the house where Fremlin was born. In the kitchen, Munro was preparing a simple meal with fragrant local herbs. The dining room is lined floor to ceiling with books; on one side a small table holds a manual typewriter. It is here that Munro works.

After a while, Munro took us to Goderich, a bigger town, the county seat, where she installed us in the Bedford Hotel on the square across from the courthouse. The hotel is a nineteenth-century building with comfortable rooms (twin beds and no air-conditioning) that would seem to lodge a librarian or a frontier schoolteacher in one of Munro's stories. Over the next three days, we talked in her home, but never with the tape recorder on. We conducted the interview in our small room at the hotel, as Munro wanted to keep "the business out of the house." Both Munro and her husband grew up within twenty miles of where they now live; they knew the history of almost every building we passed, admired, or ate inside. We asked what sort of literary community was available in the immediate area. Although there is a library in Goderich, we were told the nearest good bookstore was in Stratford, some thirty miles away. When we asked whether there were any other local writers, she drove us past a ramshackle house where a man sat bare-chested on the back stoop, crouched over a typewriter, surrounded by cats. "He's out there every day," she said. "Rain or shine. I don't know him, but I'm dying of curiosity to find out what he's up to."

Our last morning in Canada, supplied with directions, we sought out the house in which Alice Munro had grown up. Her father had built the house and raised mink there. After several dead ends, we found it, a pretty brick house at the very end of a country road, facing an open field where an airplane rested, alighted temporarily it seemed. It was, from our spot, easy to imagine the glamour of the air, the pilot taking a country wife away, as in "White Dump" (1986), or the young aviation stuntsman who lands in a field like this in "How I Met My Husband" (1974).

Like the house, like the landscape of Ontario, which resembles the American Midwest, Munro is not imposing. She is gracious, with a quiet humor. She is the author of seven books of short stories, including the forthcoming *Open Secrets* (1994), and one novel, *Lives of Girls and Women* (1971); she has received the Governor General's Award (Canada's most prestigious literary prize), and is regularly featured in Best American Short Stories (Richard Ford recently included two Alice Munro stories in the volume he edited) and Prize Stories: The O. Henry Awards; she also is a regular contributor to *The New Yorker*. Despite these considerable accomplishments, Munro still speaks of writing with some of the reverence and insecurity one hears in the voices of beginners. She has none of the bravura or bluster of a famous writer, and it is easy to forget that she is one. Speaking of her own work, she makes what she does sound not exactly easy, but possible, as if anyone could do it if they only worked hard enough. As we left, we felt that contagious sense of possibility. It seems simple—but her writing has a perfect simplicity that takes years and many drafts to master. As Cynthia Ozick has said, "She is our Chekhov, and is going to outlast most of her contemporaries."

INTERVIEWER

We went back to the house where you grew up this morning. Did you live there your entire childhood?

ALICE MUNRO

Yes. When my father died, he was still living in that house on the farm, which was a fox and mink farm. It's changed a lot though. Now it's a beauty parlor called Total Indulgence. I think they have the beauty parlor in the back wing, and they've knocked down the kitchen entirely.

INTERVIEWER
Have you been inside it since then?

MUNRO

No, I haven't, but I thought if I did I'd ask to see the living room. There's the fireplace my father built and I'd like to see that. I've sometimes thought I should go in and ask for a manicure.

INTERVIEWER

We noticed a plane on the field across the road and thought of your stories "White Dump" and "How I Met My Husband."

MUNRO

Yes, that was an airport for a while. The man who owned that farm had a hobby of flying planes, and he had a little plane of his own. He never liked farming so he got out of it and became a flight instructor. He's still alive. In perfect health and one of the handsomest men I've ever known. He retired from flight instruction when he was seventy-five. Within maybe three months of retirement he went on a trip and got some odd disease you get from bats in caves.

INTERVIEWER

The stories in your first collection, *Dance of the Happy Shades* (1968), are very resonant of that area, the world of your childhood. At what point in your life were those stories written?

The writing of those stories stretched over fifteen years. "The Day of the Butterfly" (1956) was the earliest one. That was probably written when I was about twenty-one. And I can remember very well writing "Thanks for the Ride" (1957) because my first baby was lying in the crib beside me. So I was twenty-two. The really late stories were written in my thirties. "Dance of the Happy Shades" (1961) is one. "The Peace of Utrecht" (1960) is another. "Images" (1968) is the very latest. "Walker Brothers Cowboy" (1968) was also written after I was thirty. So there's a really great range.

INTERVIEWER

How do they seem to hold up now? Do you reread them?

MUNRO

There's an early one in that collection called "The Shining Houses" (1968), which I had to read at Harbourfront in Toronto two or three years ago for a special event celebrating the history of *Tamarack Review*. Since it was originally published in one of the early issues of that magazine, I had to get up and read it, and it was very hard. I think I wrote that story when I was twenty-two. I kept editing as I read, catching all the tricks I used at that time, which now seemed very dated. I was trying to fix it up fast, with my eyes darting ahead to the next paragraph as I read, because I hadn't read it ahead of time. I never do read things ahead of time. When I read an early story I can see things I wouldn't do now, things people were doing in the fifties.

Do you ever revise a story after it's been published? Apparently, before he died, Proust rewrote the first volumes of *Remembrance of Things Past.*

MUNRO

Yes, and Henry James rewrote simple, understandable stuff so it was obscure and difficult. Actually I've done it recently. The story "Carried Away" was included in *Best American Short Stories 1991.* I read it again in the anthology, because I wanted to see what it was like and I found a paragraph that I thought was really soggy. It was a very important little paragraph, maybe two sentences. I just took a pen and rewrote it up in the margin of the anthology so that I'd have it there to refer to when I published the story in book form. I've often made revisions at that stage that turned out to be mistakes because I wasn't really in the rhythm of the story anymore. I see a little bit of writing that doesn't seem to be doing as much work as it should be doing, and right at the end I will sort of rev it up. But when I finally read the story again it seems a bit obtrusive. So I'm not too sure about this sort of thing. The answer may be that one should stop this behavior. There should be a point where you say, the way you would with a child, This isn't mine anymore.

INTERVIEWER

You've mentioned that you don't show your works in progress to friends.

MUNRO

No, I don't show anything in progress to anybody.

INTERVIEWER

How much do you rely on your editors?

MUNRO

The New Yorker was really my first experience with serious editing. Previously I'd more or less just had copyediting with a few suggestions—not much. There has to be an agreement between the editor and me about the kind of thing that can happen. An editor who thought nothing happened in William Maxwell's stories, for example, would be of no use to me. There also has to be a very sharp eye for the ways that I could be deceiving myself. Chip McGrath at *The New Yorker* was my first editor, and he was so good. I was amazed that anybody could see that deeply into what I wanted to do. Sometimes we didn't do much, but occasionally he gave me a lot of direction. I rewrote one story called "The Turkey Season" (1980), which he had already bought. I thought he would simply accept the new version but he didn't. He said, Well, there are things about the new version I like better, and there are things about the old version I like better. Why don't we see? He never says anything like, We will. So we put it together and got a better story that way, I think.

INTERVIEWER

How was this accomplished? By phone or by mail? Do you ever go into *The New Yorker* and hammer it out?

MUNRO

By mail. We have a very fruitful phone relationship, but we've only seen each other a few times.

When did you first publish in *The New Yorker*?

"Royal Beatings" was my first story, and it was published in 1977. But I sent all my early stories to *The New Yorker* in the fifties, and then I stopped sending for a long time and sent only to magazines in Canada. *The New Yorker* sent me nice notes, though—penciled, informal messages. They never signed them. They weren't terribly encouraging. I still remember one of them said, The writing is very nice, but the theme is a bit overly familiar. It was, too. It was a romance between two aging people—an aging spinster who knows this is it for her when she's proposed to by an aging farmer. I had a lot of aging spinsters in my stories. It was called "The Day the Asters Bloomed." It was really awful. And I didn't write this when I was seventy—I was twenty-five. I wonder why I wrote about aging spinsters. I didn't know any.

And you married young. It's not as though you were anticipating a life as an aging spinster.

I think I knew that at heart I was an aging spinster.

Were you always writing?

Since about grade seven or eight.

Were you a serious writer by the time you went to college?

Yes. I had no chance to be anything else because I had no money. I knew I would only be at university two years because the scholarships available at that time lasted only two years. It was this little vacation in my life, a wonderful time. I had been in charge of the house at home when I was in my teens, so university was about the only time in my life that I haven't had to do housework.

Did you get married right after your two years?

I got married right after the second year. I was twenty. We went to Vancouver. That was the big thing about getting married—this huge adventure, moving. As far away as we could get and stay in the country. We were only twenty and twenty-two. We immediately set up a very proper kind of middle-class existence. We were thinking of getting a house and having a baby, and we promptly did these things. I had my first baby at twenty-one.

And you were writing all through that?

I was writing desperately all the time I was pregnant because I thought I would never be able to write afterward. Each pregnancy spurred me to get something big done before the baby was born. Actually I didn't get anything big done.

INTERVIEWER

In "Thanks for the Ride," you write from the point of view of a rather callous city boy who picks up a poor town girl for the night and sleeps with her and is alternately attracted to and revolted by the poverty of her life. It seems striking that this story came from a time when your life was so settled and proper.

MUNRO

A friend of my husband's came to visit us the summer when I was pregnant with my eldest daughter. He stayed for a month or so. He worked for the National Film Board, and he was doing a film up there. He told us a lot of stuff—we just talked the way you do, anecdotally about our lives. He told the story about being in a small town on Georgian Bay and going out with a local girl. It was the encounter of a middle-class boy with something that was quite familiar to me but not familiar to him. So I immediately identified strongly with the girl and her family and her situation, and I guess I wrote the story fairly soon afterward because my baby was looking at me from the crib.

INTERVIEWER

How old were you when that first book came out?

MUNRO

I was about thirty-six. I'd been writing these stories over the years and finally an editor at Ryerson Press, a Canadian publisher that has since been taken over by McGraw-Hill, wrote and asked me if I had enough stories for a book. Originally he was going to put me in a book with two or three other writers. That fell through, but he still had a bunch of my stories. Then he quit but passed me on to another editor, who said, If you could write three more stories, we'd have a book. And so I wrote "Images," "Walker Brothers Cowboy," and "Postcard" (1968) during the last year before the book was published.

INTERVIEWER

Did you publish those stories in magazines?

MUNRO

Most of them got into *Tamarack Review*. It was a nice little magazine, a very brave magazine. The editor said he was the only editor in Canada who knew all his readers by their first names.

INTERVIEWER

Have you ever had a specific time to write?

MUNRO

When the kids were little, my time was as soon as they left for school. So I worked very hard in those years. My husband and I owned a bookstore, and even when I was working there, I stayed at home until noon. I was supposed to be doing housework, and I would also do my writing then. Later on, when I wasn't working every day in the store, I would write until everybody came home for lunch and then after they went back, probably till about two thirty, and then I would have a quick cup of coffee and start doing the housework, trying to get it all done before late afternoon.

INTERVIEWER
What about before the girls were old enough to go to school?

MUNRO
Their naps.

INTERVIEWER
You wrote when they had naps?

MUNRO
Yes. From one to three in the afternoon. I wrote a lot of stuff that wasn't any good, but I was fairly productive. The year I wrote my second book, *Lives of Girls and Women*, I was enormously productive. I had four kids because one of the girls' friends was living with us, and I worked in the store two days a week. I used to work until maybe one o'clock in the morning and then get up at six. And I remember thinking, You know, maybe I'll die, this is terrible, I'll have a heart attack. I was only about thirty-nine or so, but I was thinking this. Then I thought, Well even if I do, I've got that many pages written now. They can see how it's going to come out. It was a kind of desperate, desperate race. I don't have that kind of energy now.

INTERVIEWER
What was the process involved in writing *Lives*?

I remember the day I started to write that. It was in January, a Sunday. I went down to the bookstore, which wasn't open Sundays, and locked myself in. My husband had said he would get dinner, so I had the afternoon. I remember looking around at all the great literature that was around me and thinking, You fool! What are you doing here? But then I went up to the office and started to write the section called "Princess Ida," which is about my mother. The material about my mother is my central material in life, and it always comes the most readily to me. If I just relax, that's what will come up. So, once I started to write that, I was off. Then I made a big mistake. I tried to make it a regular novel, an ordinary sort of childhood adolescence novel. About March I saw it wasn't working. It didn't feel right to me, and I thought I would have to abandon it. I was very depressed. Then it came to me that what I had to do was pull it apart and put it in the story form. Then I could handle it. That's when I learned that I was never going to write a real novel because I could not think that way.

INTERVIEWER
The Beggar Maid (1978), too, is a sort of a novel because it's interconnected stories.

MUNRO
I don't want to second-guess things too much, but I've often wanted to do another series of stories. In my new book, *Open Secrets*, there are characters who reappear. Bea Doud in "Vandals" (1993) is mentioned as the little girl in "Carried Away"

(1991), which is the first story I wrote for the collection. Billy Doud is the son of the librarian. They're all mentioned in "Spaceships Have Landed" (1994). But I mustn't let this sort of plan overtake the stories themselves. If I start shaping one story so it will fit with another, I am probably doing something wrong, using force on it that I oughtn't. So I don't know that I'll ever do that kind of series again, though I love the idea of it. Katherine Mansfield said something in one of her letters like, Oh, I hope I write a novel, I hope I don't die just leaving these bits and pieces. It's very hard to wean yourself away from this bits-and-pieces feeling if all you're leaving behind is scattered stories. I'm sure you could think of Chekhov and everything, but still.

INTERVIEWER

And Chekhov always wanted to write a novel. He was going to call it "Stories from the Lives of My Friends."

MUNRO

I know. And I know that feeling that you could have this achievement of having put everything into one package.

INTERVIEWER

When you start writing a story, do you already know what the story will be? Is it already plotted out?

MUNRO

Not altogether. Any story that's going to be any good is usually going to change. Right now I'm starting a story cold. I've been working on it every morning, and it's pretty slick. I don't really like it, but I think maybe, at some point, I'll be into it. Usually, I have a lot of acquaintance with the story before I start writing it. When I didn't have regular time to give to writing, stories would just be working in my head for so long that when I started to write I was deep into them. Now, I do that work by filling notebooks.

You use notebooks?

I have stacks of notebooks that contain this terribly clumsy writing, which is just getting anything down. I often wonder, when I look at these first drafts, if there was any point in doing this at all. I'm the opposite of a writer with a quick gift, you know, someone who gets it piped in. I don't grasp it very readily at all, the *it* being whatever I'm trying to do. I often get on the wrong track and have to haul myself back.

How do you realize you're on the wrong track?

I could be writing away one day and think I've done very well if I've done more pages than I usually do. Then I get up the next morning and realize I don't want to work on it anymore. When I have a terrible reluctance to go near it, when I would have to push myself to continue, I generally know that something is badly wrong. Often, in about three-quarters of what

I do, I reach a point somewhere, fairly early on, when I think I'm going to abandon this story. I get myself through a day or two of bad depression, grouching around. And I think of something else I can write. It's sort of like a love affair—you're getting out of all the disappointment and misery by going out with some new man you don't really like at all, but you haven't noticed that yet. Then, I will suddenly come up with something about the story that I abandoned. I will see how to do it. But that only seems to happen after I've said, No, this isn't going to work, forget it.

INTERVIEWER
Can you always do that?

MUNRO
Sometimes I can't, and I spend the whole day in a very bad mood. That's the only time I'm really irritable. If Gerry talks to me or keeps going in and out of the room or bangs around a lot, I am on edge and enraged. And if he sings or something like that, it's terrible. I'm trying to think something through, and I'm just running into brick walls. I'm not getting through it. Generally I'll do that for a while before I'll give it up. This whole process might take up to a week, the time of trying to think it through, trying to retrieve it, then giving it up and thinking about something else, and then getting it back, usually quite unexpectedly, when I'm in the grocery store or out for a drive. I'll think, Oh well, I have to do it from the point of view of so-and-so, and I have to cut this character out, and of course these people are not married, or whatever. The big change, which is usually the radical change.

INTERVIEWER

That makes the story work?

MUNRO

I don't even know if it makes the story better. What it does is make it possible for me to continue to write. That's what I mean by saying I don't think I have this overwhelming thing that comes in and dictates to me. I only seem to get a grasp on what I want to write about with the greatest difficulty. And barely.

INTERVIEWER

Do you often change perspective or tone?

MUNRO

Oh yes, sometimes I'm uncertain, and I will do first person to third over and over again. This is one of my major problems. I often do first person to get myself into a story and then feel that for some reason it isn't working. I'm quite vulnerable to what people tell me to do at that point. My agent didn't like the first person in "The Albanian Virgin" (1994), which I think, since I wasn't perfectly sure anyway, made me change it. But then I changed it back to first again.

INTERVIEWER

How consciously, on a thematic level, do you understand what you're doing?

MUNRO

Well, it's not very conscious. I can see the ways a story could go wrong. I see the negative things more easily than the positive things. Some stories don't work as well as others, and some stories are lighter in conception than others.

INTERVIEWER

Lighter?

MUNRO

They feel lighter to me. I don't feel a big commitment to them. I've been reading Muriel Spark's autobiography. She thinks, because she is a Christian, a Catholic, that God is the real author. And it behooves us not to try to take over that authority, not to try to write fiction that is about the meaning of life, that tries to grasp what only God can grasp. So one writes entertainments. I think this is what she says. I think I write stories sometimes that I intend as entertainments.

INTERVIEWER

Can you give an example?

MUNRO

Well, I think that "The Jack Randa Hotel" (1993), which I quite like, works as an entertainment. I want it to, anyway. Although a story like "Friend of My Youth" (1990) does not work as an entertainment. It works in some other way. It works at my deepest level.

INTERVIEWER

Do you agonize just as much over those pieces you consider entertainments as over your central material?

Yes, that's true.

Are there stories that haven't been any trouble at all
to write?

I actually wrote "Friend of My Youth" very quickly.
From an anecdote. There is a young man I know
who works in the library in Goderich and researches
things for me. He was at our house one night and he
began to talk about neighbors of his family, neighbors who lived on the next farm. They belonged to
a religion that forbade them to play card games, and
so they played crokinole, which is a board game. He
just told me about that, and then I asked him about
the family, their religion, what they were like. He
described these people and then told me about the
marriage scandal—the young man who comes along
who is a member of their church and gets engaged
to the older daughter. Then, lo and behold, the
younger sister was pregnant so the marriage has to
be switched. And they go on all living together in the
same house. The stuff about fixing the house, painting it over is all true, too. The couple painted their
half, and the older sister didn't—half the house got
painted.

Was there really a nurse?

No, the nurse I invented, but I was given the name.

We had a fund-raising event at the Blyth Theatre, about ten miles away from here. Everybody contributed something to be auctioned off to raise money, and somebody came up with the idea that I could auction off the right to have the successful bidder's name used for a character in my next story. A woman from Toronto paid four hundred dollars to be a character. Her name was Audrey Atkinson. I suddenly thought, That's the nurse! I never heard from her. I hope she didn't mind.

INTERVIEWER

What was the inception of that story?

MUNRO

When I started to write the story we were on one of our trips from Ontario to British Columbia. We drive out every year in fall and drive back in spring. So I wasn't writing, but I was thinking about this family in the motels at night. Then the whole story of my mother closed around it, and then me telling the story closed around my mother, and I saw what it was about. I would say that story came easily. I didn't have any difficulty. I've done the character of my mother so often, and my feelings toward her, I didn't have to look for those.

INTERVIEWER

You have several mothers in your work. That particular mother appears in other stories, and she seems very real. But so does Flo, Rose's stepmother in "The Beggar Maid."

But Flo wasn't a real person. She was someone very like people I've known, but she was one of these composite characters that writers talk about. I think Flo was a force because I wrote that story when I had just come back to live here after being away for twenty-three years. The whole culture here hit me with a tremendous bang. I felt that the world I had been using, the world of my childhood, was a glazed-over world of memory once I came back and confronted the real thing. Flo was an embodiment of the real thing, so much harsher than I had remembered.

INTERVIEWER

You obviously travel a great deal, but your work seems fundamentally informed by a rural sensibility. Do you find that stories you hear around here are more resonant for you, or did you use just as much material from your life when you lived in cities?

MUNRO

When you live in a small town you hear more things, about all sorts of people. In a city you mainly hear stories about your own sort of people. If you're a woman there's always a lot from your friends. I got "Differently" (1989) from my life in Victoria, and a lot of "White Dump." I got the story "Fits" (1986) from a real and terrible incident that happened here—the murder-suicide of a couple in their sixties. In a city, I would only have read about it in the paper. I wouldn't have picked up all the threads.

Is it easier for you to invent things or to do composites?

I'm doing less personal writing now than I used to, for a very simple obvious reason. You use up your childhood, unless you're able, like William Maxwell, to keep going back and finding wonderful new levels in it. The deep, personal material of the latter half of your life is your children. You can write about your parents when they're gone, but your children are still going to be here, and you're going to want them to come and visit you in the nursing home. Maybe it's advisable to move on to writing those stories that are more observation.

Unlike your family stories, a number of your stories could be called historical. Do you ever go looking for this kind of material, or do you just wait for it to turn up?

I never have a problem with finding material. I wait for it to turn up, and it always turns up. It's dealing with the material I'm inundated with that poses the problem. For the historical pieces I have had to search out a lot of facts. I knew for years that I wanted to write a story about one of the Victorian lady writers, one of the authoresses of this area. Only I couldn't find quite the verse I wanted—all of it was so bad that it was ludicrous. I wanted to have it a little better than that. So I wrote it. When I was writing that story I looked in a lot of old newspapers, the kind of stuff my husband has around—he does historical research about Huron County, our part of Ontario. He's a retired geographer. I got very strong images of the town, which I call Walley. I got very strong images from newspaper clippings. Then, when I needed specific stuff, I'd sometimes get the man at the library to do it for me. To find out things about old cars or something like that, or the Presbyterian Church in the 1850s. He's wonderful. He loves doing it.

INTERVIEWER

What about those aunts, the wonderful aunts who appear?

MUNRO

My great-aunt and my grandmother were very important in our lives. After all, my family lived on this collapsing enterprise of a fox and mink farm, just beyond the most disreputable part of town, and they lived in real town, in a nice house, and they kept up civilization. So there was always tension between their house and ours, but it was very important that I had that. I loved it when I was a little girl. Then, when I was an adolescent, I felt rather burdened by it. My mother was not in the role of the lead female in my life by that time, though she was an enormously important person. She wasn't there as the person who set the standards anymore. So these older women moved into that role, and though they didn't set any standards that I was at all interested in, there was a constant tension there that was important to me.

Then you didn't actually move into town as the mother and daughter do in "Lives of Girls and Women" (1971)?

MUNRO

We did for one winter. My mother decided she wanted to rent a house in town for one winter, and she did. And she gave the ladies' luncheon party, she tried to break into society, which was totally impenetrable to her. She couldn't do it. There was just no understanding there. I do remember coming back to the farmhouse that had been occupied by men, my father and my brother, and you couldn't see the pattern on the linoleum anymore. It seemed as if mud had flowed into the house.

INTERVIEWER

Is there a story you like that others don't? Are there any stories your husband doesn't like, for instance?

MUNRO

I liked "The Moon in the Orange Street Skating Rink" (1986) a lot, but Gerry didn't like that story. It was from anecdotes he'd told me about his childhood, so I think he expected them to come out quite differently. Because I thought he would like it, I didn't have qualms. And then he said, Well, not one of your best. That's the only time we ever had trouble about anything I wrote. Since then he's been really careful about not reading something until I'm away, and then if he likes it he will mention it, but maybe he won't mention it at all. I think that's the way you have to manage in a marriage.

Gerry's from here, less than twenty miles from where you grew up. Are his anecdotes and his memories more useful to you than those of Jim, your first husband?

MUNRO

No, Jim was from near Toronto. But he was from a very different background. He lived in a sort of upper-middle-class commuter town where most of the men worked in Toronto and were professional. Cheever wrote about towns like that around New York. I'd never known people of this class before, so the way they thought about things was interesting as hell, but it wasn't anecdotal. I guess I was too hostile for a long time to appreciate it. I was more left-wing then. Whereas the things that Gerry tells me are further extensions of all the stuff I remember from growing up—though there's an entire difference between a boy's life in town and a girl's life on the farm. The greatest part of Gerry's life was probably between the ages of seven and fourteen, when the boys roamed the town in gangs. They weren't delinquents or anything, but they did more or less as they pleased, like a subculture within the town. Girls were not part of that, I don't think ever. We were always in little knots of girlfriends, we just didn't have the freedom. So it was interesting to learn all this.

INTERVIEWER

How long did you live outside of this region?

I got married the end of 1951, went to live in Vancouver, and stayed there until 1963, and then we moved to Victoria, where we started our bookstore, Munro's. And I came back, I think it would be, in the summer of 1973. So I had only been ten years in Victoria. I was married for twenty years.

Did you move back east because you met Gerry, or for work?

For work. And also because I had been living with my first husband in Victoria for ten years. The marriage was unraveling for a year or two. It's a small city. You have a circle of friends who all know each other, and it seems to me that if a marriage is breaking up, it's very hard to stay in the same environment. I thought it would be better for us, and he couldn't leave because he had the bookstore. I got an offer of a job teaching creative writing at York University outside of Toronto. But I didn't last at that job at all. I hated it, and even though I had no money, I quit.

Because you didn't like teaching fiction?

No! It was terrible. This was 1973. York was one of the more radical Canadian universities, yet my class was all male except for one girl who hardly got to speak. They were doing what was fashionable at the time, which had to do with being both incomprehensible and trite. They seemed intolerant of anything else. It was good for me to learn to shout back and express some ideas about writing that I hadn't sharpened up before, but I didn't know how to reach them, how not to be an adversary. Maybe I'd know now. But it didn't seem to have anything to do with writing—more like good training for going into television or something, getting really comfortable with clichés. I should have been able to change that, but I couldn't. I had one student who wasn't in the class, who brought me a story. I remember tears came into my eyes because it was so good, because I hadn't seen a good piece of student writing in so long. She asked, How can I get into your class? And I said, Don't! Don't come near my class, just keep bringing me your work. And she has become a writer. The only one who did.

INTERVIEWER

Has there been a proliferation of creative-writing schools in Canada as in the United States?

MUNRO

Maybe not quite as much. We don't have anything up here like Iowa. But careers are made by teaching in writing departments. For a while I felt sorry for these people because they weren't getting published. The fact that they were making three times as much money as I would ever see didn't quite get through to me.

INTERVIEWER

It seems the vast majority of your stories are based in

Ontario. Would you choose to live here now, or was it circumstance?

Now that I've been here I would choose to. It was Gerry's mother's house, and he was living there to take care of her. And my father and my stepmother lived in the region, too. We felt that there was a limited period of time when we would be at the service of these old people, and then we would move on. Then, of course, for various reasons, that didn't happen. They've been gone a long time, and we're still here. One of the reasons to stay now is that the landscape is so important to both of us. It's a great thing that we have in common. And thanks to Gerry, I appreciate it in such a different way. I couldn't possess any other landscape or country or lake or town in this way. And I realize that now, so I'll never leave.

INTERVIEWER

How did you meet Gerry?

MUNRO

I had known Gerry when we were in university together. He was a senior, and I was a freshman. He was a returned World War II veteran, which meant that there were seven years between us. I had a terrific crush on him when I was eighteen, but he did not notice me at all. He was noticing other people. It was a small university so you sort of knew everybody and who they were. And he was one of that small group of people who seemed—I think we called them bohemian, when they still said *bohemian*.

They wrote poetry for the literary magazine, and they were dangerous, got drunk and so on. I thought he was connected with the magazine, and when I wrote my first story, part of my plan was that I would take this manuscript to him. Then we would fall into conversation, and he would fall in love with me, and everything would go on from there. I took the story to him, and he said, John Cairns is the editor, he's down the hall. That was our only exchange.

That was your only exchange all through your years in college?

Yes. But then, after I had published the story, he had left university. I was working as a waitress between my first and second years, I got a letter from Gerry. It was really a wonderful letter all about the story. It was my first fan letter. But it wasn't about me at all, and it didn't mention my beauty, or that it would be nice for us to get together or any of that. It was simply a literary appreciation. So that I appreciated it less than I might have if it had been from anybody else because I was hoping that it would be more. But it was a nice letter. Then, after I moved back to London and had the job at Western, he somehow heard me on the radio. I did an interview. I must have said where I was living and given the impression that I was not married anymore, because he then came to see me.

And this was twenty-some odd years later?

Easily. More than twenty years later, and we hadn't seen each other in the meantime. He didn't look at all as I'd expected. He just called me up and said, This is Gerry Fremlin. I'm in Clinton, and I was wondering if we could have lunch together sometime. I knew his home was in Clinton and I thought he had probably come home to see his parents. I think by this time I knew that he was working in Ottawa, I'd heard that from somebody. And I thought the wife and children were back in Ottawa, and he's home to visit his parents and he thought he'd like to have lunch with an old acquaintance. So this is what I expected until he turned up and I learned that he was living in Clinton and there was no wife and no children. We went to the faculty club and had three martinis each, at lunch. I think we were nervous. But we rapidly became very well acquainted. I think we were talking about living together by the end of the afternoon. It was very quick. I guess I finished out that term teaching at Western and then came up to Clinton, and we started living together there in the home where he had moved back to look after his mother.

You hadn't made the decision to come back here for writing.

I never made a decision with any thought of my writing. And yet I never thought that I would abandon it. I guess because I didn't understand that you could have conditions for writing that would be any better than any other conditions. The only things that ever stopped me writing were the jobs—when I was defined publicly as a writer and given an office to work in.

INTERVIEWER

That seems reminiscent of your early story "The Office" (1962), about the woman who rents an office in order to write and is so distracted by her landlord she eventually has to move out.

MUNRO

That was written because of a real experience. I did get an office, and I wasn't able to write anything there at all—except that story. The landlord did bug me all the time, but even when he stopped I couldn't work. This has happened anytime I've had a setup for writing, an office. When I worked as writer in residence at the University of Queensland in Australia, I had an office there, in the English department, a really posh, nice office. Nobody had heard of me, so nobody came to see me. Nobody was trying to be a writer there anyway. It was like Florida—they went around in bikinis all the time. So I had all this time, and I was in this office, and I would just sit there thinking. I couldn't reach anything. I meant to, but it was paralyzing.

INTERVIEWER

Was Vancouver less useful for material?

MUNRO

I lived in the suburbs, first in North Vancouver, then in West Vancouver. In North Vancouver, the men all went away in the morning and came back at night, all day it was housewives and children. There was a lot of informal togetherness, and it was hard to be alone. There was a lot of competitive talk about vacuuming and washing the woollies, and I got quite frantic. When I had only one child, I'd put her in the stroller and walk for miles to avoid the coffee parties. This was much more narrow and crushing than the culture I grew up in. So many things were forbidden—like taking anything seriously. Life was very tightly managed as a series of permitted recreations, permitted opinions, and permitted ways of being a woman. The only outlet, I thought, was flirting with other people's husbands at parties. That was really the only time anything came up that you could feel was real, because the only contact you could have with men, that had any reality to it, seemed to me to be sexual. Otherwise, men usually didn't talk to you, or if they did they talked very much from high to low. I'd meet a university professor or someone, and if I knew something about what he knew, that would not be considered acceptable conversation. The men didn't like you to talk, and the women didn't like it either. So the world you had was female talk about the best kind of diet, or the best care of woollies. I was with the wives of the climbing men. I hated it so much I've never been able to write about it. Then in West Vancouver, it was more of a mixed suburb, not all young couples, and I made great friends there. We talked about books and scandal and laughed at everything like high school girls. That's something I'd like to write about and haven't, that subversive society of young women, all keeping each other alive. But going to Victoria and opening a bookstore was the most wonderful thing that ever happened. It was great because all the crazy people in town came into the bookstore and talked to us.

INTERVIEWER

How did you get the idea to start the bookstore?

MUNRO

Jim wanted to leave Eatons, the big department store in town. We were talking about how he wanted to go into business of some kind, and I said, Look, if we had a bookstore I could help. Everybody thought that we would go broke, and, of course, we almost did. We were very poor, but at that time my two older girls were both in school, so I could work all the time in the store, and I did. That was the happiest period in my first marriage.

INTERVIEWER

Did you always have the sense that the marriage wouldn't last?

MUNRO

I was like a Victorian daughter. The pressure to marry was so great, one felt it was something to get out of the way—Well, I'll get that done, and they can't bug me about it, and then I'll be a real person and my life will begin. I think I married to be able to write, to settle down and give my attention back to the important thing. Sometimes now when I look back at those early years I think, This was a hard-hearted young woman. I'm a far more conventional woman now than I was then.

Doesn't any young artist, on some level, have to be hard-hearted?

It's worse if you're a woman. I want to keep ringing up my children and saying, Are you sure you're all right? I didn't mean to be such a ... Which of course would make them furious because it implies that they're some kind of damaged goods. Some part of me was absent for those children, and children detect things like that. Not that I neglected them, but I wasn't wholly absorbed. When my oldest daughter was about two, she'd come to where I was sitting at the typewriter, and I would bat her away with one hand and type with the other. I've told her that. This was bad because it made her the adversary to what was most important to me. I feel I've done everything backward—this totally driven writer at the time when the kids were little and desperately needed me. And now, when they don't need me at all, I love them so much. I moon around the house and think, There used to be a lot more family dinners.

You won the Governor General's Award for your first book, which is roughly equivalent to the Pulitzer Prize in our country. It happens only very rarely in the States that a first book wins such a big prize. When it does, the writer's career often seems to suffer afterward.

Well, I wasn't young, for one thing. But it was difficult. I had about a year when I couldn't write anything because I was so busy thinking I had to get to work on a novel. I didn't have the burden of having produced a huge best seller that everyone was talking about, as Amy Tan did with her first book, for instance. The book sold very badly, and nobody—even though it had won the Governor General's Award—nobody had heard of it. You would go into bookstores and ask for it, and they didn't have it.

INTERVIEWER

Do reviews matter much to you? Do you feel you've ever learned from them? Have you ever been hurt by them?

MUNRO

Yes and no, because really you can't learn much from reviews, but you can nevertheless be very hurt. There's a feeling of public humiliation about a bad review. Even though it doesn't really matter to you, you would rather be clapped than booed offstage.

INTERVIEWER

Were you a big reader growing up? What work if any had an influence?

MUNRO

Reading was my life really until I was thirty. I was living in books. The writers of the American South were the first writers who really moved me because they showed me that you could write about small towns, rural people, and that kind of life I knew very well. But the thing about the Southern writers that interested me, without my being really aware of it, was that all the Southern writers whom I really loved were women. I didn't really like Faulkner that much. I loved Eudora Welty, Flannery O'Connor, Katherine Anne Porter, Carson McCullers. There was a feeling that women could write about the freakish, the marginal.

INTERVIEWER
Which you've always done as well.

MUNRO
Yes. I came to feel that was our territory, whereas the mainstream big novel about real life was men's territory. I don't know how I got that feeling of being on the margins, it wasn't that I was pushed there. Maybe it was because I grew up on a margin. I knew there was something about the great writers I felt shut out from, but I didn't know quite what it was. I was terribly disturbed when I first read D. H. Lawrence. I was often disturbed by writers' views of female sexuality.

INTERVIEWER
Can you put your finger on what it was that disturbed you?

MUNRO
It was, How I can be a writer when I'm the object of other writers?

What is your reaction to magic realism?

I did love *One Hundred Years of Solitude*. I loved it, but it can't be imitated. It looks easy but it's not. It's wonderful when the ants carry off the baby, when the virgin rises into the sky, when the patriarch dies, and it rains flowers. But just as hard to pull off and just as wonderful is William Maxwell's *So Long, See You Tomorrow*, where the dog is the character. He's dealing with a subject that potentially is so banal and makes it brilliant.

Some of your newer stories seem to mark a change in direction.

About five years ago, when I was still working on the stories that were in *Friend of My Youth*, I wanted to do a story with alternate realities. I resisted this because I worried it would end up as *Twilight Zone* kind of stuff. You know, really junky stuff. I was scared of it. But I wrote "Carried Away," and I just kept fooling around with it and wrote that weird ending. Maybe it's something to do with age. Changing your perceptions of what is possible, of what has happened—not just what can happen but what really has happened. I have all these disconnected realities in my own life, and I see them in other people's lives. That was one of the problems—why I couldn't write novels, I never saw things hanging together any too well.

What about your confidence? Has that changed over the years?

In writing, I've always had a lot of confidence, mixed with a dread that this confidence is entirely misplaced. I think in a way that my confidence came just from being dumb. Because I lived so out of any mainstream, I didn't realize that women didn't become writers as readily as men, and that neither did people from a lower class. If you know you can write fairly well in a town where you've hardly met anyone else who reads, you obviously think this is a rare gift indeed.

You've been a master at steering clear of the literary world. Has this been conscious or largely circumstantial?

It certainly was circumstantial for a long time, but then became a matter of choice. I think I'm a friendly person who is not very sociable. Mainly because of being a woman, a housewife, and a mother, I want to keep a lot of time. It translates as being scared of it. I would have lost my confidence. I would have heard too much talk I didn't understand.

So you were glad to be out of the mainstream?

This is maybe what I'm trying to say. I probably wouldn't have survived very well otherwise. It may have been that I would lose my confidence when I was with people who understood a lot more than I did about what they were doing. And talked a lot about it. And were confident in a way that would be acknowledged to have a more solid basis than mine. But then, it's very hard to tell about writers—who is confident?

INTERVIEWER

Was the community you grew up in pleased about your career?

MUNRO

It was known there had been stories published here and there, but my writing wasn't fancy. It didn't go over well in my hometown. The sex, the bad language, the incomprehensibility... The local newspaper printed an editorial about me, "A soured introspective view of life... And, A warped personality projected on..." My dad was already dead when they did that. They wouldn't do it while Dad was alive, because everyone really liked him. He was so liked and respected that everybody muted it a bit. But after he died, it was different.

INTERVIEWER

But he liked your work?

MUNRO

But he liked my work, yes, and he was very proud of it. He read a lot, but he always felt a bit embarrassed about reading. And then he wrote a book just before he died that was published post-humously. It was a novel about pioneer families in the southwest interior, set in a period just before his life, ending when he was a child. He had real gifts as a writer.

Can you quote us a passage?

In one chapter he describes what the school was like for a boy who lived a little earlier than he did—"On other walls were some faded brown maps. Interesting places like Mongolia were shown, where scattered residents rode in sheepskin coats on small ponies. The center of Africa was a blank space marked only by crocodiles with mouths agape and lions who held dark people down with huge paws. In the very center Mr. Stanley was greeting Mr. Livingston, both wearing old hats."

Did you recognize anything of your own life in his novel?

Not of my life, but I recognized a great deal of my style. The angle of vision, which didn't surprise me because I knew we had that in common.

Had your mother read any of your work before she died?

My mother would not have liked it. I don't think so—the sex and the bad words. If she had been well, I would have had to have a big fight and break with the family in order to publish anything.

Do you think you would have done it?

I think so, yes, because as I said I was more hard-hearted then. The tenderness I feel now for my mother, I didn't feel for a long time. I don't know how I would feel if one of my daughters wrote about me. They're about at the age now where they should be coming out with a first novel that is all about childhood. It must be a dreadful experience to go through, becoming a character in your kid's novel. People write carelessly wounding things in reviews like, oh, that my father was a seedy fox farmer, and things like this, reflecting on the poverty. A feminist writer interpreted "My Father" (1971), in *Lives of Girls and Women*, as straight autobiographical representation. She made me into someone who came out of this miserable background, because I had a "feckless father." This was an academic at a Canadian university, and I was so mad, I tried to find out how to sue her. I was furious. I didn't know what to do because I thought, It doesn't matter for me, I've had all this success, but all my father had was that he was my father. He's dead now. Is he going to be known as a feckless father because of what I did to him? Then I realized she represented a younger generation of people who had grown up on a totally different economic planet. They live in a welfare state to a certain extent—Medicare. They're not aware of the devastation something like illness could cause to a family. They've never gone through any kind of real financial trouble. They look at a family that's poor and they think this is some kind of choice. Not wanting to better yourself is fecklessness, it's stupidity or something. I grew up in a house that had no indoor toilet, and this to this generation is so appalling, truly squalid. Actually it wasn't squalid. It was fascinating.

INTERVIEWER

We didn't ask you questions about your writing day. How many days a week do you actually write?

MUNRO

I write every morning, seven days a week. I write starting about eight o'clock and finish up around eleven. Then I do other things the rest of the day, unless I do my final draft or something that I want to keep working on, then I'll work all day with little breaks.

INTERVIEWER

Are you rigid about that schedule, even if there's a wedding or some other required event?

MUNRO

I am so compulsive that I have a quota of pages. If I know that I am going somewhere on a certain day, I will try to get those extra pages done ahead of time. That's so compulsive, it's awful. But I don't get too far behind, it's as if I could lose it somehow. This is something about aging. People get compulsive about things like this. I'm also compulsive now about how much I walk every day.

INTERVIEWER

How much do you walk?

MUNRO

Three miles every day, so if I know I'm going to miss a day, I have to make it up. I watched my father go through this same thing. You protect yourself by thinking if you have all these rituals and routines then nothing can get you.

INTERVIEWER

After you've spent five months or so completing a story, do you take time off?

MUNRO

I go pretty much right into the next one. I didn't use to when I had the children and more responsibilities, but these days I'm a little panicked at the idea of stopping—as if, if I stopped, I could be stopped for good. I have a backlog of ideas. But it isn't just ideas you need, and it isn't just technique or skill. There's a kind of excitement and faith that I can't work without. There was a time when I never lost that, when it was just inexhaustible. Now I have a little shift sometimes when I feel what it would be like to lose it, and I can't even describe what *it* is. I think it's being totally alive to what this story is. It doesn't even have an awful lot to do with whether the story will work or not. What happens in old age can be just a draining away of interest in some way that you don't foresee, because this happens with people who may have had a lot of interest and commitment to life. It's something about the living for the next meal. When you travel you see a lot of this in the faces of middle-aged people in restaurants, people my age—at the end of middle age and the beginning of old age. You see this, or you feel it like a snail, this sort of chuckling along looking at the sights. It's a feeling that the capacity for responding to things is being shut off in some way. I feel now that this is a possibility. I feel it like the possibility that you might get arthritis, so you exercise so you won't. Now I am more conscious of the possibility that everything could be lost, that you could lose what had filled your life before. Maybe keeping on, going through the motions, is actually what you have to do to keep this from happening. There are parts of a story where the story fails. That's not what I'm talking about. The story fails but your faith in the importance of doing the story doesn't fail. That it might is the danger. This may be the beast that's lurking in the closet in old age—the loss of the feeling that things are worth doing.

INTERVIEWER

One wonders though, because artists do seem to work to the very end.

MUNRO

I think it's possible that you do. You may have to be a little more vigilant. It's something I never would have been able to think of losing twenty years ago—the faith, the desire. I suppose it's like when you don't fall in love anymore. But you can put up with that because falling in love has not really been as necessary as something like this. I guess that's why I keep doing it. Yes, I don't stop for a day. It's like my walk every day. My body loses tone now in a week if I don't exercise. The vigilance has to be there all the time. Of course it wouldn't matter if you did give up writing. It's not the giving up of the writing that I fear. It's the giving up of this excitement or whatever it is that you feel that makes you write. This is what I wonder—What do most people do once the necessity of working all the time is removed? Even the retired people who take courses and have hobbies are looking for something to fill this void, and I feel such horror of being like that and having that kind of life. The only thing that I've ever had to fill my life has been writing. So I haven't learned how to live a life with a lot of diversity. The only other life I can imagine is a scholarly life, which I probably idealize.

INTERVIEWER

They are very different lives, too, the life of a single pursuit as opposed to the serial.

MUNRO

You go and play golf and you enjoy that, and then you garden, and then you have people in to dinner. But I sometimes think, What if writing stops? What if it just peters out? Well, then I would have to start learning about something. You can't go from writing fiction to writing nonfiction, I don't think. Writing nonfiction is so hard on its own that it would be learning a whole new thing to do, but maybe I would try to do that. I've made a couple of attempts to plan a book, the sort of book everybody's writing about their family. But I haven't got any framework for it, any center.

What about the essay "Working for a Living" (1981), which appears in *A Grand Street Reader*? That reads like a memoir.

MUNRO

Yes. I'd like to do a book of essays and include it.

INTERVIEWER

Well, William Maxwell wrote about his family in that way in *Ancestors*.

MUNRO

I love that book, yes. I asked him about it. He had a lot of material to draw on. He did the thing you have to do, which is to latch the family history onto something larger that was happening at the time— in his case, the whole religious revival of the early nineteenth century, which I didn't know anything about. I didn't know that America had been practically a godless country, and that suddenly all over the country people had started falling down in fits. That was wonderful. If you get something like that, then you've got the book. It would take a while. I keep thinking I'm going to do something like this, and then I get the idea for one more story, and that one more story always seems so infinitely more important, even though it's only a story, than the other work. I read that interview in *The New Yorker* with William Trevor, when he said something like,

And then another little story comes along and that solves how life has got to be.

(1994)

Jeanette Winterson

THE ART OF FICTION NO. 150

Interviewed by Audrey Bilger

I cannot recall a time when I did not know I was special," writes Jeanette Winterson at the beginning of her fictionalized autobiography *Oranges Are Not the Only Fruit* (1985). And, indeed, the facts of her life have supported that view. Born in Manchester in 1959, Winterson was adopted by Pentecostal evangelist Constance Brownrigg and her husband, John William Winterson, a factory worker. From her earliest years she was groomed by her mother and church to be a missionary, and her first forays into the world of letters were the sermons she began preaching at the age of eight. Her awareness of herself as different from others was heightened when she attended Accrington Girls' Grammar School, a place that her mother dubbed the "breeding ground" because it put young Jeanette in contact with the ordinary girls of the industrial Midlands, who were more interested in embroidering platitudes on samplers than in saving souls at tent meetings.

At fifteen, Winterson had a love affair with a woman that was discovered and condemned by her church, leading to her expulsion from the community and to her leaving home to support herself. Working variously as an ice-cream van driver, a funeral parlor makeup artist, and a domestic worker in a mental institution, she studied at Accrington College of Further Education and then went on to obtain her B.A. in English from St. Catherine's College at Oxford in 1981.

Between 1981 and 1987, Winterson worked at the Roundhouse Theatre in London and then in publishing. During that time she wrote her first book, *Oranges Are Not the Only Fruit*, a semiautobiographical account of coming of age as a lesbian and a writer, interwoven with elements of the mythical and the fantastic. *Oranges* earned her the Whitbread Award for a first novel, and in 1990, when Winterson adapted it for television, the series won a number of international awards, including BAFTA Best Drama and the Prix Italia. In 1985, she also published *Boating for Beginners*, a light revisionist romp through the Book of Genesis that she now categorizes as a "comic book."

In 1987, with the publication of *The Passion*, Winterson began to support herself as a full-time writer. *The Passion*, an intricate tale, loosely set in the Napoleonic era, garnered the John Llewelyn Rhys Memorial Prize. The reiterated phrase of Henri, one of the two narrators, crystallizes Winterson's vision of the indissolubility of fact and fiction: "I'm telling you stories. Trust me."

Sexing the Cherry (1989), with its time-transcending characters and fairy-tale magic, won the E. M. Forster Award from the American Academy of Arts and Letters. *Written on the Body* (1992) challenged readers' traditional assumptions about gender and identity by refusing to categorize the narrator as male or female.

Winterson's experimentalism as a novelist has continued in *Art and Lies* (1994) and, most recently, in *Gut Symmetries* (1997). In 1995, she published *Art Objects*, a collection of essays—part art criticism, part manifesto—in which she applauds risk-taking as a measure of greatness: "The riskiness of Art, the reason why it affects us, is not the riskiness of its subject matter, it is the risk of creating a new way of seeing, a new way of thinking." According to Winterson, "The rebellion of art is a daily rebellion against the state of living death routinely called real life."

This interview took place on a brisk autumn London day in an editor's office at *Granta*. Over the course of several hours, Winterson responded to questions with unflagging intensity and polish. Her speaking presence conveys the kind of quiet magnetism that would no doubt have led to spectacular conversions had she pursued a missionary path.

INTERVIEWER

Why did you leave London?

JEANETTE WINTERSON

I didn't want to live there anymore. It became untenable for me in all sorts of ways. After having two very bad experiences with the press, both with *Written on the Body* and *Art and Lies*, I just didn't want to be in the fishbowl. I thought, I want to get away from here because it's not going to do me or my work any good to stay. So I went and hid myself in the woods.

But that doesn't mean that I don't have a very powerful relationship with this city. I have just bought myself a mad, derelict, fallen-down Georgian house in one of the older parts of London, because I need to return here, and, like Dickens, I love to walk the streets in the night and see what is happening, see what's going on. So in me there is that tension between needing the space and peace and also wanting to be where humanity is concentrated at its worst and its best.

INTERVIEWER

What happened with the press to make you feel so exposed in London? Did it have to do with reviewers?

WINTERSON

I don't read reviews. I stopped reading them after *Sexing the Cherry* because I thought there was really no point. I don't have to sit down and listen to these ravings or even these praises, because there are very few people actually reviewing now whose authority I respect or who I think have got anything to say. I take the Ezra Pound view that you shouldn't take any notice at all of anybody who has not written a significant work themselves. Then, what they have got to say is worthwhile whether you like it or not. If they haven't, it isn't. So that's my view. And I stick with it. But at the time I got fed up with being continually thrashed to bits and having my personal life exposed in ways that were vicious and designed to destroy. I thought, I don't have to stand here any longer. I can go. Which I did. That made me feel a lot better.

INTERVIEWER

Do you see yourself as a recluse now?

WINTERSON

Well, I always was, which is a bit bizarre living in London, because I never go anywhere except silently, secretly, by myself. I like to go up and down anonymously. I don't like to be known or recognized, and so living in London was a little bit absurd. I wanted it for the culture. My house was very conspicuous, and there was at one time a lot of envy—who is she and why should she have it? And there was a notorious made-up interview where someone pretended they had been in my house, and in fact they had just been looking through the window. I can't live with that! So I decided that I didn't want to be looked at any longer.

Now I have my little house hidden away in the woods, and a little house here, which I am rebuilding, and I shall come and go secretly between the two, and that will suit me very well.

INTERVIEWER

It's not surprising that you want to retain some contact with London since cities play such an important role in your works.

WINTERSON

I am interested in the tension between the built environment and the natural environment and how the two can coexist, given that they have to coexist, and how at the moment our dreams of bliss are a kind of invented Arcadia. Everyone wants to escape to the hills and leave behind the swarming cities, which are disease and crime. Clearly, this is just as crazy as everyone wanting to leave the hills and rush to the cities to get jobs. It's as though people are always uneasy in the place where they are and think that the extreme alternative will provide the solutions. But we know that there aren't any. I like to focus on the nightmare city so people don't become too used to it, too happy to live with it.

INTERVIEWER
Do you take part at all in a community of writers?

WINTERSON
I am more on my own. Obviously I know writers. Kathy Acker is a very close friend. But I'm not clubbable, you see. I don't like literary parties and literary gatherings and literary identities. I'd hate to join anything, however loosely. Remember, I come at it from the outside in every sense because, whatever people say, working-class women don't get on in this job. If they do, where are they? People come at me with a very middle-class consciousness. They look at me and they think, Well, she went to Oxford, she has obviously done all right. So they put me in their own pigeonholes. But they can't understand what it means to come from a house with no books and no bathroom and your father a factory worker, not being in school much because you're traveling around in a gospel tent. No encouragement and no education, because it's not important, especially not for girls, and having to choose to leave home in order to carry on. And not getting any money to go to university with, and having to work all the way through. I mean, people do that now, but they didn't when I was there. So,

there was nothing anticipated about me or for me. What I did was unusual. That's why, I think, from the start I felt on the outside, and to a large extent, I have remained so. I wouldn't change that because I think my temperament and my character are pretty solitary. I view with suspicion any insider activities. I suppose I am a bit of an anarchist at heart.

In spite of your emphasis on your own working-class roots, your books are not particularly marked by class.

No, they're not. I'm not interested in it. I know it exists, and I know what I am, and I know that to some extent that never changes. I think if you're British, you view the class system perhaps rather differently than if you are not. Because you have always known it. It's not that it isn't a problem, it's not that it isn't something that I want to deal with, but it is not something that is useful to me in my fiction. It's why I use an archetype. My characters all have something of the hero archetype about them, in that they are largely stripped of context. But they offer a kind of operatic salvation, for themselves and for the reader, in that through their lives one's own struggles can be experienced without being overly definitive, without pinning them down too much, which I wouldn't want to do. And obviously I have been able to escape that by setting something in an imagined past or in an imagined present, tinkering with place and time so that the reader can't quite say, Oh yes, I know where this is, I can identify here. I want them rather to identify with a being, with a state of consciousness, with a particular kind of imaginative value rather than some sort of TV character.

INTERVIEWER

From the outset of your career, you've had trouble with readers trying to pin things down on a more concrete level. After the publication of *Oranges Are Not the Only Fruit* you were caught in a backlash of people trying to delve into your personal life, to assess the extent of its autobiographical content in spite of comments within the work itself about the impossibility of separating fiction from fact.

WINTERSON

Oh, I'll never escape from that, will I? I think I spent the best part of ten years saying, This is not autobiography in the way that you understand it. It is simply a way of using raw material ... because one always uses raw material from one's own life. There is as much of me in *Sexing the Cherry* as there is in *Oranges*. It is simply the way that I disguise and translate the direct experience and, I hope, make it rather more permanent than it would be otherwise. Writers always put themselves into their work, constantly. But you can't just untangle it and take it back to its source. It's not simple. In *Art and Lies*, I say something about how you can't reconstruct the bunch of grapes from the bottle of wine. They are not the same in the last analysis nor would one want them to be. So I do try to keep these strict definitions ... because I know that the whole push at the moment of saying that this is about a writer's life is a way of minimizing the work and trying to make it controllable, handleable. It is to say, Well, this isn't really art, whatever art is—not that they have any idea—but it is about experience. I get rather tired of that. What matters is what writers do with the experience, whatever the experience is. Now whether it took place in my imagination or in my psyche or whether it took place in my physical body, do we really have to split hairs like that?

INTERVIEWER

Since there are autobiographical elements in *Oranges* that involve other people, there were, no doubt, readers who did care about whether or not you were making things up. What did your mother think of the book?

WINTERSON

She did read it. That was the last letter I got from her. She wrote rather bitterly that it was the only time she had ever had to order a book in a false name—that was clearly the big problem. Of course, she was deeply angry. Interestingly, she was angry for the right reasons. She kept saying, But this isn't true, it didn't happen like that. I'd say, No, that's right, you should become a reviewer for the national press. Autobiography reverses the positions because normally it's parents who tell children the stories, not children who tell the story to their parents.

INTERVIEWER

Oranges Are Not the Only Fruit does celebrate the triumph of the protagonist over the narrow-mindedness of her community. Her ability to imagine a way out is a decisive factor in her success. To what extent has the imagination helped you to overcome obstacles in your life?

It has been a bridge for me away from a particular background, but I suppose the preliminary to that was education, because I put all my faith in that. I thought, If I can get out of here, get myself to Oxford, get myself educated, things will be better. Which is very much a *Jude the Obscure* dream. And it's equivocal, of course. You do it and then you realize that it wasn't at all what you thought.

It was actually books that started to make those pockets of freedom, which I hadn't otherwise experienced. I do see them as talismans, as sacred objects. I see them as something that will protect me, I suppose, that will save me from things that I feel are threatening. I still think that—it doesn't change. It doesn't change, having money, being successful. So from the very first, if I was hurt in some way, then I would take a book—which was very difficult for me to buy when I was little—and I would go up into the hills, and that is how I would assuage my hurt. That is still the case, for me. Whatever has happened to me, if it is difficult for me to deal with, or if I cannot deal with it at all, then I'll take a book, probably something like *Four Quartets*, and go out on my own—I would much rather do that than talk to anyone—and read it, and it becomes a salve, an ointment in a very real way. To me, the words are things, living things. For me they work far more potently than any other method, and, I dare say, that will go on until I die.

INTERVIEWER

When did you start to write?

WINTERSON

I always wrote sermons, but I'm not sure that really counts. I didn't write any fiction or anything that you would call *creative writing*—to use a term I loathe beyond measure—until I sat down to write *Oranges*. That was a journey for me, an investigation. One whose results were unpredictable. I didn't know that I was writing a book that would be published, I just knew that I was following a particular line of energy, which had to be followed, and at the end of it, there really was a book, which was something of a surprise to me.

INTERVIEWER

Did writing sermons as a child and having direct contact with an immediate audience affect your later fiction writing?

WINTERSON

Writing sermons is very good discipline because you have a limited amount of time and a chosen subject, and you have to convince your audience. And if you fail, you fail—I mean, you can see you've failed by looking out at them. So it teaches you a particular economy of style. It not only teaches you tricks of the trade, of ordinary rhetoric and how to use language for a very specific purpose to make sure that you are saying exactly what you want to say, but also to use images and symbols. One of the good things, I think, about the Christian faith is that it draws on such a wealth of images and symbols, which even the least church-minded of us still recognizes. We are two thousand years of Western Christianity. That's in our body and our blood, which is partly why the symbolism of the East, although it expresses the same truths just as well, doesn't work for us quite as it ought to. You have to have your own symbols and myths to express your collective past. That's why I am a bit dubious about ransacking the East, as we're so fond of doing at the moment, because there is something rather desperate and also rather faddish in it, as though we feel that we've made redundant all our own pictures and metaphors, which is simply not true. They still have that depth charge. I think it is a question of writers using them.

INTERVIEWER

You have said that you see yourself as an evangelist for the word.

WINTERSON

Yes, I suppose once an evangelist, always an evangelist. We have to be careful of the word *evangelical*. I think it can have positive value, but for most people it means something that is intrusive and low-minded and bigoted. Not that I have a particular doctrine, something narrow and confined that I want to get across, but what one has to be careful of, of course, is not becoming too dogmatic or too soapboxy in the approach. I do have a very vigorous attitude to life and I want to change things. That is my character. I don't know whether I was drawn into those kinds of church processes because I have this kind of character or whether those processes formed my character. Who knows? But I like energy. I like to see people who are committed to something and are prepared to go out and say, Look, this really matters to me and maybe it would matter to you. Maybe it would make a difference. For me it's art, particularly words, particularly language. I suppose if I pursue it with the same kind of enthusiasm with which I once stood up and spoke for God, people will have to forgive me . . .

INTERVIEWER

At the end of *Oranges Are Not the Only Fruit*, the narrator tells us that she could have been a priest, but she is going to be a prophet instead. This change in vocation seems to be connected to her evolution into a writer. Do you see the connection between your own upbringing and your writing as being one of translating the evangelical spirit into art?

WINTERSON

What I really want to do is to persuade people to experience for themselves what I believe to be present in art, which is this extraordinary releasing power. I suppose where the great divide comes between true evangelicals and what I do is that I want to hand the process entirely over to the individual and say, There's no book. There are no rules. You must find it for yourself. But I hope it will be invigorating, and I hope it will be empowering.

INTERVIEWER

One continuing legacy from your training as a missionary is a close relation to the Bible. Do you see the Bible as a foundational text?

It is for us in the West, yes. I sometimes wonder about the younger generation, but I still feel that everyone knows a few Bible stories and knows about the central Christian myth of miraculous birth, the life, the Crucifixion, the Resurrection. I think you could ask anyone and they would have some idea what you were saying. And therefore from that you can construct a kind of central archetype around which our ideas are formed. The stories all say the same thing. Every country has a hero narrative, which always begins with the strange and miraculous birth of a child who is threatened, and then the person grows to adulthood and does extraordinary deeds, and then is usually killed by their enemies, but nevertheless has an effect on consciousness that is profound. Those stories are everywhere. Just as when you look at the human body and there are certain overriding physical characteristics that we all share, whether here or in deepest Africa, so in the unconscious, in the subconscious, there are elements of myth that remain the same across peoples.

INTERVIEWER

In *Oranges* you engaged in revising the Bible or revising aspects of the Bible, but in *Gut Symmetries* you appear to accept the Bible as part of a larger tradition. Has your view of the Bible changed?

WINTERSON

I don't think my journey is an untypical one in that if you have been immersed in something, there will come a point when you have to rebel against it. It was necessary for me to leave behind my entire early background—physically, emotionally, and intellectually ... to have nothing to do with it. *Oranges* was a way of cleansing myself from all that, of saying, No, this is what I am. Not this other thing, this made thing. Now I am going to make myself, I'll be self-invented. Over the years—since I wrote *Oranges* eleven years ago—I have continued to think long and deeply about those issues that I suppose I have thought about since I was a very small child. Now I feel comfortable again to use the Bible as one source book amongst many others, but as a very important one. It is something that I know so very well that it would be ridiculous for me to try to do without it. And there's no point. I don't accept the God myth of the church. I think it's hogwash. But that doesn't mean that I don't accept the essential mystery of the scriptures and of the religious faith.

INTERVIEWER

But you don't feel the need to fight against it at this point?

WINTERSON

Absolutely not. It's of much more use to me as an ally. But that's only because of this relationship whereby it was everything, then it had to be nothing, and now I have come back to a point where it is as though a friend walks beside you, neither in front nor behind.

INTERVIEWER

Does the Bible have, then, the status of other texts that inhabit your work and your life?

Yes, very much so. I like to know a lot of stories and myths. That is extremely important to me. It helps me think about things, it helps me piece things together. It makes a bridge. I think it's one of the ways human beings have always understood their environment and the challenges that environment has posed.

In your earlier works you play around with myths and fairy tales, revising them and making new ones. Is this a way of offering up new plots for people to think about?

Yes. A lot of people knew these stories somewhere, or a version of them. It's a question of coaxing these stories back into conscious memory from where they have been lost. I think I have spoken before about the writer, the artist being a kind of dredging net going down into the rich silt of the mind, of the spirit, to bring up things that are normally out of reach or not accessible to consciousness. It's the duty of the writer—and indeed of all artists— to think long and deeply and to be able to drill down into those substrata so that these contents are released. Also, I think that as you drill down there is a release in all of the senses because great pressures build up in people and they don't know why. Quite often something very simple, a way of elucidating it, a way of telling the story, can release that and relieve it and make them feel, Yes, that's what is happening to me, or, This is how I feel. Then immediately one is taken off that horrible little rock

of chaos where one is entirely alone and brought
back into the community.

In your writing, you forge ties with the people who
are your friends in the realm of letters—Virginia
Woolf, T. S. Eliot, William Blake, and others—by
alluding to them, quoting them, playing around with
their words in your text. Do you see that as a tribute
or as the inevitable result of your life as a reader?

WINTERSON
I think it's both. I have a very good memory. Being
brought up without books, it was perhaps more
urgently necessary to memorize things than it is for
most people. I'd also been brought up to memorize
large chunks of the Bible. So I know just stacks and
stacks of stuff by heart, which I continually mutter
to myself as I go about my business. I shall probably
turn into some frightful old woman who mutters all
the time. I think I am already. It's a lifeline to me. It's
a kind of rosary, isn't it, these chants of mine? They're
full of sacred text, and so naturally they occur in my
work. It's simply that they do, insomuch as I think
about them while I'm writing, and I think, Yes, that
fits. It then suggests an allusion, which the reader can
gather or not, according to what they bring to the
book. The more I can stuff in it, the more layers there
are in my work, the more there is for people to mine.

INTERVIEWER
You've written, "I cannot do my own work without
known work." Do you have any sort of program for
yourself, certain texts that you immerse yourself in,

in order to write, or is it less structured than that for you?

It's both. Obviously I'm rather a great troller of secondhand bookshops. Fortunately, I live near Oxford, a very good place to search for secondhand books. I like fishing about, seeing what I can find. Which has always seemed to me part of the sinister side of the computer revolution. Because there will be no more fishing. A terrible way of confiscating knowledge, these computer indexes. That really worries me. I like to crawl around secondhand bookshops, and indeed libraries, and just see what's there. So there's that part of it that is haphazard. Except, strangely enough, when I am about to write a book, I always find exactly what I want as if by chance. But it isn't chance, it's one of those synchronicities. Otherwise, I'll choose something that I want to read, and I'll read it a lot. A couple of winters ago I wanted to read all of Shakespeare again. So I thought, Right, that's what I'll do from October to March, and it will be something I do every day. At the moment, I'm on the last eight volumes of the collected works of Jung, because I did the other nine last winter.

INTERVIEWER

Book collecting is something that you have said you did even when you didn't have the resources for it. Are you able to indulge in this passion more freely now?

WINTERSON

Yes. I did an interview for CBC on the radio, and the chap interviewing me asked me what was the most

I'd ever spent on a first edition. I said that I never spent more than three thousand pounds, and he nearly fainted. He said, Well, that is like six thousand Canadian dollars! That really horrified him. Why would anybody in their right mind ...? And I said, Look, people spend that on a holiday to Barbados. People spend that on a fancy piece of hi-fi equipment or a new computer. God help us, people spend that on a dress. I could go to Donna Karan in Knightsbridge and I could spend that. Nobody would find that particularly surprising. But they do find it surprising when I say that I've spent that on a book. But, to me, it's not. It's lovely to be able to do that. It's a great thrill, and I don't think I shall ever tire of it ... to be able to buy things that come up in catalogues that then go into my own little sanctuary.

INTERVIEWER

In *Art and Lies* you deal with the book as artifact, as a kind of bearer of history in and of itself. Is that one of your fascinations—books as having passed through various hands and times?

WINTERSON

Yes. I love that. I love to think about the secret life of the book and where it's been and who's had it. The associations there are very compelling. Also, the period I collect, which is modernism, 1900 to 1940, is a nostalgic period because it's probably the last great period of the book as we shall know it, insomuch as books were still being very well produced, often on rag paper with extremely interesting people doing the covers, some making beautiful things. But now that only happens in a way that is extremely self-conscious—specialist private-press editions that are aimed at the collector. They're not aimed at me, I don't want to collect anything that is made for collecting. What a world we are! That you have things that you can collect like that!

A great friend of mine, who was one of the most important collectors in Britain, died recently. His collection has now been broken up, as he wished. These books must now go back into the market to become part of someone else's collection. So, rather than left to the Bodleian—and we are talking about millions of pounds' worth of books—it's the most wonderful thing that they have gone back. There is a kind of rightness to that, isn't there? It's rather like Excalibur being dragged back into the lake. I think I'll do that, too, so they will appear again. Which is rather nice, so one only has them for a time.

INTERVIEWER

How do you see your own books as artifacts? Do you take an active part in designing their appearance?

WINTERSON

I think the time I like best, in a lazy kind of way, is in between finishing the book and publishing it, because you've done all the work that you can, and you know that it's gone to a good home. I like getting on with the nuts and bolts of the book after that. How are we going to make it look beautiful? How are we going to sell it, and how can we use it as an image tool? Those things interest me. I am not the kind of writer who simply puts the final post off and then says, I don't want to know anything else about what happens. I used to be in publishing, and that side of life is still one that I like to be involved with and work closely with.

I would hate to see books and publishing become shabby second cousins to the rest of the media. There is a bit of a danger that books and publishers, and perhaps even writers, will take the view that it doesn't matter what our product looks like because we'll have readers anyway. It's a very defensive attitude—no, we mustn't go out and make new readers. People who buy CDs or videos or go to movies don't normally read. There's an attitude that says if you don't like reading, if you don't love books, you never will, so we don't have to care about that. I care about that very much. I think you have to build bridges and help people simply to open the book and start reading it. Because as soon as they do that you are fifty percent there.

INTERVIEWER

You've written elsewhere about the need for people to raise themselves to the level of art, rather than art bringing itself down to the level of people.

WINTERSON

That's definitely what I feel. But I feel you can help people, perhaps people who are a bit nervous of books. The word still has power even in the multimedia age, and people who are not used to the word can be a bit scared by it, especially if they haven't had a particular kind of education. They feel that books are somehow not for them because they didn't grow up with them. You have to help them to feel that a book is not going to explode in their face, and that's where packaging and image and really clever publishing can help. There is nothing wrong with that, nothing to be ashamed of.

For whom do you write?

I don't ever think of it. I simply do the work that I need to do without imagining an audience at all. I am always surprised when I do meet readers or when I do public appearances, where I see people from all walks of life, a great cross section, a great variety. One of my personal aims has been to try to bring the word back to people who are dispossessed of it. So when people come along and say, I don't normally read, but somebody gave me one of your books and now I have read all of them, that, for me, is a great victory. Because, of course, they won't stop with my books. They'll read other people's, too.

So you hope in some way to transform people's lives through your writing?

Very much so, yes. It's not that I set out with that in mind. I never sit down and think that now I want to write something with a high moral tone or with a particular seriousness or a relevancy to today's gender issues. I never think like that. It's rather more a smuggling, a kind of contraband, wanting to get something across frontiers, places where it's not normally allowed.

I think people are often quite unaware of their

inner selves, their other selves, their imaginative selves, the selves that aren't on show in the world. It's something you grow out of from childhood onward, losing possession of yourself, really. I think literature is one of the best ways back into that. You are hypnotized as soon as you get into a book that particularly works for you, whether it's fiction or a poem. You find that your defenses drop, and as soon as that happens, an imaginative reality can take over because you are no longer censoring your own perceptions, your own awareness of the world. Most of us spend a lot of time censoring everything that we see and hear. Does it fit with our world picture? And if it doesn't, how can we shut it out, how can we ignore it, how can we challenge it? We are continually threatened in life, it's true. But once you are alone with a book, and it's also true with a picture or with music, all those defenses drop and you can enter into a quite different space where you will learn to feel differently about yourself.

INTERVIEWER

There was a time when you were writing and working to support yourself, and now the writing supports you. How have things been different for you since you've been writing full-time?

WINTERSON

It has been a long time—I have been doing it since 1987. When I sold *The Passion* here, I decided that I would just live on the money. My needs are fairly simple. Of course, one just spends as much money as one has. Very peculiar that! You never actually have any money. You think, If I had this much money ten

265

years ago, I would have thought I was amazingly rich, but I still manage to spend it all and not have any left. At the moment, speaking purely financially, I get a good price in the marketplace. I am published in a lot of countries, so I do well. But I don't imagine, and I can't expect, that will always be the case. A writer's life is very much a high-wire act, especially with huge changes of market forces now—whether there are going to be any books at all and what it will be like in twenty years. So I think that's why it's very important simply to care about the work and to do the best work you can, and not to worry about the market or the audience or any of those considerations.

INTERVIEWER

Do you have more freedom now than you did before in terms of editors and publishers accepting your experimental style?

WINTERSON

Well, if my books didn't sell, I wouldn't be published. That's for sure. I have always had a very personal relationship with the people who publish me. Frances Coady, now at *Granta*, published me at Random House. I have had to move quite a bit, but I think that is because my own career coincided with the strange phenomenon in the eighties when publishing houses kept being bought and sold. So I have had to move around, much more than is usual. That's been a bit strange. But I think I can pretty much do what I want now. I do it anyway, you know, and I'm not bothered. If they won't pay me, they won't pay me. I'm still doing it.

You have alluded to a dislike for the computer age, and you also mentioned that you have a fondness for your typewriter. Does this mean that you don't use a word processor?

WINTERSON

Yes. It does mean that. I don't. I love my typewriter. It's electric, of course, but it's one of those wonderful old-fashioned models that never, never break down. It'll just go on forever. I have written everything on it since *The Passion*. It's a friend of mine. I know all its little ways, and I wouldn't want anything else.

I like the physicality of the piece of paper. I like cutting up my bits of paper if I want to change it around. I am very messy in that respect. My original manuscript of *Gut Symmetries* has all the corners cut off because I had to repaginate it. I thought, What is the quickest way of doing it? So I just cut all the corners off and then photocopied it and redid the photocopies, so mine has got these stupid triangles. But I like that. It's my manuscript. I can do what I want with it. I don't care what it looks like, as opposed to that kind of self-publishing where people hand in these amazing word-processed things and you just think, Well, that looks very nice, but ...

INTERVIEWER

Do you compose at the typewriter?

WINTERSON

Yes, straight on the typewriter. I don't like doing it any other way. I don't even like doing it with pen and paper. I will if I have to. But I tend not to at all.

How do your books come to you? Do you think first
of a character?

Well, every book has been different. Each touching-
off point tends to come as a surprise and is unlooked
for. I have a pact with myself about my work—I
simply go to my study every day and wait. I read, I
write things, but when I'm not writing a book, I don't
necessarily expect anything to happen. But I still go
there. It seems to create the necessary psychic space
and also the necessary tension out of which something will be formed. With *Gut Symmetries* it took an
awfully long time. The book collapsed on me three
times. I had to throw away three drafts well into
two-thirds, because I hadn't quite got to the point
where I could actually write it. You really have to
have faith then—and it is a question of faith—and
you do have to believe, because there is no other way.
There is nothing objective about this. It is faith and
it is belief. There is nothing to say that because you
have covered pages in the past that you will cover
them in the future. Or that they will be any good.
There are no guarantees. But I had some idea of the
characters, and I knew what I wanted to deal with
in terms of physics and what that might say. It was a
question of finding a structure that would be in fact
simple enough to hold some very complex material
and direct enough to get across things that are very
elusive. I needed to set up a contrast, so that the form
and the material could be best presented without
either getting tangled in the other. That was in fact
extraordinarily difficult to do.

INTERVIEWER

Once you had the structure, did the book come quickly, or was it still an uphill climb?

WINTERSON

When it's written, of course, it could never have been written any other way. You just think, What was all the fuss about? Yes, it was difficult. It's like stoking a fire. To start with you must tend it very carefully—it won't burn anything you throw on it. By the time it's a big blaze you can chuck old tires and sofas on it and it will burn. But to start with, that will just put it out. I kept putting out my fire by throwing on too much unwieldy, unsuitable material before it was blazing. Then I would have to start the whole thing painfully again with little twigs and bits of paper, and nurse it and make it go until I got to that point where I thought, Right, I'll just chuck the lot on there and it will be incandescent.

INTERVIEWER

In your own works, do you see philosophy as driving the plots, or are philosophy and plot so interconnected that it's hard to separate them?

WINTERSON

It's really to do with thinking. Sometimes I look at my work, and I think, Oh God, my characters don't do anything except think! But that is what I do. I have to think about things constantly, ceaselessly. So that leads to abstract speculation, but always I hope to pull it through some very concrete experiences. I like to think that my work is tangible, something that you can touch, taste, smell, feel. I wouldn't want to become so lost in philosophizing or abstractions that it didn't have any relevance anymore, which again is why I try to use stories in particular ways to concretize the image ... to express it in terms such that people will feel it is alive with color rather than an abstract thought. I myself don't really need things concretized, but that's the way I want to pass things on. I love abstract paintings, and I find pictures of things rather distressing. That's not because I despise them, or that they are less than the sort of stuff I like. It's simply what feeds you, what works for you in a particular way. I like to look at harmonies of color or sound or language in a way quite separate from their meaning, that is, their superficial meaning.

INTERVIEWER

This goes along with your dislike of realism?

WINTERSON

I dislike it simply because the narrative function of the novel has been overtaken and done much better now by television and cinema. For instance, when photography was invented, a great many painters thought that they would be out of a job, and a great many of them were. But not painters like Picasso, who rejoiced in photography and took a lot of pictures himself, who thought that this would lead to a new freedom for painters because they would no longer have to represent what was there. Instead, they could paint much more subjectively and, as he thought, more honestly. They would no longer be bound to the narrative of fact. Now I can't see why for us as writers it shouldn't be the same thing. If television and cinema can mop up that need for narrative drive, for life as it is lived, for a picture of the every-day, then great! Let it. Because it is a function and people need it, that should free up words into something far more poetic, something about the inner life, the imaginative life ...

You have criticized contemporary writing for being too focused on narrative, and you even say that you don't write "novels." Do you believe that the novel as a genre is dead?

Yes, I do think so, because *novel* is a historical word from a historical period. The novel is a nineteenth-century construct, and I don't see what place it has now on the borders of the twenty-first. I prefer to talk about *fiction* because, to me, the novel means something very specific, and comes out of a particular nineteenth-century sensibility. I love those books and wouldn't want to be without them. I wouldn't want anybody not to read them. I shall have my little goddaughter on Dickens as soon as I ever can. But it's this business of reproduction furniture. You cannot keep producing the things that have been successful in the past or that have expressed the human condition in the past. You have to move forward, you have to make it new for every couple of generations, because otherwise it is not a living thing anymore. Books shouldn't be printed television, they should be something in their own right.

You express a kind of self-consciousness about the

novel as a genre, which hearkens back to the eighteenth century, a period in which novelists were very self-conscious about the newness of the form.

Yes. In fact, the eighteenth century is a century of which I am particularly fond. I have a Georgian house, I like things eighteenth century. I like that sense of liberty and anarchy along with mathematical preciseness and civility and ridiculously artificial manners. I like the self-consciousness of the century, which I feel disappears in the nineteenth century into a kind of debased moralizing, where self-consciousness becomes self-righteousness. You can see it in the art, you can see it in the social constructs. I think of the apotheosis of the novel as a nineteenth-century phenomenon, and something that was not present in that particular form in the eighteenth century or again by the early twentieth. It seems to me to be something that belongs to a particular period, and should be understood in its period. I wouldn't call *Orlando* a novel—and neither did Virginia Woolf—and I don't mean that's because she called it a biography. I mean it simply isn't. It in no way resembles a nineteenth-century product. It's closer, if anything, to an eighteenth-century piece. So it's really about trying to use words precisely so that we know what we are talking about, rather than saying that I hate novels. I don't. But I want to know what it is we're writing now, and I don't see that they are novels. Or they shouldn't be.

If moving beyond the concept of the novel allows

you greater scope for creating a more authentic form, how do you proceed to do this? Does the form of a work develop organically or is it something that you impose on the work from outside?

I think the two things come together. Just as if you were painting a picture, you would want to use particular colors depending on your subject matter, depending on what emotional intensity you wanted to express. So it is with the written work—the form must somehow be created organically from within, not so much the content, but the mood that you want to create.

I suppose sometimes you're really lucky and you hit something that works together beautifully, and then other times you have literally to make it up as you go along. You say, What can I try now? Will this work? Will that work? Can anybody help me? And that's when you go back desperately to your private ancestors to see how they've solved a particular problem. There is a whole technical side about what you need to know in order to write well—which is continually overlooked, though never overlooked when people talk about pictures and music. Unless you are absolutely and thoroughly soaked in English language and literature, if you are writing in English, you will never know what you need to know. The funny thing about creative-writing courses is that they busily rush around teaching people how to express their banalities without teaching them how to source the things that they need to discover. If you go and study music or painting, you learn about the past. You learn where to look, you learn what to look at, how to look things up. You need creative-reading courses, not creative-writing courses. Then people would have something that they could actually use in a positive way instead of rushing in thinking, How can I express myself?

INTERVIEWER

In *Art and Lies*, you write, "It is right to question standards but wrong to assume that there aren't any." Where do the standards come from?

WINTERSON

You have to choose the best of the past—and the standards are very high in the English language—and ask yourself, Where do I figure in this, do I come anywhere near it? If not, you may as well stop. If you really think that you are nowhere compared with the people you admire—and that has to be a very ruthless and honest self-examination and not simply flattery—then really you should stop. It's only by thoroughly knowing those other writers and daring to challenge them, even, that you would ever write. So there's always this paradox of respect and challenge, of recognizing that work exists that you should always be striving toward, which you have to look up to, which is fantastic and which probably you will never reach. It is almost a balance—either you have got it or you haven't. I don't know how you really teach it to people who want to write, because there is always too much of the one or the other, too much reverence or too much audacity. Either, I know I can do it all, or, I'm so timid, I'm just going to copy.

Would you say that some people experiment by simply disregarding standards without fully understanding them?

Yes. You can't know what to challenge unless you know what you are up against. You have to know the rules, and then you can break them. But if you don't know them, then you are working in a kind of formless chaos, which is not to say that you might not accidentally produce something interesting. It will certainly mean that you can't repeat the trick, and it will mean that you yourself are utterly unshored from what it is you are trying to do. It makes you a kind of pinball in a great pinball machine. You fire around the game, and maybe you will hit something and maybe you won't.

So you agree with what T. S. Eliot says in "Tradition and the Individual Talent" about an artist's relation to the past being one of altering tradition even as he or she absorbs and enters into it?

Yes, oh yes. I think Eliot was also right to be very wary about people who want to express their personality. It is important, first of all, to be sure that you do have something to express, but also to show a care for language that suggests that it comes first, before you, before your personality, before your own ambitions. There is always that level of humility. Whenever we talk about writing, we start to talk about paradoxes.

We've talked about respect and challenge. Now we are talking about chutzpah and humility. The writer is at once the most abject of people and the most arrogant. Because the person who really knows, knows the glories of the past and how significant they are to him or her, is at the same time prepared to say, And now I will add to them.

INTERVIEWER

How would you describe your own relation to language?

WINTERSON

I like to use lots of different words, and the accusation has always been leveled against me, Why do you use these strange words? The answer is because they're there. If you have a very refined and subtle instrument such as the English language, which has been in use for many hundreds of years, it will do almost anything you want it to do. But it is also an old language, so you need continually to be refreshing it, revitalizing it, and putting it together in surprising ways, which it will allow you to do if you will take the time. That's part of my challenge, to make sure that the language I'm using is fresh and revived and isn't in any sense a clichéd language or one that doesn't demand any thought from me. I try hard to get not only the right word but a word that's got buried in it lots of other associations.

INTERVIEWER

And sometimes you offer up etymologies for words, such as *invent* or *metaphor*, in order to recover their lost meanings?

Yes. Again, to take those words back through the history of the word and history of the individual using it so that we can see how its meanings have accreted over time, and therefore how it might be able to freeze up. Because there are small words with so much in them, and to loosen one out and put it back into common consciousness, I think, is a good idea. Because then when people see the word somewhere else, maybe it will have more meaning for them.

INTERVIEWER

Does your attempt to do this rely more upon poetry or prose? Does poetry lift language higher somehow than prose can, away from the realm of everyday speech?

WINTERSON

I think it depends who is using it. In the past, poetry has had that function of crystallizing and expanding the possibilities of language because of its preciseness. But I don't think that has to be the case. It is possible, and we have seen it many a time, for prose to work on the same levels that poetry does. Not all the way through, because you can't sustain that kind of intensity. The pieces have to be slacker. I don't mean that they should be thoughtless, but while parts of them are intense and fused and hard in every sense, others should allow the readers some space so that their own minds can relax a little bit. You have to be in control to bring in the densities of poetry and understand, too, that you need places—passing places, pausing places—where you and the reader can sit down for awhile.

Do you see literature as making demands on readers to take some sort of responsibility for their own lives? Does your work challenge readers to see themselves in new ways?

Yes, I do think so, at least I hope so. It would be a failure if someone were to come at my books and not be able to take away something like that about their own lives. I want my books to make them think, How could I do it differently? How could I have made more sense of it? But not everything works for every person. Some things that move me very much would leave other people cold. Which is why you need so much variety in art and why you need a lot of it as well. We can never have enough. The idea that there is a limit and you can't have any more or you don't need any more, which people cite from time to time. We've got enough now, surely. That will be all right. Some people hate, say, Kathy Acker's work, really hate it. And yet, a lot of kids really love her stuff—it means something to them, it means something particular. It helps them to understand who they are in a very formless society. Which is great.

I get very tired of people endlessly slagging off work by writers when they don't know what's happening out there. If anything, the writers have a better idea than any critics or single readers because they at least get more feedback from a wide variety of people—they know whether or not things are getting across. There is something absurd about books being praised or dismissed by one person reading it in their front room and then writing up what they think in a newspaper. In a way, nothing could be more ridiculous, because while a book has to be a one-to-one relationship, it's also going to be a relationship with thousands of people, each of whom will have a different experience. One reason why I don't worry too much about reviews is because in the end the book has to survive on its own terms and on its own merits. There is a lot of patronizing reviewer criticism that suggests people want to read things that are easy or about themselves in a very obvious way. That has not been my understanding or experience at all. It always makes me laugh when I do a public reading. For instance, I usually do one at the National Theatre when I publish, and it's always sold out. There are always about fourteen hundred people there. They all turn up and pay their three quid. Now, what do they do it for, if they are not getting anything out of it? No reviewer—because they are so high and mighty—would ever go to an event like that. So, they don't see the people who come in off the street and want to know about books. It's the same with pictures, it's the same with music. I think reviewing is very isolated from the string of people who are actually going out and paying to experience this and wanting it in their lives.

INTERVIEWER

You mentioned in *Art Objects* that students are demanding your works in their classes. Why do you think your themes appeal to young readers?

WINTERSON

I think it is really to do with the kinds of characters that I use to get at particular situations. I have talked about the hero motif. That is something that is true for every young person—they have to be the hero in their own lives. They have to kill a certain number of monsters, usually escape from a wicked overbearing parent, leave home and go into the big wide world to seek their fortune. So, the hero motif is very powerful. It's in their own lives, and it's something that they can readily identify with when they see it reflected back to them in a way that tries to get across both the dangers, the perils, as well as the great pleasures of that sort of individuation.

But growing up isn't necessarily to do with young people. It is to do with anybody who simply hasn't done it. There are a lot of much older people who refuse to be the hero in their own lives, who put it off—a lot of women, for whom that was not seen to be appropriate, which is very sad. You always see young girls, full of life, launching themselves on the world, and then so quickly getting smacked down in the way that young men are not smacked down. Obviously, women are beginning to find that they really won't put up with that. They want to see what it is they can achieve for themselves. So, I think that's a large part of the appeal of my work. Because all my characters are on a quest. They're all looking for something that they don't have, and then, of course, they find that it is within themselves. But not until the end of the book.

All of your works involve a love plot. And yet, things don't usually work out for your characters. You seldom allow them to have a kind of a perfect bliss in love.

Well, I don't do happy endings, do I? They always end ambiguously by the water. I do not think that the endings are depressing, but I don't think that they are contrived in human terms either. Things are continually beginning again—they're never really resolved, you know. They are only resolved temporarily. We live in a society that peddles solutions, whether it's solutions to those extra pounds you're carrying, or to your thinning hair, or to your loss of appetite, loss of love. We are always looking for solutions, but actually what we are engaged in is a process throughout life during which you never get it right. You have to keep being open, you have to keep moving forward. You have to keep finding out who you are and how you are changing, and only that makes life tolerable.

INTERVIEWER

You are often concerned with journeys in your books, the space traveled—physically and metaphysically—between two points. You repeatedly circle around the idea that travel can take place on different levels. Do you see travel as a metaphor for narrative? What do journeys represent to you?

WINTERSON

Well, I am a bit obsessed with them. I have noticed this. I have also noticed how most of my books end at the sea or by a river, always some water at the end. Once you start recognizing your own obsessions, you know you're getting old. I suppose I am fascinated by journeys because—and my partner complains about this enormously because she loves to travel—I loathe travel. I will do anything not to travel. She says, Let's go to this place, and so we get all the books, and I read about it and then I make up stories and describe it all. Finally she says, You don't want to go now because you've been, haven't you? Unfortunately, this is true.

I wrote *The Passion* before I had been to Venice. I just imagined it. I hadn't been to New York for seven years when I wrote *Gut Symmetries*, but it didn't make any difference. I do travel in my head. It's the old joke about the magic carpet or the broomstick. That's how poor people used to make journeys, because they couldn't afford to make them literally. Certainly when I was a kid, it was one of the games we used to play. We invented places we would go, describing them to each other because none of us could ever afford to go anywhere. I didn't go to London until I was twenty-one.

It may be that because it gave me all that pleasure when I was a child it continues to give me pleasure now. But it now works on a different level. It's something more profound to me, because it's one of those good metaphors, isn't it, the idea of the journey? Everyone understands it straightaway. They also understand that you are talking about an inner journey and an outer journey at the same time. It's quite a simple trope for conveying some very complex information. That is what I try to do—to choose something that is simple and yet works as an enormously powerful conductor. That is what the journeys in the books are really about, trying to get somebody away from victim status.

INTERVIEWER

One might say that your writing is characterized by

a kind of excess. Have you gotten different responses to that aspect of your work?

If you want something to be clear straightaway then it's probably better not to read my books. Read somebody else's. I don't really feel that I should be held accountable for writing the kinds of books that I want to write just because some reader I can't imagine or will never know doesn't want to read them. It seems a bit unfair. You can't win in the art stakes, because there is always somebody who is cross with you. So that's why it is better not to care and instead think, Well, I must really do my work, hope that it reaches people, and leave the rest to chance. That's often mistaken for arrogance, but it isn't. You have to believe that you are good, because if you think you are rubbish, why are you doing this stuff anyway? And what are you doing chucking it out there for people to buy? I think that would be the true arrogance—if you thought your stuff was rubbish and still got people to pay good money to read it.

INTERVIEWER

Have you been accused of being arrogant?

WINTERSON

Yes, largely because I do insist on doing my own work in my own way. I suppose it is a take-it-or-leave-it attitude, but then people are at liberty to leave it. That's their choice. I can't second-guess those choices. You can't tie yourself up in knots trying to please all of the people, and you can't make a kind of computer-generated product that is just meant to target an interest group. I suppose that is what, to some extent, the publishers would like, because that's where the money is. But writers don't work like that and can't. If it is arrogant to wish to do the best that you can in your own way, then, sure, I'm arrogant.

You frequently represent gender as a plot that we're handed. Do you see gender as something flexible and fluid?

Obviously society doesn't see gender as unimportant. I see it as extremely important indeed. And thereby many injustices are caused. I see it as less important as I get older. I no longer care whether somebody's male or female. I just don't care. Which is strange, because I used to care very much, especially because my emotional and sexual affinities are with women. That was obviously a very specific choice and, again, there is this business of having to define something clearly and really know what it is that you feel before you can relax. I defined myself very clearly as somebody who preferred the company of women and wanted to arrange my life as such. It's not that I'm not that person anymore, because my partner is a woman, and I hope we will stay together because we are very happy. But I have many more male friends, say, than I used to, and I feel much more relaxed about the whole issue—it's changed. But that doesn't mean I don't know exactly what's going on out there.

Characters in your novels often cross-dress or play

around with gender. Villanelle does this in *The Passion*. Jordan in *Sexing the Cherry* dresses as a woman, and is able to gain access to women's ways of talking when men aren't around. Do you see gender as a kind of performance?

WINTERSON

I think I do. If we can do a hop and a skip out of the nineteenth century and land ourselves back, we find that it very much is so. The eighteenth century is a century where there is much more flexibility. Men could wear makeup, for instance. Byron wore makeup, and nobody thought anything about it. He was the last man to wear makeup like that. The eighteenth-century dandy is not a figure who exists in the nineteenth century until you get to Oscar Wilde, and you know what everyone thought of him.

In opera in the eighteenth century, the composer—say Handel or Mozart—would simply write for a particular voice. He wouldn't think, Is this a man or a woman? He liked that voice and would write a part. So when the person got on stage, sometimes they'd have to be a man and sometimes a woman. This does not happen in the nineteenth century. You don't see it again until Strauss's *Rosenkavalier* in 1911, which is extraordinary. It does tell us so much about the nineteenth-century sensibility about gender, a huge fear of anything crossing over. Men are men and women are women. But it is a distortion. Take the plays of Shakespeare, for example. You are meant to believe that a man is falling in love with another man. You're not meant to see it as pantomime. You are meant to see and feel that element of risk and fear and danger and trespass. In *As You Like It* when

Rosalind cross-dresses, you're meant to believe that she becomes a boy. You should not see through the disguise, any more than the people around her can see through the disguise. I am quite glad now, because in present productions of Shakespeare that ambiguity, that tease is really coming back ... that people are meant to have their own affections and feelings dislocated from their normal seat into something a bit more threatening.

Do you see yourself as taking part in a tradition of women's writing explicitly, or is that something that you eschew in favor of a broader sense of tradition?

It's both. I feel that the broad tradition is mine—it has to be because I claim it. It's an inheritance, which is given to you, but you have to be worthy of it. You have to win it to make it your own, then you have to use it. It's rather like the parable of the talents in the Bible. The great lord gives out the various bags of money to his servants and says, What are you going to do with it? and then goes off. Some invest it, and one person buries it in the ground. We are given this enormous literary heritage—certainly you are as a writer—but then you have to make it work for you. You have to use it. If you just bury it in the ground, it's dead. So for me it is vital constantly to use the broadest tradition and to get as much from it as I can. But at the same time, within that, I recognize that strand in women's writing of which I am directly a part and which speaks to me in a very personal way. It has to, because I am part of that struggle.

As well as being a writer neither male nor female, I am a writer who is a woman. I am very conscious of that. I am conscious that the voice does get stronger all the time, the voice of the woman writing. Which is why I feel I have to continue, and do a bit more and take the baton a little bit further, if possible. Otherwise, I am letting down the past as well as the future. You're insulting those women who did it absolutely to the best they could, making huge sacrifices at the time. There is a passage at the end of *A Room of One's Own* where Virginia Woolf says we have to work for women writers so that they will appear. My work is to do that work.

INTERVIEWER

Do you feel a pressure from your audience to be a spokesperson for women, for lesbians?

WINTERSON

Oh, yes! But it would be a very bad thing indeed if I were to do that. The best I can do is the best I can do, which is my work. I have no objection to all of this stuff being pumped out—there really is a place for it. But I don't want to do it. I don't want to be a political writer, or a writer whose concern is sexual politics.

INTERVIEWER

Virginia Woolf in *A Room of One's Own* faults Charlotte Brontë for allowing politics to come into *Jane Eyre*. Specifically, she points to the passage in which Jane is reflecting on the limitations of her life as a woman and raging against the boxes into which she has been put. Woolf sees Brontë's introduction of this anger into the text as an artistic flaw. What is your view of the relation between political engagement and artistic creativity?

I think Virginia Woolf was speaking quite rightly from her own anxieties, something that she personally was very worried about, but I don't think that she was right. It may be better to try to speak honestly, even if that anger to some extent flaws part of the work, than to try to suppress and possibly dampen down your own rocket fuel in the process. I think it's better to take the risk. You can edit it out later if you want to, and if you can't—because it would be sort of an amputation, or a surgery that would damage the rest—then leave it in, and let the passages speak for themselves. And let people say, Well, this passage doesn't work. I mean, it annoys me in D. H. Lawrence when he starts his working-class rant. I have written about that. I know I do it as well. But it probably doesn't matter, because no work is perfect. We can't endlessly be worrying about how to write a perfect work. We can only do the best we can. So it may not be worth wasting energy on.

INTERVIEWER

A large body of people want to read your work strictly as lesbian literature. Is that a problem for you?

WINTERSON

No, it's not. There is nothing I can do about it, so it can't be a problem for me. That's another one of the obsessions we're in at the moment. We will pass through it, and if the book lasts, then it will cease to be a problem. I have to take the long view and really not mind. Because it's only a slightly more extreme version of anybody reading the text in a way that they like ... that it has become a group rather than an individual identity with the book.

Do you think that lesbian relationships in your fiction come across as superior to heterosexual relationships?

WINTERSON

Yes, probably. But they don't in *Gut Symmetries*, no. And we don't really know what's going on in *Written on the Body*, do we?

INTERVIEWER

The single most discussed aspect of *Written on the Body* is that we don't know what the gender of the narrator is. Did you intend for *Written on the Body* to be completely ambiguous in terms of gender?

WINTERSON

Well, no, I just couldn't be bothered. I didn't want to pin it down. I thought, There is no need to do so, so I won't do so. If I put in a gender then it weights my story in a way that I don't want it to be weighted. So I didn't. I didn't expect that a huge furor would arise. I must say that took me totally by surprise.

INTERVIEWER

What do you think of the fact that some reviewers of *Written on the Body* praise your understanding of the male psyche based on their reading of the narrator as a man?

WINTERSON

That's a bit weird. But that's all right. It's an open text. To some extent when you read a book that you care about, you do build it again as your own text. That's inevitable. We all do that. You set up a very jealous and personal relationship with it, and then it can only be your text, and the last thing you want to be told is that there is another way of reading it.

INTERVIEWER

What is your view of heterosexuality now? *Oranges Are Not the Only Fruit* presents heterosexuality as something that can only oppress women. However, at the end of *Gut Symmetries*, it is not really clear who will end up with whom, or whether any of them will end up with any of the others. That is, you don't seem to be promoting the same-sex relationship at the expense of the heterosexual one.

WINTERSON

I didn't want to have a clear winner in this book. It is more complex than that. I think men can really get in the way when you are trying to sort your life out and get on with it. Because they just take up so much space. I'm not under any illusions that I could have been where I am now in literary terms if I had been heterosexual. I really believe I would not be. Because—and this has gotten me into huge trouble before, but I suppose I may as well get into trouble again—I can't find a model, a female literary model who did the work she wanted to do and led an ordinary heterosexual life and had children. Where is she? I am no fool, I mean I looked at this at the time. I don't think people's sexuality is really that fixed. I had various boys at various times as well as various girls. There was a part of me that instinctively knew that in order to be able to pursue my life, which was going to be hard enough anyway, I would be much better off, either on my own or with a woman. A man would simply get in the way, and I would have to use up energy that I didn't have to spare. I do believe that to be the case. It probably wouldn't be the case now, say, if I changed to a new partner, because I am sufficiently established. But I do think that when you are young and you are trying to make your way in the world it really is an issue.

Women who have tried to push it aside as an issue say things like, Well, I won't even think about having children until I am forty. Then of course they are completely knackered. It seems to me difficult enough to have children when you have got all the energy of being twenty-one. Some of the people I know who had children quite late, pushing forty, are exhausted. They are not the women they were twenty years ago, and they can't manage not to have any sleep for two years. So by pushing the problem into the future you don't solve it. The issue of how women are going to live with men and bring up children and perhaps do the work they want to do has in no way been honestly addressed. It is simply being made into a problem that you have when you're forty instead of when you are twenty.

In your last few books, you have taken up the topic of disease. It comes up in *Written on the Body* and then again in *Art and Lies*, in which Handel is a surgeon, and you allude to it in *Gut Symmetries*, as well. How do you see disease functioning as a metaphor, and does it connect to other ideas that you have about the body in general?

It's one of those useful metaphors that everyone understands. People are rather terrified by the idea of a degenerative disease, whether it's cancer or AIDS, that will hijack the entire healthy organism and ruin it. Even the dimmest people can see that this is not only to do with their own bodies but a kind of metaphor for the state crumbling away. So it's one that writers can easily use for their own purposes. I used it because I wanted to exploit that fear, to make people really sit up and take notice and try to fit the inner body onto the outer body, as it were. To say, What is it that is really going on with you? What do you know about your body and your psyche, your sanity? It goes back to the idea of people continually being at the mercy of things that they don't recognize because they refuse to recognize them. As we know, cancer and AIDS in their early stages are virtually undetectable unless you're lucky. By then the damage is done. I feel very strongly that people—because they shut so much out—are prey to destructive forces that take them over, gut them as human beings, leave them as nonfunctioning shells, and by the time they discover this it is too late. So that's why some of the stuff in *Written on the Body* and *Art and Lies* is not necessarily for the squeamish. I wanted people to recoil and to have to think about it.

INTERVIEWER
You often present forgiveness as an important gate-

way to healing. That's something that Picasso in *Art and Lies* must learn to do. She thinks about the abuse she suffered at the hands of her family and feels that she has to forgive herself for being complicit in her own suffering. Could you discuss your view of forgiveness?

WINTERSON
Well, there are only three possible endings to any story, aren't there? Revenge, tragedy, or forgiveness. That's it. All stories end like that. There aren't any that don't. I suppose it depends temperamentally on which ones you want to choose. I have noticed that for me forgiveness is important. I have had quite a rackety life. I knew that my parents would never forgive me for what I had done but there came a point where I had to forgive them. That was a choice I made, knowing that it could not be reciprocated, and perhaps not even wanting it to be anymore. It wasn't reconciliation, it was about forgiveness ... simply for me to try to look at them honestly and recognize what they were and not judge them and not be angry with them anymore. So, for me, finding in myself that kind of compassion was partly to do with—*Oranges*, which is in many ways a very loving portrait of a monster.

In a sense, that's where autobiography does come in—my relationship with my mother was operatic, it was Wagnerian and tempestuous. She was this huge, huge creature, physically and emotionally demanding, and I am quite small physically. So immediately there was this contrast and this tension ... this great thing constantly bearing down on this very small thing, along with the manipulations and the brutal-

ities. I am wondering what one does with all that—
and this comes up in *Art and Lies*—in that you can't
spend the rest of your life saying, Look how I've been
treated. I am a terrible victim. This is Picasso's great
saying, too. I will find something else. I will put that
behind me. It is only possible if you can forgive and
let the bitterness go. I have found that most resolutely
in my own life, which is why I am actually happy
now. That was the first lesson to me—of learning to
forgive other people, and I have had to do it quite a
lot since. I don't mean that's because I'm a saint, but
I mean you have to choose. In the end it is better to
say, I can't change them, but I can forgive them and
I can change myself.

INTERVIEWER

Is it a way of changing the stories that one tells about
oneself?

WINTERSON

Very much so, yes. The way you depict your own life
is important. For some people, it's either revenge—
they're always looking for someone else to blame
and to get back at—or it's tragedy because the whole
thing is such a bloody mess and they'll never get out
of it. But the moment that you can forgive, you take
back the power and the healing waters flow. I know
that personally, and I find it in literature. It's the end
of the Shakespearean comedies where in the fifth
act everyone comes together and sees each other for
what they are. You get it in *As You Like It*, where
at the end of the play the characters return from the
Forest of Arden, all rather sobered by their experience. None of them are what they thought they were

or perhaps even what they would like to be, but there is a great deal of acceptance, and then, of course, the play's joyous ending. Even in the tragedies you find this. What else is there at the end of *The Winter's Tale* when Hermione steps down from the statue, and she and Leontes find in each other a reconciliation and forgiveness of all that is past? What was stonelike, her mirroring his stolid heart, is suddenly fluid and warm again.

INTERVIEWER

There is also a potential for a new beginning there, a clearing of the way for the future. You have written that "to continue to do new work is to continue a development of style that allows the writer to surprise herself." How have you surprised yourself lately and do you have ideas of what you will be doing in the near future?

WINTERSON

Well, *Gut Symmetries* was a very different book from *Art and Lies*, and yet it concerns all the things that have always concerned me. It's obviously my book. It couldn't be anybody else's book. It's important to be able to construct for yourself a new book that you didn't expect and something that moves away from what you have done immediately before. I have tried to do this. But I can't be sure that I will be able to go on doing it. No one can know that. In the short stories I am writing now, there is a kind of straightforward happiness and ease, which I always get when I have finished a book ... an extra run of energy, which can turn into other things. That's a very nice time. So I am enjoying that. But I know perfectly well that the real work will begin in about a year when I'll have to start another piece of fiction, and I have absolutely no idea ... That's a lie. I have a very tiny idea, which is not really an idea at all, which is something very deep in the water, which has a light, but not a very bright light. But I'll get it. So it's there, but it's going to take a long time to come up, and it will be about a year. It may be hell, it may be like *Gut Symmetries*, to get started on it. It may feel like utter defeat rather than something new.

There was very much, after I left London, after *Art and Lies*, a period of retreat and breakdown. Not in a sense of nervous or mental breakdown, but a breakdown of what I had become at that point because it was no longer of any use to me. In a sense, I was having to remake myself in order to be able to write *Gut Symmetries*. That process will have to continue. If I stop, if I stop remaking myself, I won't be able to do any good work anymore. So the challenge is to continue to do it, to continue to keep sane. Also, to remember what I'm here for, no matter how many voices tell me I am really here for other things or really here for nothing at all.

There is a fairy story about the prince and the black stones. On top of a crystal mountain is a princess, the thing of highest worth, the thing desired. The prince, the hero, the questing self, wants to get to the princess, the thing of highest worth. He starts to climb the mountain, which is crystal and therefore extremely slippery, difficult. On the way, he does all right for a bit. Then these black stones in his path start to speak and they say, You are a fool. Why are you going up this mountain? You will never get to the top. In any case when you get to the top it won't be worth it, there is nothing there. Or, You're going to die of thirst, you're going to die of hunger. This continues all the way up. He becomes more and more depressed, and he thinks, I will never, never get to the top. Then, of course, eventually the hero does get to the top and frees the princess. He looks back and realizes that the black stones were the souls of all the people who had failed before and therefore didn't want anyone else to succeed, because the only thing that justified them was their own failure. That's a useful story if you are a writer, because the way is full of black stones. All you know is that there is this thing of highest value, of great worth, that you want to keep trying to achieve. Every time, up the slippery rock, with no sense of being able to get there, you simply have to stuff your ears and keep climbing.

(1997)

Wendy Wasserstein

THE ART OF THEATER NO. 13

Interviewed by Laurie Winer

Wendy Wasserstein was born in Brooklyn, New York, on October 18, 1950, the youngest of four children. Her mother, an amateur dancer, grew up in Poland and moved to the United States when her father was suspected of being a spy. Wasserstein's father was a textile manufacturer. When she was eleven, the family moved to the Upper East Side of Manhattan, where she attended a series of young women's schools before enrolling in Mount Holyoke College.

Wasserstein received her B.A. from Mount Holyoke in 1971 and earned her M.A. from New York's City University in 1973, where she studied creative writing with Israel Horovitz and Joseph Heller. The same year saw Wasserstein's first professional production, her play *Any Woman Can't*, presented by Playwrights Horizons, a small off-Broadway theater that has played a large role in her career. But it was at the Yale School of Drama,

in which she enrolled the next year, that Wasserstein found her métier as a playwright. She was the
lone woman among a dozen men studying playwriting—a "kind of bizarre macho class," her classmate and friend Christopher Durang remembers it.
"There were an awful lot of would-be Sam Shep-
ards, and Wendy felt a little left out." At the first
reading of her play *Uncommon Women and Others*
(1977), a male classmate complained, "I just can't
get into this." The play was later filmed as part of
PBS's *Theatre in America* series.

After receiving her M.F.A. from Yale in 1976,
Wasserstein returned to New York, where she has
lived ever since. During the next several years, her
plays were produced in various off-Broadway the-
aters. Her eighth play, *The Heidi Chronicles* (1988),
was produced off-Broadway by Playwrights Horizons; in 1989, within weeks of moving to Broadway, the play won both the Pulitzer Prize and the
Tony Award for best play. Her next play, which
was produced in 1992, was *The Sisters Rosensweig*.
Wasserstein has also written a collection of essays,
Bachelor Girls (1990); a children's book, *Pamela's
First Musical* (1996); and several screenplays—
although she considers these things that happen
while she is "waiting for the next play."

Soon after *The Sisters Rosensweig* opened
on Broadway, we met in the breakfast room of
Wasserstein's apartment overlooking Central Park
in New York City. "I don't use it much; I'm not
good enough," she laughed. A second interview
was conducted this spring during rehearsals for her
latest play, *An American Daughter* (1997).

INTERVIEWER

What do your sisters think of *The Sisters Rosensweig*?

WENDY WASSERSTEIN

I didn't show anyone in my family the play. The problem with writing plays is that everyone has an opinion. And you don't want those opinions. You want people to say, I love you no matter what. I'm a forty-two-year-old woman. What would my mother say? Oh, it's nice, Wendy, and I notice the mother is dead? I really didn't want any of them to see it until the opening, but my sister Sandy kept saying she wanted to come, so finally I said, You can come but you can't call me tomorrow and make any comments, because if you call me and don't say anything, I'll know you think it's bad. So no comment, either way. She saw it and sent me flowers the next day. They came with a note that said, No Commitment. I realized that either the florist had made this Freudian slip or he was the florist to some Upper West Side bachelor who regularly sends out no-commitment flowers.

But my mother is indefatigable. I hear her talking to my nieces and saying things like, You want to marry young. You know, you don't want to grow old like Wendy. She's fascinating. She is not a schooled person—my grandfather wrote plays and was the head of a school district in Poland, but my mother went to high school in New Jersey and then stopped. But she is deeply funny and, for someone who has not read, verbal and witty and an original thinker. She never cooked and she took great pride in having no skills at all. She had four children and then my two cousins came to live with us. And she danced. By the time I got to high school she

301

was going to dancing lessons. That woman is over eighty and she's still dancing. Her name is Lola and when she walks down the street, chorus boys stop her to say hello. She wears leather! She's older now and so looks more like a grandmother, but if you had hit her when I was in college—she was a number. She's from that generation of mothers who had intelligence and creativity and no place to put that except into family. If the circumstances were different I'm sure she would have been a dancer or set designer. She thinks she's marvelous in every way. If you said, Wendy is so talented, she'd say, Of course, she's my daughter. My love of the theater comes from her.

My dad doesn't talk very much. He's very gentle and sweet, and my suspicion is that he's extremely bright and reflective. He invented the process that put wires into ribbons, which I guess is a little like being a furrier. They are really a yin and yang, those two.

INTERVIEWER

Did you have fun growing up?

WASSERSTEIN

I did because my mother was eccentric. In Brooklyn a lot of mothers really did play mah-jongg and have their hair done. My mother looked like Bertolt Brecht when I was growing up. She had extremely short hair. She'd say to the hairdresser on Kings Highway, You know how I like it, so it looks like you made a mistake. When I went to yeshiva, the rabbi's daughter would come to dinner and my mother would give us hamburgers and string beans with butter sauce. You're not supposed to have milk with meat and she'd lie and say it was lemon juice.

Also, being so close to my brother was fun. We went exploring a lot. My sister Sandy got married when I was six. She was nineteen. My aunt Kiki fell through the floor at her wedding. She was dancing and fell through, which I thought was fabulous. Sandy eventually got divorced and went to live in England for eight years. She came back, and one day my mother had her pick me up from the June Taylor School of Dance. So there I was, a yeshiva girl, going to dance school on Saturdays—my mother had me lying to the rabbi about that. Between the lemon juice and the lying to the rabbi, I'm going straight to hell. Anyway, she told Sandy to take me to Howard Johnson's and Radio City. So Sandy took me to the House of Chen, where we had shrimp dishes—and I knew your lips fall off from the shrimp but I was too scared to tell her, I can't eat this. And then, instead of going to Radio City, she took me to see *Expresso Bongo*, which was one of those English art movies. I remember a scene where the girl was wearing kilts with suspenders and no top. And then Sandy made me lie about it all to my mother.

When I was in second grade, I made up a play that I was in. I told my mother that I was in this play and the lie got larger and larger. Finally, arbitrarily, I said, My play is on tomorrow, and she got me a velvet dress and made my hair in ringlets, and off I went to school. And she came to school and there was no play. She covered for me and said, I must be confused, it must be another one of my children. Then she came home and told me I was a fibber. She must have yelled at me because to this day I have trouble with fibbing.

Would you call *The Sisters Rosensweig* your first well-made play?

Yes, in terms of structure. When I see the play, I feel I'm seeing a Broadway play in 1958, or what I wish those plays had been. I remember going to them and thinking, I really like this, but where are the girls? *The Sisters Rosensweig* is like those plays—the curtain goes up and there's one set, and the play is well-made, you know, beginning, middle, and end. It takes place over a weekend, the stars get applause, the stars get exit applause, they each tell their stories, it arcs in the second act, all of that. It was much harder to write than any of my other plays.

Did your other plays prepare you for it?

In a way. *The Sisters Rosensweig* seems a combination of *Isn't It Romantic* (1981) and *Uncommon Women*. But those other plays are episodic and this was a deliberate decision not to be episodic. Also, I decided not to write another play about my generation. Even though it has autobiographical materials, the focus of the play is not me. I wanted to do all those things and also evoke a fondness for plays that I love, including Chekhov. On the day I finished it I thought, This was a lot of effort just to prove to myself what a good writer Chekhov is.

You sound as if you didn't get emotionally involved.

Ending *The Sisters Rosensweig* was hard, and when I finish plays I tend to get emotional and weepy. I remember the day I finished it I got weepy and then I realized it wasn't right. When we were doing the workshop in Seattle, I got weepy again and I realized it still wasn't right and I thought, How many times am I going to get weepy? Today in a taxi ride I was thinking that I would like to fix the speeches between Sara and Merv in the last scene. In the first draft, Sara sang for Merv. Then Merv sang "For Me and My Gal" in return. I was thinking, They slept together once and they're singing and running off together? What kind of play is this?

When Sara does sing for herself—that song about Moishe Pupick, about being the only Yiddish girl in MacNamara's Band—it's an amazing moment. Jewish audiences respond to Sara's need to assimilate and her need not to. For a larger audience the moment is about identity and reconnecting with yourself after being lost for some time. When Sara first starts to sing those lyrics, the audience laughs because she's singing Yiddish words. But it's actually a deeply serious moment.

This play is thought of as a comedy, which is great, but to me this is a very serious play, and what you touched on in that moment is almost tonality, the heart of the play.

INTERVIEWER

One of the most moving moments in the play is when Gorgeous receives a real Chanel suit as a gift. Why is that so moving?

WASSERSTEIN

I think it comes from when I was in high school and I first realized there were people who wore real Pappagallo shoes and then there were people who wore imitation Pappagallo shoes from Chandlers. So I became very interested in this idea of what was real and what was imitation and what it felt like to wear the imitation and finally get the real.

INTERVIEWER

The Chanel suit touches on something that isn't seemly to speak of, which is that material things can give you almost a spiritual sense of happiness. It's almost like being loved in a way because it makes you feel safe and secure and beautiful or whatever, and that's something that very few people write about.

WASSERSTEIN

It was odd—we hired a rabbi as the religious adviser on the play, Rabbi Shnier, whom I kept calling Rabbi Schnorrer. We did this because Madeline didn't want to light the Sabbath candles unless she was doing it right. She didn't want to be offensive. A friend of mine was dating a rabbi, so I went to speak at his temple. We were talking about Jewish women and self-image, and I said that I never thought of myself as undesirable or unattractive, frankly, until I turned twelve and began watching these movies in which none of the men ever fell in love with anybody who looked remotely like me. No one was ever Jewish, no one was hardly ever brunette. I never thought of that before, but in retrospect it really makes me angry. Maybe that will change now. Just like when I was growing up and there were no smart girls in plays. Or if they were smart, were sort of these really mean career people.

You know what's interesting? *The Sisters Rosensweig* is a play that men like. Mort Zuckerman came up to me and said, I love your play, and I looked at him and I said, You do?

INTERVIEWER

I notice that you use the word *girl* a lot.

WASSERSTEIN

I've been called on the table for years on that. I call myself a Jewish girl. Maybe it's because you can't correct semantically who in your heart you know you are. But in the last five years feminism has opened up to humor. Women who are a bit older can believe in something and also see it ironically. And younger women who once thought that to be a feminist you had to be antimarriage, have no sense of humor, and have hairy legs are changing. When I saw Marilyn Quayle speak at the convention in 1992, I thought, Everything I do is anathema to this woman. She thinks I will rot and boil in hell. But I think of her exactly what she thinks of me—Poor woman.

Feminism has affected me more in my writing than in a specifically political way. Sitting down to write a play that has three parts for women over forty, I think, is political.

Do you feel you are doing something important by making images of older, complete women?

I do in a way. When Gorgeous returns the Chanel suit she is in some way heroic. For a woman to be heroic she doesn't have to save the planet. My work is often thought of as lightweight commercial comedy, and I have always thought, No, you don't understand, this is in fact a political act. *The Sisters Rosensweig* had the largest advance in Broadway history, therefore nobody is going to turn down a play on Broadway because a woman wrote it or because it's about women.

How has the theater changed since you started out?

It's interesting that the two most successful straight plays the year *Sisters Rosensweig* came out were mine and Tony Kushner's *Angels in America*—a play about three women over forty and an epic about a gay fantasia. Even five years before, that wouldn't have happened.

In conversation you sometimes are angrier and more provocative than you seem in your plays.

My plays are my art and not just self-revelation. Creating a well-made play means you have to round the edges so they fit into the form. Also, the plays are deliberately comedic. Humor masks a lot of anger, and it's a means of breaking up others' pretenses and of not being pretentious yourself.

INTERVIEWER
You started out in the early seventies at Playwrights Horizons with Christopher Durang, Bill Finn, and all those other people. What do you remember about the early days?

WASSERSTEIN
When I was at Yale, I sent a play called *Montpelier Pizz-zazz* (1974) to Playwrights Horizons about a week after they moved to Forty-Second Street. Upstairs was still the Sex Institute of Technology. Downstairs it smelled of urine and there were pictures of the dancers on the walls. It was not a glamour spot. That's where I met André Bishop. I sent *Uncommon Women* to Playwrights Horizons and they did a reading of it and wanted to do it. But I eventually gave it to the Phoenix Theatre instead. I thought it would get a better production and better exposure. It was because of losing that play that André decided he would turn Playwrights into the kind of theater no playwright would turn down.

INTERVIEWER
How did Playwrights attract so much raw talent when it was new?

WASSERSTEIN
It mostly had to do with André Bishop. What André managed to do was diminish the sense of

competition—we all thought this was our theater. I don't know if any other theater has been able to accomplish that—maybe the Manhattan Theatre Club with Terrence McNally and Donald Margulies, but it's not quite the same. I don't know whether it was because a lot of us had gone to school together—Christopher Durang, Alfred Uhry, and Ted Tally, who writes screenplays and won an Oscar for *Silence of the Lambs*—or because André was so gentle and sweet. It was also cockamamy because it was on Forty-Second Street between Ninth and Tenth. When we did the first reading of *Uncommon Women*, my dad, when he left the theater, gave André a fifty-dollar bill and said, Take care of yourself, son. He could not understand why this nice boy from Harvard was next to a massage parlor.

INTERVIEWER

Did you have an immediate rapport with Christopher Durang?

WASSERSTEIN

What Peter Patrone says in *The Heidi Chronicles* Christopher said to me, "You look so bored, you must be very bright." I remember in a class at Yale, E. L. Doctorow said that he was very sad because a girl at Sarah Lawrence had committed suicide. Christopher asked, Was it for credit? Alfred found it offensive, but I just started laughing, and I thought, This guy is great! I've never met anyone like him.

The thing about this whole group of people was that no one said, I've got to win the Pulitzer by the time I'm thirty. That was never what it was about. It was almost like they were too eccentric, and still are,

I think. They were not a slick group—they didn't go to the right parties or work a room or anything like that. But these are the people I feel aesthetically close to, as some sort of gauge of myself.

INTERVIEWER

It was André who brought you all together?

WASSERSTEIN

Well, he gave us a place where we could hear our plays read. My first play was read at Playwrights before I even went to Yale. *Any Woman Can't.*

INTERVIEWER

I've never seen it.

WASSERSTEIN

And you never will. It's an awful play. I wrote it when I took Israel Horovitz's playwriting course up at City College. My mother was walking down the street and she ran into the receptionist from the June Taylor School of Dance, where I went as a child. The receptionist asked, How's Wendy? My mother said, Well, I don't know. She's not going to law school, she's not dating a lawyer, and now she's writing plays. She's cuckoo. The receptionist said, Give me Wendy's play because I work across the hall from a new theater called Playwrights Horizons. So my mother gave her *Any Woman Can't.* Bob Moss was running the theater, and they did a reading.

INTERVIEWER

You're all funny and you all tend to write rather episodically. Durang had more acts in a play than anyone had ever seen and Bill Finn wrote musical vignettes that came together as a whole in the end.

WASSERSTEIN

I think we were the next generation after Terrence McNally, Lanford Wilson, and John Guare—who were all breaking form, too, from Edward Albee and Arthur Miller. I guess someone could say we were the first generation who grew up watching television and also going to the theater.

INTERVIEWER

While the previous generation only went to the theater.

WASSERSTEIN

That's right. The next generation will go to the theater even less. So the episodic writing was something that came to me. I thought writing a full-length play was something I didn't want to do and didn't know how to do. It seemed old fogyish. But I was on a committee to evaluate the Yale School of Drama, and there was this young woman, a directing student, who told me that what she wanted to do was explode text. I thought of Miss Julie exploding over the Yale School of Drama saying, There goes *The Sea Gull*! I thought, Well, before you explode it you should know how to do it. I thought, I would just like to try to do this. If in fact playwriting is like stained glass, if it becomes more and more this obscure craft, then it would be interesting to know how to do that craft.

INTERVIEWER

Did you learn by going?

WASSERSTEIN

Yes. When you write in an episodic mode, you know that the scene will be over. The hardest part, what's really boring, is getting people on and off the stage. You can't just bring the lights down and bring them up again. Someone has to say, I'm leaving now.

INTERVIEWER

And there's got to be a good reason for it, too. Not, Oh, there's the phone!

WASSERSTEIN

Exactly. That's very hard to do. I always think structurally. But for *The Sisters Rosensweig* it was very hard going. In that play there are four scenes in the first act and three in the second. I should have combined the first two scenes.

INTERVIEWER

You expressed some dissatisfaction about the end of the play. You didn't want to end with Merv and Sara singing to each other. Did that feel wrong to you?

WASSERSTEIN

I did do it originally, and it was great when Merv sang "For Me and My Gal." But suddenly this play became Mervyn the Magician, this man who came into these three sisters' lives and turned the place upside down. It made the play smaller, instead of larger.

INTERVIEWER

Because it narrowed the question of whom the play was about or who got what?

Yes, because it was about getting a guy. For Sara, Mervyn is an agent of change. But he's not the answer.

INTERVIEWER

Do you ever see actors when you write?

WASSERSTEIN

Sometimes, but they never end up doing the play. You think Julie Andrews or people you don't even know.

INTERVIEWER

You once said that you look forward to writing because you can't wait to leave yourself.

WASSERSTEIN

Well, I was very sad when *The Sisters Rosensweig* opened the first time. People like Merv and Gorgeous are fun to write. They're nice to have in your apartment. They're really good company. So when you discover those people, they're talking and you're not talking anymore. I remember the day I wrote the line for Gorgeous about Benjamin Disraeli being a Jewish philanthropist. I started laughing because I thought, That's Gorgeous, there you go. The character, not my sister. If you stay with the actual people in your real life, it won't work. It's too constraining.

INTERVIEWER

What about when you are developing a character similar to yourself? Do you write what you know about yourself or do you find out things about yourself while you're writing the character?

It's closer to writing yourself as if you were these other people. I think the voice of the author in this play is in Geoffrey's speech to Pfeni about making the best art and the best theater. That's me, Wendy, the writer speaking, and it's interesting that I put the words into the mouth of a bisexual British man.

INTERVIEWER

Can you explain that?

WASSERSTEIN

I think because in some ways it's less inhibiting. But you're always writing different aspects of yourself into different characters. You are never writing yourself. There are aspects of me in Pfeni—the distancing aspect, the vulnerability, and the need to wander. And the ability to get involved with a bisexual. Hey—when's the mixer? There are aspects of me in Sara, too. I am a Jewish girl who's been in these Waspy institutions all my life. Ed Kleban used to say that what was interesting about me was that the family moved very quickly from being middle-class Brooklyn to upper-middle-class Upper East Side and all the pretentions of it.

INTERVIEWER

Do you tend to write about what you know?

WASSERSTEIN

I think yes. I learn things from watching and listening to people. I'm not much of a reader. I'm slightly dyslexic. Take Merv—he is someone I knew when I was eight years old. I don't run into a whole lot of

Mervs right now. Nor do I run into a lot of the Gorgeouses of life. But I remember these colorful people and their language. I remember going to someone's bar mitzvah in Brooklyn with my mother and young niece. And you know when they take the Torah out? My mother said to Samantha, Quick, kiss the Torah before the rabbi takes it out for cookies and lunch. It was such a crazy image to me.

INTERVIEWER

It sounds like a dream.

WASSERSTEIN

It was like a dream or a Philip Roth short story. But I always have this terrible memory for what people said. You always remember what someone said yesterday, so you hold them accountable—maybe that's why I tend to write about people I know.

INTERVIEWER

Where do you write?

WASSERSTEIN

I used to write in a garage out in Bridgehampton that was literally a UPS drop-off. My brother lived on fifty acres on the water, and I wrote in this place with a garage underneath, two rooms upstairs and just a little typewriter. I wrote there in the summers. I also write in this little typing room at the Society Library on Seventy-Ninth Street. A friend gave me an office at Comedy Central on Fifty-Seventh and Broadway, but the problem there is that a telephone is there and I get on the phone a lot. But when I'm alone in one of these small rooms and I'm working—if I'm in the middle of something, of a play—it's fun. That's kind of nice. I don't feel this way if I'm in the middle of something that I don't really want to be writing. That's less fun.

You use a typewriter?

I've always used a typewriter or, because I go to libraries, I write longhand in a notebook. Spiral-bound, on the sides. I tend to write longhand and then I'll start typing it on an IBM. I'll type it myself. This is why it takes me too long to write a play. Finally, I'll get it to a typist or to various young assistants, young playwrights or whomever, who type it up for me afterward.

Do your plays start with an image?

My plays start with a feeling. *The Sisters Rosensweig* started when I was living in London writing *The Heidi Chronicles*. I thought about Americans abroad, and somebody said to me, You're terribly Jewish, just like my brother-in-law. It was that same feeling I had at Mount Holyoke, a little bit uncomfortable with myself. Like wherever I went I was always wearing a tiara with chinchilla.

What were you doing in London?

I was there on a grant from the British American Arts Association. It was for midcareer stimulation. I loved that grant. I lived in this one room at the Nell Gwynn House. I am better in one room with a hot plate. I'm not really good at working in fancy places or in places that you're supposed to write in, like your study. I don't think I'd ever write in a room that was lined with lovely curtains.

INTERVIEWER

Why is that? Does it strike you as pretentious?

WASSERSTEIN

Or maybe too perfect. Maybe writing reminds me of school. Also, I want to shut out the other things from my life.

INTERVIEWER

So you were in London writing *Heidi*, and *The Sisters Rosensweig* was germinating?

WASSERSTEIN

The play had been germinating since the night I got this message to call my brother's secretary in New York to set up dinner with him in London that night. Here I was on a $4,000 grant from these good socialist girls. Now maybe that doesn't sound too odd, but at the time it sounded nuts. So I called Bruce—he was turning forty at the time—and we had dinner in London. It was the night of Thatcher's election. He was going to Annabel's to celebrate while my friends were having a wake somewhere. So that started me thinking about Americans in London.

INTERVIEWER

What about the genesis of *An American Daughter*?

WASSERSTEIN

I always think of new plays when I'm finishing one. I was finishing *The Sisters Rosensweig* and was prompted by Nannygate—by what happened to Zoë Baird, what happened to Lani Guinier, what is happening to Hillary Clinton. It was also a reaction to turning forty-two—to midlife decisions, to not having children. It was both personal and political. This is a darker play than *The Sisters Rosensweig*. My plays tend to skip a generation—this one is closer to *The Heidi Chronicles*, though it is also darker than that play.

INTERVIEWER

An American Daughter seems to be your most overtly political play. Does that come partly out of your several White House invitations in the past few years?

WASSERSTEIN

It comes from going to plays, from being on panels, from being involved with arts funding. It also comes from the assumption that artists are always liberal, and that the politics of the theater are never surprising. I thought it was time to look inward. To use the theater to do that. And yes, I've been to the White House.

INTERVIEWER

Do you think that artists are unlike other people, with different needs?

Well, I don't know. There is something about the happiness I feel in that garage when Merv and Gorgeous are talking to me. Sitting in the garage in a nightgown with a typewriter—it might be the only time I'm calm. It's an ageless sort of happiness. It's what made me happy when I was twenty-seven and writing *Uncommon Women*, and what made me feel happy last summer. I'm a pretty nervous gal. So there is always the anxiety of writing, which is awful, but at those moments I do feel at one.

Can you compare the feeling of writing alone in the library to the moment when the production begins and you're suddenly surrounded by people with very intense deadlines . . .

It's exhausting. You have to get dressed and show up. And behave yourself. You can't eat all the food on the plate because there are other people there, too. But it's the best part of doing plays, if the actors are asking intelligent questions, and someone like Robert Klein is telling you how good your play is. The other difference for me is Dan Sullivan, the director, who is one of those rare creatures with a wonderful analytical and theatrical mind. That's why I go to every rehearsal. I'm not gifted visually—I can only fix my plays by hearing them. Dan will turn to me and say, This line doesn't work, and I'll rewrite it while I'm there. So I am always on my feet.

INTERVIEWER

What stage will a play be in before you show it to someone else?

WASSERSTEIN

I always finish a draft before I show it to anybody. I'll rewrite a scene thirty-seven times before I show it to anyone. Maybe it's from insecurity. I enjoy the process of polishing until finally I set a deadline and meet it. I finished both *Heidi* and *Rosensweigs* by my birthday. On my birthday I said to myself, I will put this in the mail to Dan Sullivan today, I'm so sick of it.

INTERVIEWER

Where were you when you heard you won the Pulitzer Prize?

WASSERSTEIN

I was home in my nightgown writing an essay about my mother that is in *Bachelor Girls*. I had heard a rumor that David Hwang was going to win it for *M. Butterfly*. I'd never been someone who won prizes. Perhaps I wasn't pretentious enough or academic enough. I never thought of myself as an intellectual or good at school. So I just assumed I wouldn't win, which would be fine. I was home and Marc Thibodeau, the press agent for *The Heidi Chronicles*, called up and said, You won the Pulitzer. I said, That's not funny. He said, No, no, I'm serious. You won the Pulitzer Prize. I kept saying, You're the queen of Romania, Marc, don't do this to me. He told me to call my mother, so I did, because I thought, This woman's going to hear my name on the radio and think I died or something. I called her. She asked me, Is that as good as a Tony? I thought, That's my mother, undermine it, don't say congratulations, just pull the rug out from under me. I wasn't in the mood, so I said, Why don't you just call my brother and he'll explain it to you. Then the phone started ringing off the hook, it was like the phone went up and started spinning around the room. I went out that afternoon and had champagne at the Four Seasons with my brother Bruce and sister Sandra and Walter Shapiro and André Bishop. Then I went to the theater. Edward Albee was there. He told me to go on stage and take a bow. I said I was too shy. He said that I never knew when it was going to happen again. So I did it.

INTERVIEWER

Did winning the Pulitzer mean more than winning the Tony?

WASSERSTEIN

It's hard to say, because they're different. Winning the Pulitzer was never a goal of mine but it meant a great deal to me in terms of self-esteem. Getting the Tony was quite different because I knew that for the sake of the play and its commercial life that it was very important. I remember sitting in the audience with André Bishop thinking, Should I go up with the scarf, without the scarf? When I went up, there were so many men standing behind me, I wanted to say, So many men, so little time. I just couldn't do it because I was the first woman to win the Tony for best play alone, and I felt the need to dignify the occasion in some way. Because what's hard about being a playwright is, as Christopher Durang would say, it's all so random—getting your play done, how it's going to be reviewed ...

INTERVIEWER

Is it any more random than other commercial art?

WASSERSTEIN

If you want to write for television, for instance, there is a supply and demand—you can make a living. Even if you're commissioned to write a play, you are not going to get paid in the same way.

INTERVIEWER

Does that make the motives of playwrights purer?

WASSERSTEIN

In a sense. It also depends on how you think, whether you think in terms of plays. I am most interested in how people talk. If I went to a movie studio and said I wanted to do a movie about three sisters over forty with a romantic lead who is fifty-four, they'd ask me to rewrite it for Geena Davis, and then they'd probably hire Beth Henley to make them all Southern. In film the voice gets taken out of it unless you're the director.

INTERVIEWER

Are you saying that screenwriters are less writers than playwrights?

WASSERSTEIN

No, it's just a different craft. Most screenwriters I know would like to be directors so that they could have some sort of control.

Many writers detest the public life brought on by success, the awards, the speeches. I get the feeling that
you enjoy it. Do you think of it as a reward for all the
time you spend alone?

There is a part of me that thinks that playwrights
deserve as much recognition as novelists or screenwriters. I also know that if you want people to come
to your plays, it helps to go on David Letterman's
show. One creates a persona. I'm actually a shy person. Michael Kinsley is also a shy person, and there
he is on TV every night. I was talking to him about
this, that fame is not about getting a restaurant reservation. It's about walking up Madison Avenue on
the way to your therapist, and you're thinking, My
God, I'm worthless, what am I doing with my life,
I'm horrible . . . Then some woman comes up to you
and says, You're Wendy Wasserstein. I can't tell
you how much you mean to me. I want to say to this
person, I'm glad I mean something to you because I
mean nothing to me. Thank you very much. Then I
think, What is wrong with me?

I like to think that those are the people who
I write for—the matinee ladies at *The Sisters
Rosensweig*. I guess it is something of a release from
being alone and working. It's odd for me to have
chosen this profession because I'm not very good at
being alone and I'm not very good at sitting still. But
at the same time, I find my work very comforting.

INTERVIEWER

You are known for being nice. Can a woman afford to be too nice?

WASSERSTEIN

I have a great interest in being ladylike, but there is also something to be said for being direct. What I hate about myself and would like to change is that I get hurt very easily. I'm too vulnerable and always have been. I don't look vulnerable. I always think vulnerable girls should have Pre-Raphaelite hair, weigh two pounds, about whom everybody says, Oh, she's so sensitive. I admire aggressiveness in women. I try to be accommodating and entertaining, and some say that's what's wrong with my plays. But I think there are very good things about being a woman that have not been taught to men—not bullshit manners but true graciousness. I think there is real anger in life to be expressed, there is great injustice, but I also think there is dignity. That is interesting, and part of the plays I want to write.

INTERVIEWER

Did you always know you were a playwright?

WASSERSTEIN

I always loved the theater, but it would have been odd to proclaim it as my vocation. I did, however, play with my Ginny doll and imagine plays for my dolls. I thought I'd be a lawyer and get married and not practice. I find it interesting how affected one is by the time in which one comes of age. I'm sure if I had gone to Mount Holyoke in 1955, I would have gotten married my sophomore year because that's

325

what everybody did. I think of Hillary Clinton as being of that generation as well. When I went to college there was a saying, Holyoke to wed and Smith to bed. So my mother sent me to Mount Holyoke. I grew up reading the Arts and Leisure section, thinking that I would be like Celeste Holm in *All About Eve* and that it would be the husband who was the playwright and I would be the well-educated person who loved the theater. In those four years all of that changed—a transitional generation. The fact that I am the playwright has to do with that time.

INTERVIEWER

Was there any anti-Semitism at Mount Holyoke?

WASSERSTEIN

I do remember one girl at Mount Holyoke did not want me to come to her house over vacation because her father didn't particularly like Jews. They lived in Newton, Massachusetts. I came from Brooklyn, where everybody was Jewish or black or they were parochial-school kids, but I didn't know them. When we moved to the Upper East Side, there were people who weren't Jewish, who went to Trinity and those fancy schools, but I didn't know them. Mount Holyoke was the first time I was ever in a house with a Christmas tree. So you did have a sense that you were Jewish and everybody else wasn't—that you were an outsider. While this could be alienating, it affected me for the better, I think. It made me feel I did not need to be anyone else. My close friends there were largely Catholic. I had one Jewish friend there from New Jersey who became a Marxist-Leninist gynecologist. How could you not love such a person? Those are the sorts of people you're supposed to meet in college.

INTERVIEWER

Who are the playwrights you most admire?

WASSERSTEIN

Chekhov, Ibsen, Wilde, Shakespeare, Chris Durang, Lanford Wilson, August Wilson, Tina Howe. I also have admiration for the women who write musicals—Betty Comden, Carolyn Leigh.

INTERVIEWER

One last question. Did you ever sit through a play of yours with your mother?

WASSERSTEIN

You mean sitting beside her? God no!

(1997)

Luisa Valenzuela

THE ART OF FICTION NO. 170

Interviewed by Ksenija Bilbija*

L uisa Valenzuela, the eldest daughter of a prominent Argentine writer, Luisa Mercedes Levinson, was born in Buenos Aires in 1938. The Levinson home was a gathering place for Argentina's literary community—Jorge Luis Borges and Julio Cortázar, among others, were frequent guests—and Valenzuela, an omnivorous reader, started writing at an early age. She published her first story, "Ese canto," in 1958.

Later that year, having married a French sailor, Valenzuela moved to Paris, where she worked as a correspondent for the Argentine newspaper *El Mundo*. Her daughter, Anna Lisa Marjek, was born in France. In 1961, Valenzuela returned to Buenos Aires and went to work at another Argentine newspaper, *La Nación*. She penned a regular feature on

---

* Sarah Lee also contributed to the interview.

the provinces, "Images for the Argentine Interior," for the paper, and continued to write fiction—her first novel, *Hay que sonreír*, was published in 1966, and a collection of stories, *Los Heréticos*, appeared the next year. The two books were translated into English and published as *Clara: Thirteen Short Stories and a Novel* in 1976.

Having been awarded a Fulbright grant to participate in the International Writing Program at the University of Iowa, Valenzuela left Argentina again in 1969. While in the program, she wrote *El Gato eficaz* (1972)—portions of that novel have been published in the States as *Cat-o-Nine Deaths*. After Iowa, she spent a year in Mexico and a year in Barcelona. "I am traveling everywhere. I am too much a gypsy," the author has said. She returned to Buenos Aires in 1974—the year of Juan Perón's death and Isabel Perón's ascent to power—and published a second collection of stories, *Aquí pasan cosas raras* (*Strange Things Happen Here*), in 1975. With the 1976 military coup, the political situation deteriorated further—repression became more pervasive, and Valenzuela, whose work until then had escaped the ire of the military, found her next novel, *Como en la guerra* (*He Who Searches*) (1977), censored.

Valenzuela moved to New York City in 1978, but her fiction continued to be informed by Argentina and the political turmoil of the seventies. She lived in the city for the next decade teaching at Columbia and New York Universities. *Cambio de armas* (*Other Weapons*), which includes the autobiographical novella "Fourth Version," was published in 1982. In 1981 she started work on *Cola de lagartija* (*The Lizard's Tail*), a roman à clef based on the life of

Perón's minister of social welfare, José López Rega, who appears in the novel as the Sorcerer, a man with three testicles. The novel was published in 1983, and was met with immediate and fervent praise.

Valenzuela settled in Argentina again in 1989, and currently lives in the Belgrano neighborhood of Buenos Aires where she grew up. Her living room is open and warm, its ocher walls adorned with numerous paintings by Puppo, Raul Alonso, Batteplanos, and Lea Lubins. In the background, the patio—overgrown with tangles of vines, roses, and ficus—looks out onto looming skyscrapers. Off of the living room is Valenzuela's study, where she does all her writing when in Buenos Aires. Two walls of the study are lined with books—written in Spanish, English, and French. Another wall is covered with masks, which Valenzuela has collected over her years of travel. Her desk occupies the heart of the room, and seems almost alive with the words and images encased under the glass cover. A computer, as well as piles of open books and letters, sits on top of the desk.

This interview took place over several meetings during the past year. Valenzuela has a beautiful, expressive face, which is framed by dark, unruly hair; she speaks slowly and deliberately, with an unmistakable Argentine accent marked with both sophistication and grit. The first conversation was conducted last September in Wisconsin, when Valenzuela was the guest lecturer at the Mid-America Conference. (A multimedia performance based on her story "Other Weapons" (1982) premiered there.) Additional conversations took place during Valenzuela's frequent visits to New York City: at a restaurant in SoHo, over several glasses of sake; at a Chinese restaurant in Midtown; and over a brief breakfast in the East Village this September, when she came to the city to write about the World Trade Center attacks for *La Nación*. In between the meetings, occasional emails were exchanged, some in English and some in Spanish, all of them signed *abrazos*—hugs.

INTERVIEWER

When did you start writing?

LUISA VALENZUELA

I dictated my first poem to my mother at age six. It was about death. Funny I would connect so early with the one unavoidable subject. The poem describes a beautiful woman with all the obvious metaphors of the time. Then a bird comes to her window and says, *Hacia ti viene la muerte*, "Death comes toward you." It came to me just like that—influenced by Poe, no doubt—and my mother wrote it down. My older sister used to read scary stories aloud to make me eat, so maybe that's where I got the inspiration. In my early years I never thought I would become a writer. Maybe those tales of terror made me decide to write—after all, it's always better to be on this side of the production line.

I published my first story at age twenty—which was also about death. Death is the ultimate mystery, which, alas, love isn't, so it's more enticing as subject matter. We are always trying to have the last word over what will finally have the last word over us.

INTERVIEWER

Your mother was a well-known Argentine writer.

What was it like to grow up surrounded by literary figures?

VALENZUELA

One time my mother and Borges composed a story together. I remember the laughter coming from the room they were working in. The story, "La Hermana de Eloísa," was published in 1955, but neither one of them liked that story much after a certain time, and it was never reprinted in a book. My mother said that the experience taught her how to edit. Borges would come out of the dining room where they were writing and laughing, and say, Today we made significant progress—we wrote one full line. Now I am grateful for that experience—they were so happy writing the story that it impressed upon me that writing is a joyous activity. And it is, for the most part.

INTERVIEWER
What was Borges like?

VALENZUELA
He was a walking system of thought. You could see the way his mind worked, since he was offering it so generously—also in a self-centered way, because he didn't care to listen much. He monologued in the most splendid and humorous fashion—he seemed so serious, but was full of wit and naughty humor.

I remember the last days we spent in New York with him. Daniel Halpern would be driving us back and forth from NYU to Columbia, and Borges would be posing impossible questions. In what version of what year of this poem did Auden change such-and-such word for another? Things like that.

We took care of the frail old man, protecting him from the students, and then in the evenings his future wife, María Kodama, would call and say, Borges wants to go listen to some jazz, or, Borges wants to take a ride in the park. By the end of the stay we were exhausted.

INTERVIEWER

As a child, were you aware of his greatness?

VALENZUELA

Not then. The people who surrounded him—the group that visited our home during those years—were all great. Borges didn't stand out among the rest. He was so shy. What I do remember are his lectures. I went to every one of them. At times, there would be sudden and long silences—the public suffered, thinking he had lost the thread, but he was simply searching. The minute he opened his mouth again, the exact term emerged like a gem.

INTERVIEWER

His talks were on literature?

VALENZUELA

Yes. Those were Peronist times, and Perón felt threatened by intellectuals. Borges was transferred from his obscure job at a municipal library to inspector of poultry in municipal markets. And since intellectuals do need to earn a living—in spite of the common belief—an organization called Pro Arte organized lectures and courses in private homes such as my mother's. The feeling was great in spite of the fear—everybody felt like conspirators, keeping all the windows closed, the meetings secret.

Could you say a little more about the Pro Arte movement?

Things here get lost so easily. There is virtually no trace now of Pro Arte, an association born— honoring the name—to help the artist. Pro Arte started by organizing exhibits, concerts, and lectures in public spaces in the forties. During Perón's regime, they had to go underground, or at least into the private domain. Many of the great writers were involved—Borges, Ernesto Sábato, Eduardo Mallea, Manuel Peyrou, Conrado Nalé Roxlo, the poets Amelia Biaggioni, Ana Emilia Lahitte, and Eduardo González Lanuza. Also the émigrés from the Spanish Civil War—Arturo Cuadrado, the publisher of *Botella al mar*, and Clemente Cimorra and Amparo Arbajal. I was very young at the time, but remember them vividly. It was a moveable, motley crowd. They were an impressive lot.

At least once a week they would get together, sometimes until the wee hours of the morning. Empanadas, sandwiches, and red wine was the usual fare. I remember the ongoing arguments between Borges and Sábato—around politics, around the value of the short story versus the novel. I remember at some point—because of politics and, perhaps, a secret literary rivalry—the situation got out of hand. Pipina Diehl offered a splendid peacemaking dinner, at the end of which she urged Georgie—Borges was called by his nickname while his mother was alive—to apologize. I wasn't aware that we had quarreled, he answered for everyone to hear, and went on sipping his soup.

INTERVIEWER

How would you compare contemporary literary life in Argentina to literary life back then?

VALENZUELA

Literary life then was passionate. Literature was really alive—it was something to be taken into account, both in the media and the public sphere. Now we run with the times. Individualism is rampant among the writers, and the media pays much more attention to politicians, starlets, and comedians—one and the same—than to intellectuals.

INTERVIEWER

Having lived for many years outside of Argentina, what is your conception of home?

VALENZUELA

I lived for over three years in France, one in Normandy and then in Paris. Practically a year in Barcelona. And ten glorious years in New York, from where I moved back and forth to Mexico and, at least once a year, with trepidation, home to Buenos Aires. I don't miss anything anymore, neither people nor places.

Many writers say that language is their real home. I am all for that notion. During the last military dictatorship it was said that the writers who had left the country would progressively distance themselves from their roots until one day they would no longer be Argentine writers. It was a way of dismissing those voices, the only ones capable of being critical and objective about the regime. I, for one, don't need my roots deep in the ground. I carry them with me—like the aerial roots of our local *clavel del aire*.

Anyhow, you can never really return home. Buenos Aires has changed so much that it is no longer my city. It is a good place to clam-in and write, and the mother tongue is crucial. One thing I discovered in coming back is the importance of your own intonations as background noise. I left New York when I started dreaming in English, talking to myself in English, thinking in English. The Argentine language is a home I don't want to lose.

INTERVIEWER

How has your identity as a writer been influenced by having homes in both New York and Argentina?

VALENZUELA

I always have written on that bridge between two places. For me, it is a necessary position—the displacement and decentering of a single perspective. I often write about Buenos Aires when I am away from it. I know for sure that *Clara* came to life because I was missing Buenos Aires so much. That novel is so Buenos Aires of the forties—the lowlifes, prostitutes, and pimps, the carnivals. Being away gives me a good perspective. Now I am elated writing about New York in Buenos Aires. It's a way of being in two places at the same time, ubiquity being one of my big dreams in life.

When you lived in New York in the eighties, you taught creative writing at New York University. What was that experience like, considering the fact that you were teaching in your second language?

VALENZUELA

I enjoyed my classes in New York precisely because of the strangeness with the language. It was good both for me and for the students, since we were sharing a frontier. We were breaking boundaries together.

INTERVIEWER

Would you say that Argentine writers—Latin American writers in general—have a different way of writing fiction than their American counterparts?

VALENZUELA

Oh, yes. I always am quite disturbed when American reviewers call my fiction surrealist. I consider it realist in excess. Latin American writers think of reality as having a wider span, that's all—we explore the shadow side of it.

But the real difference has to do mostly with the origins of language. Spanish grammar is different from English grammar. This means that we have a different approach not only to the world, but to the word. At times it is something very subtle, a more daring immersion into the unknown. *Un día sorprendente*, to give a very specific example, doesn't mean exactly the same as *un sorprendente día*. In English, you cannot even turn around a phrase or leave a dangling participle. Joyce needed to explode the English language to allow its occult meaning to emerge.

Cortázar just plays around with Spanish words and grammar for the same purpose. Ours is a much more elastic grammar. English is onomatopoeic, beautifully strict, clear-cut. Spanish, on the other hand, is more baroque and allows for ambiguity and metaphor. Does it have to do with the speaker's character, or is character, as we may surmise, a construction of language?

INTERVIEWER

What do you think about the idea of women's language?

VALENZUELA

I openly fight for it. I think there is a different charge in the words—women come from the badlands of language. Women know a lot about ambivalence and ambiguity—which is why, I think, good, subtle political writing by women novelists is dismissed in Argentina. Women are expected to console, not disturb the readers.

INTERVIEWER

Do you consider yourself a feminist?

VALENZUELA

I think of myself as somebody who is a born feminist but doesn't like any isms. I don't want to be obliged to anything. I hate labels. But ever since I was a little girl, I fought my way as a woman. I saw the oppression too clearly. I think of myself as a casualty of that war and I bear my wounds with pride, though I avoid banner waving.

Going back to your time at NYU, what do you think a writer who teaches can offer to a writer in a creative-writing class?

You cannot make a writer—it is an innate way of seeing the world, and a love of language, and a lifetime commitment. But the students in those classes already had a writer's mind, so you could teach them to see what they didn't see in their own work and move them beyond their own limitations—force them, push them inside the darkest corridors of their imagination, and also motivate them.

Have you ever taken a creative-writing class?

Never. The streets, journalism, and travel were my classes. I love to roam on my own in the bad neighborhoods of foreign cities. But who knows, a good writer's workshop could become the equivalent of that, and it might even put you on the right path when you are blocked. Though I'm too proud, too old, and too lazy to even consider such a thing.

You started out as a journalist. Do you think journalism has contributed to your fiction?

Not necessarily. Both worlds run parallel for me, but never—as yet—converge. Journalism taught me to be very precise and brief, very attentive to language. At *La Nación* my boss, Ambrosio Vecino, was a very literary man, a real teacher. He had been Cortázar's best friend during their college years together. But journalism requires a horizontal gaze. It is absolutely factual. On the other hand, fiction requires a vertical gaze—delving deeper into the nonfacts, the unconscious, the realm of the imaginary. These are two very different ways of seeing the world.

Fiction, for me at least, is the best way to say things. I can be much more clear minded if I allow my imagination to take the lead—never loosing the reins, of course, but at full gallop. I also believe that, if you are fortunate, you can access the unconscious through fiction. In my case, elaborate ideas emerge in a very organized manner. Fiction for me is a way of "writing what you don't know about what you know," to quote Grace Paley.

Borges has this wonderful phrase in a short story, *La falta de imaginación los mueve a ser crueles*—"The lack of imagination moves them to cruelty." Though cruelty with imagination can be the worst of all— just think of certain torturers in our respective countries. As a tool, imagination should only be used by writers, in their writing.

INTERVIEWER

What was Cortázar like?

VALENZUELA

I saw Julio Cortázar for the last time in December 1983. We spent a long afternoon together, and he confessed a strong need to write a novel. I asked him if he had any idea about the plot of his future novel. No, he didn't, but he had a recurrent dream in which the publisher handed him the printed book, and he glanced through it and found it perfect—he finally had been able to say what he had wanted to say all his life. And it didn't surprise him at all that the book was written not in letters, but with geometrical figures. He died the next year, on February 14. I remember thinking that the writers who had been honored with his friendship should bring his book into existence— one writer could write the triangle, another the cube, the circle, or sphere, and so on.

INTERVIEWER

How does the writing process work for you? Do you know, for example, when you are starting a novel as opposed to a short story?

VALENZUELA

Yes, absolutely. Well, except for my first novel, *Clara*. Back then, I never thought I would be able to write a novel, and suddenly the idea I had for a short story needed to branch and develop.

Otherwise the division is clear. You inhabit another realm when you are writing a novel. It's like being in love—being "in novel." At times, the need is unbearable. During those periods, I don't want to write short stories. On the other hand, I might get a spark or an idea for a story. Then I need a certain willpower to start pulling the thread, with the exact tension and patience so as to discover what lies behind the glimpse. Cortázar said that when the moment came he had to go to the typewriter and pull the story out of himself as if he were pulling out some kind of creepy creature, *una alimaña*. It sometimes feels like that.

Do you have a writing schedule?

VALENZUELA

Each work finds its own time. For many years I wrote at night. Then I became scared of writing at night, probably on account of the ghosts that you call to mind when you are writing, mostly when dealing with the subject of torture and other dark political issues. I've returned to the night shift just recently, and am rediscovering the pleasure of total silence. But I still enjoy jumping out of bed and onto the computer—from dream to word, with no time to repent.

INTERVIEWER

You don't have any rituals or routines that prepare you for writing?

VALENZUELA

I don't have a ritual, but I like them a lot. With this postmodern contraption, the PC, I just do a few hands of solitaire as a warm-up. I wish I could play the piano instead.

INTERVIEWER

Do you write straight through from beginning to end?

VALENZUELA

In general, yes. When I don't write straight from

beginning to end, even if doing so takes a couple of years, I know I'm in deep trouble.

Do you revise much?

This last novel had many versions. It probably has to do with the fact that I write on a computer now. I find it quite degrading, but times are changing. Before, I wrote by hand with a soft fountain pen—I still regret the loss of my old Parker 51, a gift from my father when I turned thirteen. If I needed a certain rhythm, I went to the typewriter. Writing by hand forced me to retype each page at least three times, and each time I retyped it I would hear the pound of the words, and polish them until they reached the perfect intonation.

How does a book start?

El Gato eficaz, for example, just started pouring out of me. It was a very intense experience. I was a writer in residence at the International Writing Program at the University of Iowa, and after a couple of blank months, this strange text came into being—and with such unusual language, so wicked and crazy. The words I used in telling that story were so unfamiliar to me that I had to write them down the minute they came. I was writing in elevators, I was writing in the streets, I was writing all over the place, on little notebooks and pieces of paper, trying to get hold of every phrase.

INTERVIEWER

What about *Black Novel with Argentines* (1990)? How did that start?

VALENZUELA

I was in New York and I thought I wanted to write a detective novel à la Chandler, but by the second page my intentions had flopped. I already knew who the killer was and who the victim was and how he had killed her. I knew, and I couldn't lie to the reader. I realized then that the real, and only, search had to be for the motive of the crime. I went on writing, and not getting any wiser about it. Many times I thought I would have to throw the whole thing away. All the while, these flashes about repression in Argentina kept popping into the mind of my Argentine protagonist, Agustín Palant. Finally, I saw the complete picture—the return of the repressed—and knew I had to be very careful not to spell it out bluntly. Since the story deals with repression it is also about what cannot easily be said. Argentina, like Agustín, needs to know, but doesn't want to hear.

INTERVIEWER

How do you deal with politics in your writing?

VALENZUELA

When I was young and all of those literary discussions were taking place in my home, the idea of politics in writing was anathema. Only Ernesto

Sábato insisted that you could use politics in fiction. For Borges and the people around him, *politics* was a dirty word. You know, art for art's sake. So back then I thought that you shouldn't put politics where your mind was, where your writing was.

Now I know differently. Although the only way to deal with politics in literature is to avoid the message at all costs, without being self-righteous or judgmental. I learned that lesson inadvertently in the process of writing *Strange Things Happen Here* in 1975. Returning from two years of travel, I was faced with such a violent Buenos Aires that I didn't recognize my city anymore. I decided that the only way I could understand—or at least have a feeling of belonging—was by writing. I decided to write a story a day, somewhat like an AA program. So I went to the local cafés, where the paranoid feelings were so palpable that any phrase I could pick up triggered a story. Often the phrases I would over-hear had nothing to do with what people were actually saying.

INTERVIEWER

Do you mean that you misheard them, or that their speech was codified in some way?

VALENZUELA

Both. The basic idea was to work around what goes unsaid yet is there, throbbing. To grasp the underlying paranoia. Usually, I misheard the phrases—but it is true that everything more or less political was said elliptically or in a coded manner. Anyway, what was important to me then were random words that would trigger my imagination. Using black humor, the grotesque, the exasperation of language, I managed to depict the horror of oppression and torture, and reintegrate myself into the reality we were living then. I wrote thirty stories in one month. In the process, I learned how to write politics without giving a message.

INTERVIEWER

Is it important to avoid the message because it makes for better fiction, or because it more easily eludes censorship?

VALENZUELA

I don't have a real message to give. I don't know the solution. But if I believed I did, I would write an essay, a column, even a pamphlet—and never contaminate fiction with a message. On the contrary, I believe fiction is a search shared with the reader.

INTERVIEWER

Has your work ever been censored? I'm thinking of "Page Zero," from your novel *He Who Searches*.

VALENZUELA

"Page Zero" was a censored page from the Spanish original. In 1979, I was correcting the proofs. The military had taken over in March, and my editor, Enrique Pezzoni, was courageous enough to go ahead with the publication but asked for caution. In "Page Zero," an introduction that is really an epilogue, the main protagonist is interrogated and tortured. His confession is supposed to be the text of the novel. I agreed with the publisher to pull out "Page Zero," but we forgot to take it off the table of contents. No one noticed anything—the novel was experimental enough.

Those were bad times for publication. We had to play around the margins of a very diffuse, random, but lethal censorship. The publishers of a distinguished house that specialized in psychology and sociology—two very threatened disciplines at that time—went to see the colonel who was in charge of education and culture and asked him for guidelines that could be followed. The colonel was outraged. How can you ask that? You can publish whatever you want. This is a free country, with a free press and freedom of speech. Of course, he added, if some madman or other decided to plant a bomb in your publishing house, there is nothing we can do about it.

INTERVIEWER

What do you think about Joseph Brodsky's claim that good poetry can only be written under political repression?

VALENZUELA

I used to quarrel with Brodsky over that claim. Brodsky would say, with his deep voice, that censorship was bad for the writer but good for literature. That upset me to no end—it may be true in places like the former Soviet Union, where censorship was regulated, but not in countries like Argentina, where censorship was completely random. You had no idea what would not please some military or other, and if something happened to upset them they would go for the kill—your parents, your children, even your friends. I might be ready to put my life at stake for my thoughts, but not everybody else's. Brodsky would say that a writer who cannot put everybody's life at risk is not worth the name, and that censorship pushed you to produce tighter metaphors. I think that a writer who cannot find the right metaphor is not worth the name, neither under a dictatorship nor a democracy.

INTERVIEWER

Have you ever experienced exile?

VALENZUELA

Once, for a month and a half—it wasn't much, yet it was difficult to bear. In 1976, I went to New York for the launching of my second book in English, *Strange Things Happen Here*. Two days after I left Buenos Aires, the police raided my apartment where my daughter was alone with her boyfriend—they were in their teens—and searched everything. They were looking for me. I had been fighting for human rights, hiding people who were in danger, getting crucial information out of the country. Fortunately, it was the police who came and not the paramilitary. They were threatening, but they didn't take the kids away or harm them. I was advised not to come back. I remember spending a whole night with a Rubik's Cube, trying unsuccessfully to solve it, as if that would put my life back in place. Eventually, I managed to return to Buenos Aires, only to leave it again—but this time it was my decision. I became an expatriate, not an exile.

INTERVIEWER

A similar scene appears in "Fourth Version," when the character Bella goes abroad to perform her one-person show.

Yes, I do steal from my life at times! In that scene, Bella receives a phone call and is informed that some people are looking for her and that she should not come back. Her attitude and outlook change—she finally acknowledges the weight of her work—and she decides to return to a violent Buenos Aires and fight, with her own weapons, not allowing fear to paralyze her as it paralyzed others.

INTERVIEWER

Conversely, characters and events that originate in your fiction at times transgress their limits, literally invading reality. Your novel *Bedside Manners* (1990), for example, which unwittingly foretold a true military insurrection.

VALENZUELA

That was an ugly coincidence. An uprising of the rebel military took place the day after the book was launched. Since the novel speaks about just such an uprising, my friends claimed I was overdoing it with the promotion of the book.

The novel takes a very pataphysical—you know, never take serious things seriously—approach to reality. The uprisings were very real—the insurgent officers called themselves the Carapintadas, since they smothered their faces with camouflage grease. Everything in *Bedside Manners* is real—the hyper-hyperinflation, raids for food, the shantytown—except the overlapping of ridiculous situations. There are many other examples. I believe narrative knows better than we all do.

You yourself appear as a character in *The Lizard's Tail*. Why?

While I was writing *The Lizard's Tail*, I realized that the Sorcerer was taking over the novel. This had to do with his choice of words—I had given him the first person, and with it the power over language. I couldn't fight with him from the outside—it would have been a form of literary cheating—so my only possibility was to get in the novel myself.

INTERVIEWER
What do you mean by literary cheating?

VALENZUELA
I was playing a difficult, two-sided game. Not that I was writing an historical novel, but very recent history was at my doorstep, and the novel goes back and forth between the first-person character of the Sorcerer and the omniscient "I." But the real person, José López Rega, on whom the character was based was very much alive then, and I just couldn't distort the facts and kill him in fiction for my convenience. It would have been too easy, and would have spoiled the whole project.

INTERVIEWER
Have you ever thought about writing your memoirs?

VALENZUELA
Of sorts. Not literary memoirs. But I've written diaries on and off, except for the last ten years or so. I

always fantasize about writing travelogues, but then traveling gets the best of me and I don't write. Also, I'm afraid that writing diaries is a way of avoiding fiction, so when I'm into a novel or a sequence of stories, I forgo the diaries.

But I think my life is literary and adventuresome in many ways, and I would love to tell it—if I could just pass the stage of direct narrative, which bores me to no end, especially because, in this case, I already know the outcome. There is no surprise left. Sticking to facts, however interesting, doesn't allow me to delve into metaphor, to understand the deeper implications.

The novel I just finished, *La Travesía* (2001), at first was intended to be a kind of apocryphal autobiography. After a couple of versions, I moved the whole thing from the first to the third person—the protagonist sounded too savvy for my taste, so I abandoned the autobiographical pretense.

INTERVIEWER

May I ask what the new novel is about?

VALENZUELA

La Travesía has to do with secrets. What are the secrets that we want to keep from others and what happens when we try to keep them from ourselves. It's a bildungsroman of adulthood. This is the first time I've dealt with reality, and it was hard for me. The whole plot is invented, but the people surrounding the protagonist are not. I played with those disquieting feelings I used to get from Jerzy Kosinski's novels—where does autobiography stop and invention start?

Your complete short stories were published recently. How did it feel to see your stories all under one roof?

VALENZUELA

I was very excited to get in touch with my first stories again. Each story has its own independence. Each story is like its own individual, grown up and on its own. When I saw them all together, like a family, I could see the thread connecting them.

INTERVIEWER

Do you regret anything you've published?

VALENZUELA

There are so many writers who have burned or disclaimed their first books. Borges, for example. What a nuisance. I am very irreverent. I know no shame in that sense. It would mean some kind of censorship, wouldn't it? Of course, there are some books I like better than others—some books still surprise me now, as if someone else had written them. On the other hand, I often regret what I haven't written because I was too lazy or too cowardly. Writing takes real courage and commitment.

(2001)

Louise Erdrich

THE ART OF FICTION NO. 208

Interviewed by Lisa Halliday

O
nly one passenger train per day makes the
Empire Builder journey from Chicago to
Seattle, and when it stops in Fargo, North
Dakota, at 3:35 in the morning, one senses how, as
Louise Erdrich has written, the "earth and sky touch
everywhere and nowhere, like sex between two
strangers." Erdrich lives in Minneapolis, but we met
in the Fargo Econo Lodge parking lot. From there,
with Erdrich's eight-year-old daughter, Kiizh, we
drove five hours up to the Turtle Mountain Chippewa
reservation, on the Manitoba border. Every August,
when tick season has subsided, Erdrich and her sister Heid spend a week in a former monastery here
to attend the Little Shell Powwow and to conduct
a writing workshop at the Turtle Mountain Community College. One afternoon, participants took
turns reciting poetry under a basswood tree beside
the single-room house where Erdrich's mother grew
up. Another day, they ate homemade enchiladas and

sang "Desperado" and "Me and Bobby McGee," accompanied by a fellow workshopper on the guitar. In class, the writing is personal, the criticism charitable. It helps that Erdrich does the exercises, too— reading out the results in her mellifluous, often mischievous voice. In tidy fulfillment of an assignment entitled "very short fiction," she wrote, "You went out for the afternoon and came back with your dress on inside out."

Karen Louise Erdrich, born June 7, 1954, in Little Falls, Minnesota, was the first of seven children raised in Wahpeton, North Dakota, by a German American father and a mother who is half French, half Ojibwe—Ojibwe, also known as Chippewa, being one of six Native American tribes comprised by the Anishinaabe ("Original People"). Both of Erdrich's parents taught at a Bureau of Indian Affairs boarding school. For many years, her grandfather Patrick Gourneau was the Turtle Mountain Chippewa tribal chair.

Erdrich was in the first coed class to attend Dartmouth, where she studied English and met her eventual husband, Michael Dorris, another writer and the founder of the college's new Native American Studies program. Shortly after receiving an M.A. in creative writing from Johns Hopkins, Erdrich wrote "The World's Greatest Fishermen" (1982), a story about the hypothermia death of June Kashpaw, an Ojibwe divorcée whose funeral summons relatives home to a fictional North Dakota Indian reservation. "Fishermen" won the Nelson Algren short-fiction prize and became the first chapter of *Love Medicine*, Erdrich's debut novel and winner of a 1984 National Book Critics Circle Award. Since then, she has written twelve more novels (including *The Crown of Columbus* (1991), coauthored by Dorris), three books of poetry, three books of nonfiction, dozens of short stories, and five children's books. Four of these books she illustrated herself. With Dorris, who was also her first literary agent, she raised three adopted and three biological children before the couple separated in 1995; two years later, Dorris committed suicide.

Erdrich returned to Dartmouth in June 2009 to receive an honorary doctorate of letters and deliver the main commencement address; the same year, her novel *The Plague of Doves*, which centers on the lynching of four Indians wrongly accused of murdering a white family (and which Philip Roth has called "her dazzling masterpiece"), was named a finalist for the Pulitzer Prize. After invariably classifying Erdrich as a Native American writer, many reviewers proceed to compare her work to that of William Faulkner or Gabriel García Márquez: Faulkner for her tangled family trees, her ventriloquist skill, and her expansive use of a fictional province no less fully imagined than Yoknapatawpha County; García Márquez for her flirtations with magical realism. But so strange are Erdrich's narrative rhythms, and so bonded is her language to its subject matter, that it seems just as accurate to call hers a genre of one.

When the workshop was over, Erdrich drove us back to Fargo for walleye cakes at the Hotel Donaldson, and then to visit her parents, who still live in the modest house in Wahpeton where Erdrich grew up. The next day, while Erdrich attended a wedding in Flandreau, South Dakota, her sister took me the remaining two hundred miles to Minneapolis, where, three days later, Erdrich and I reconvened at her bookstore and Native American arts shop, Birchbark Books. Here, Erdrich's eldest daughter, Persia, decides which children's books to stock. Taped to most of the shelves are detailed recommendations handwritten by Erdrich herself. An upside-down canoe hangs from the ceiling, suspended between a birch-bark reading loft and a Roman Catholic confessional decorated with sweetgrass rosaries. We linger at the store, but not until we make the long walk to Erdrich's house do we finally sit down on the back porch and turn the tape recorder on.

Erdrich was wearing her driving clothes: jeans, sandals, and an untucked button-down shirt. A Belgian shepherd named Maki dozed at our feet, and Erdrich's youngest daughter came out a couple of times—once to ask whether we wanted Play-Doh ice-cream cones, later to report that a Mr. Sparky was on the phone. Then a neighboring buzz saw started up, and we moved inside: up to a small attic room pleasantly cluttered with photographs, artifacts, and many more Catholic and Ojibwe totems, including moccasins, shells, bells, dice, bitterroot, a bone breastplate, an abalone shell for burning sage, a turtle stool, a Huichol mask with a scorpion across its mouth and a double-headed eagle on its brow, and a small army of Virgin statuettes. Crowded into a bookshelf beside a worn armchair in the center of the room are the hardbound spiral notebooks in which, in a deeply slanted longhand, Erdrich still writes most of her books—sitting in the chair with a wooden board laid across its arms as a desk.

In *The Beet Queen* (1986), Dot Adare's first-grade teacher puts Dot into the "naughty box." Was there a naughty box in your own childhood?

LOUISE ERDRICH

Do I have to talk about this? It is a primal wound. Yes, I was put into the naughty box.

INTERVIEWER

What had you done?

ERDRICH

Nothing. I was a model child. It was the teacher's mistake I am sure. The box was drawn on the blackboard and the names of misbehaving children were written in it. As I adored my teacher, Miss Smith, I was destroyed to see my name appear. This was just the first of the many humiliations of my youth that I've tried to revenge through my writing. I have never fully exorcised shames that struck me to the heart as a child except through written violence, shadowy caricature, and dark jokes.

INTERVIEWER

Was your teacher anything like the one in your story "Sister Godzilla" (2001)?

ERDRICH

No, but I had Franciscan sisters for teachers later. Some were celestial, others were disturbed. My sixth-grade teacher, Sister Dominica, hit home runs at recess and I loved her, but there was no exact Sister Godzilla. As for Miss Smith, I still have her

photograph. She had cat-eye glasses, a blond bouf-
fant do, and wore a chiffon scarf tied at the tip of her
chin. I'd been reading for a while before Miss Smith,
but I'd never thought about how there's a presence
inside of words. The Ojibwe say that each word has
a spirit. Miss Smith drew eyelashes on the *o*'s in *look*,
and irises in the middle of the *o*'s, and suddenly *look*
contained the act of looking. I had a flash of pure joy.

INTERVIEWER

Is it true your father paid you a nickel for every story
you wrote as a child?

ERDRICH

Yes, he did, and he's sick of hearing about it. It's
also true that, about a year ago, he gave me a roll of
antique nickels and said, I owe you.

INTERVIEWER

What were the stories about?

ERDRICH

Lonely girls with hidden talents. At a family white-
elephant sale we auctioned off one of my early stories
for eight bucks—someone else got it. I've been trying to buy it back.

My father is my biggest literary influence.
Recently I've been looking through his letters. He
was in the National Guard when I was a child and
whenever he left, he would write to me. He wrote
letters to me all through college, and we still corre-
spond. His letters, and my mother's, are one of my
life's treasures.

What are they about?

Mushroom hunting. Roman Stoics. American Indian Movement politics. Longfellow. Stamp collecting. Apples. He and my mother have an orchard. He used to talk about how close together meadowlarks sit on fence posts—every seventh fence post. Now, of course, they are rare. When I went off to college, he wrote about the family, but in highly inflated terms, so that whatever my sisters and brothers were doing seemed outrageously funny or tragic. If my mother bought something it would be a cumbersome, dramatic addition to the household, but of course unnecessary. If the dog got into the neighbor's garbage it would be a saga of canine effort and exertion—and if the police caught the dog it would be a case of grand injustice.

How did your parents meet?

My mother is Turtle Mountain Chippewa, and she lived on her home reservation. My father taught there. He had just been discharged from the air force. He went to school on the GI Bill and got his teaching credentials. He is adventurous—he worked his way through Alaska at age seventeen and paid for his living expenses by winning at the poker table. He saved the money he made as a cook's flunky and helped out his parents. After he got his credentials, I guess he thought it would be interesting to work on a reservation. He assumed there would actually be mountains in the Turtle Mountains, so he brought his skis. In fact, on the way there, he looked north and saw cloud formations on the horizon and thought they were mountains. But when he arrived he found that the Turtle Mountains are low hills—no skiing. He met my grandfather before he met my mother.

Your mother's father.

Patrick Gourneau. Aunishinaubay was his Ojibwe name. He had an eighth-grade education, but he was a fascinating storyteller, wrote in exquisite script, and was the tribal chairman during the treacherous fifties termination era, when the U.S. Congress decided to abrogate all Indian treaties and declare Indian Nations nonexistent. My grandfather was a persuasive man who made friends with people at every level of influence. In order to fight against our tribe's termination, he went to newspapers and politicians and urged them to advocate for our tribe in Washington. He also supported his family through the Depression as a truck farmer. My father, himself a great talker, got to know Pat Gourneau as another interesting person who loved to converse. Then he saw Pat's daughter Rita and apparently she knocked his socks off. My mother has always been the reserved beauty to his smitten schoolteacher. I was born when she was nineteen and I've always loved having a young mother—she is often mistaken for my sister.

Did she speak Ojibwemowin when you were growing up?

My grandfather spoke the Red Lake dialect of the
language, as his family had originated there, but
he also spoke and wrote an exquisite English. My
mother learned words here and there, but you have
to be immersed in a language as a child to pick it up.

Why?

We are wired to have a period of language opportunity. It is harder to learn languages after the age of
eight or ten. In addition, Ojibwe is one of the most
difficult languages to learn because its verbs take on
an unusual array of forms. There's no masculine or
feminine designation to the nouns, but instead they're
qualified as animate or inanimate. The verb form
changes according to its status as animate or inanimate as well as in regard to human relationships. The
verbs go on and on. Often when I'm trying to speak
Ojibwe my brain freezes. But my daughter is learning to speak it, and that has given me new resolve.
Of course, English is a very powerful language, a
colonizer's language, and a gift to a writer. English
has destroyed and sucked up the languages of other
cultures—its cruelty is its vitality. Ojibwe is taught
in colleges, increasingly in immersion programs, but
when my grandfather went to government boarding
school he wasn't allowed to speak Ojibwe. Nor were

Indian students in Catholic boarding schools, where my mother went, as so many of our family were Catholic.

Were you raised to be devout?

Every Catholic is raised to be devout and love the Gospels, but I was spoiled by the Old Testament. I was very young when I started reading, and the Old Testament sucked me in. I was at the age of magical thinking and believed sticks could change to serpents, a voice might speak from a burning bush, angels wrestled with people. After I went to school and started catechism I realized that religion was about rules. I remember staring at a neighbor's bridal-wreath bush. It bloomed every year but was voiceless. No angels, no parting of the Red River. It all seemed so dull once I realized that nothing spectacular was going to happen.

I've come to love the traditional Ojibwe ceremonies, and some rituals, but I hate religious rules. They are usually about controlling women. On Sundays when other people go to wood-and-stone churches, I like to take my daughters into the woods. Or at least work in the garden and be outside. Any god we have is out there. I'd hate to be certain that there was nothing. When it comes to God, I cherish doubt.

What was it like to leave Wahpeton for Dartmouth?

My father, rightly, picked out a paragraph in *The Plague of Doves* as a somewhat autobiographical piece of the book. Evelina leaves for college and at their parting her parents give her a love-filled stare that is devastating and sustaining. It is an emotion they've never before been able to express without great awkwardness and pain. Now that she's leaving, that love beams out in an intense form.

As the eldest child, I often felt that I belonged more to my parents' generation than to my own. In the beginning of the book, Evelina is always scheming to watch television. My parents didn't let us watch much television. Dad had us cover our eyes when the commercials came on. He didn't want us to nurse any unnecessary desires and succumb to capitalism. Shakespeare's history plays and *The Three Stooges* were major influences.

What was Dartmouth like?

For one thing, the ratio of men to women was nine to one. And I was quite shy, so meeting people was painful. I'd be at a party and because I was so quiet, someone would say, You're stoned, aren't you, Karen? My name was Karen then. But I was only rarely stoned, just shy.

Recently I read a book by Charles Eastman, one of the first Native American physicians in Dakota, about going to Dartmouth. He described exactly how I felt, like I was being torn away. And yet, I wanted to go, I wanted to get away. Sinclair Lewis knew about the crazed feeling that you get when people think you're a pleasant person. You get all this praise for your good behavior but inside you're seething. I was fairly dutiful, and I felt that way. I've always loved that line from Flannery O'Connor's "Revelation"—"Go back to hell where you came from, you old wart hog." In Wahpeton I was a graveyard-shift waitress who wanted to destroy my customers.

At Dartmouth, I was awkward and suspicious. I was in the first year of the Native American program. I felt comfortable with Chippewas and people from the Turtle Mountains, and I felt comfortable with Dakotas because Wahpeton is part of the Dakota reservation and I knew many Dakota people. It took me a while to get to know people from other tribes. People assume there is just one sort of Native experience. No. Do the Irish immediately feel comfortable with the Chinese? I was intimidated by the mighty Mohawks. It took me a long time to get to know my serene and beautiful Navajo roommate. Certainly I didn't understand the non-Indians, the people who came from East Coast backgrounds. Until then, I had met three African American people in my entire life. I had never met an East Indian person, a Jew, a Baptist, a Muslim. I hadn't left Wahpeton so I only knew a peculiar Wahpeton mixture of people, all smashed and molded into a similar shape by small-town life. I don't have a thick skin, and I especially didn't then. I obsessed over everything people said, ran it over forever in my mind. I still do that, but it's better now.

Why did you decide to change your name to Louise?

There were so many Karens when I was born. It was the 1954 name of the year. I think there was a Mouseketeer named Karen. I was happier when I was called Louise. My grandfather was named Louis. I thought it had a good, lucky sort of writerliness to it. There were lots of Louises who were artists and writers—Louise Bogan, Louise Bourgeois, Louise Glück. The only Karen writer I knew and liked was Karen Blixen and she changed her name, so I did, too.

Were you a good literature student?

I worked hard to catch up with people. I didn't know any of the writers other Dartmouth freshmen had read. I knew the Old Testament, of course, and read indiscriminately from the local library—Leon Uris and James Michener and Ayn Rand and Herman Wouk—but nobody at Dartmouth was reading *Marjorie Morningstar*. They were reading Joyce. Who was that? I did have some Shakespeare, because in Wahpeton we'd bought a wonderful record player with green stamps, and my father brought home recordings of the plays—the tragedies, of course. And I liked James Welch, the Blackfoot writer. But otherwise, it was the Dune trilogy and Isaac Asimov and *The Prophet*.

Before coming to Dartmouth, I won a scholarship to an American Legion summer camp and was trapped with the John Birch Society. So I had a strange, brief flirtation with the Right. I voted for Richard Nixon. But then Nixon was a hero to a lot of Native people. Despite everything else, he was one of the first presidents to understand anything about American Indians. He effectively ended the policy of termination and set our Nations on the course of self-determination. That had a galvanizing effect in Indian country. So I voted for Nixon and my boyfriend wanted to kill me and I didn't know why. Why was this so important? Nixon was even running against a South Dakota boy, George McGovern. But McGovern had no understanding of treaty rights, and I also thought I was voting in accordance with my father, because he kept saying George this, George that, what a demagogue. Then about a year ago, I said, Dad, I thought we were both against George in that election. And he said, I was talking about George Wallace.

INTERVIEWER

How does your father feel about your books?

ERDRICH

He gave me those nickels, remember? It didn't occur to me that my books would be widely read at all, and that enabled me to write anything I wanted to. And even once I realized that they were being read, I still wrote as if I were writing in secret. That's how one has to write anyway—in secret. At a certain point, you have to not please your parents, although for me that's painful because I'm close to my parents and of course I want them to be happy.

INTERVIEWER

When did you start writing *Love Medicine*?

I went back to North Dakota after college and became a visiting poet in a program called Poets in the Schools. It was a marvelous gig. I went all around the state in my Chevy Nova, teaching, until I contracted hepatitis at the old Rudolf Hotel in Valley City. What did I expect for eight dollars a night? I was in my smoking, brooding phase, and I was mostly writing poetry. In time, the poems became more storylike—prose, really—then the stories began to connect. Before the hepatitis I also drank, much more than I do now, so I spent a lot of time in bars and had a number of crazy conversations that went into *Love Medicine*. I also used to go to tent revivals up in the Turtle Mountains—that experience eventually became part of *The Plague of Doves*.

INTERVIEWER

A tent revival?

ERDRICH

Where the revivalists pitch a tent and you sit under it and listen to preachers who try to convert you— bring you to Jesus right in the tent. It's like a traveling church. I went to hear that biblical language. Maybe I thought at last I'd witness a miracle. I used to listen to Jimmy Swaggart and Jack Van Impe, who are televangelists. I don't listen to TV preachers anymore because they lost their music and became political, but I used to love it. The formality of Mass was gone—it was just you and some crazy, powerful version of God. As a child, I couldn't get up in the middle of holy Mass and shout, Come down on me! Come Spirit, Spirit! The closest version was a charismatic Catholic group I joined called the God Squad—I was still a teenager then—mainly I'd heard you could go on retreats and make out.

I started writing *Love Medicine* after I realized that narrative was invading the poetry. In the beginning, I was trying to write a spare kind of poetry, like James Wright or Robert Creeley, I suppose, but it was terrible. Then I started writing poems with inner rhymes but as they became more complex they turned into narrative. I started telling stories in the poems. But the poems I could write jumping up from my desk or lying on the bed. Anywhere. At last, I had this epiphany. I wanted to write prose, and I understood that my real problem with writing was not that I couldn't do it mentally. I couldn't do it physically. I could not sit still. Literally, could not sit still. So I had to solve that. I used some long scarves to tie myself into my chair. I tied myself in with a pack of cigarettes on one side and coffee on the other, and when I instinctively bolted upright after a few minutes, I'd say, Oh, shit. I'm tied down. I've got to keep writing.

INTERVIEWER

Where were you when you wrote *Love Medicine*?

ERDRICH

I had come back to Fargo again and was living downtown. I worked in a little office space with a great arched window on the top floor. It was seventy bucks a month. It was heaven to have my own quiet, beautiful office with a great window and green linoleum floors and a little desk and a view that carried to the outskirts of Fargo. The apartment I lived in over Frederick's Flowers belonged to my brother and had no windows, only a central air shaft that was gloomy and gray. That apartment also got into the book. It was a peculiar apartment—you couldn't stay in it all day or you'd go nuts. It cost fifty dollars a month, so all I had to pay every month was one hundred and twenty bucks in rent. I had a bicycle. I ate at the Dutch Maid café. I was living well.

INTERVIEWER

What did you do for money?

ERDRICH

My best job was working for a man named Joe Richardson who had a small-press outfit called Plains Distribution. He managed to get funding for a fancy traveling RV stuffed with small-press books. We distributed work by writers like Ted Kooser, Linda Hasselstrom, Mark Vinz, Tom McGrath. In the middle of all of this I found myself at the trial of Leonard Peltier. It was all taking place right near the sinister apartment I lived in. I was surprised to see neighbors from Wahpeton and a lot of other people I'd grown up with. They were passionate about the American Indian Movement. They got me into the courtroom every day. After listening to all that was said, I was astounded when Peltier was convicted. There was simply no evidence that convicted him. He was convicted out of fear. We know how that goes.

At last, I ran out of money. I applied to the Yaddo and MacDowell writers' residencies. I got some time there, and I was able to finish "Scales" (1982). Then I thought I'd better write a real novel. So I left everything else and wrote a book called *Tracks* (1988). I started it at Johns Hopkins, where I received a teach-

371

ing stipend. I got a lot of encouragement there from John Barth, a genius, a superb teacher, and Edmund White, whom I adored—a man of tender intelligence, and a daring writer. I also got to study with Richard Howard. What luck. He would set one of my poems aside and say, "This one we'll allow to leech away into the sands of discourse." So some of my poems leeched away into the sands of discourse. Then Richard looked at other poems and responded from his sublime knowledge, but he always spoke with a natural sort of kindness. I also met C. Michael Curtis at Johns Hopkins, but he wouldn't have remembered me. Later, he was the first person who accepted a story of mine—"Saint Marie" (1984)— into a glossy magazine. That was a huge moment for me. I still have his acceptance letter. I stared at it for hours and days. After the story was published I got two letters. One from an outraged priest who said I'd written nauseating phantasms of convent life. The other was from Philip Roth. He sent me a letter out of the blue just to say that he liked the story. I stared at his letter for a long time as well. I think I was too shy to answer it, but I wrote the rest of the book.

INTERVIEWER
What happened with *Tracks*?

ERDRICH
It continued to be rejected. It was rejected all over the place. And thank God for that—it was the kind of first novel where the writer tries to take a high tone while loads of mysterious things happen, and there was way too much Faulkner in there. People would find themselves suddenly in cornfields with

desperate, aching anguish over the weight of history. I kept it though, the way people keep a car on blocks out in the yard—for spare parts.

The *Tracks* I've read is a short book.

That's because all of the spare parts got used in other vehicles. And of course I rewrote *Tracks* entirely by 1989, but before that I had withdrawn it from consideration by publishers and started again on *Love Medicine*.

One of the characters in *Love Medicine* says, "You know Lulu Lamartine if you know life is made up of three kinds of people—those who live it, those afraid to, those in between. My mother is the first." Which category is yours?

I suppose I've always wanted to be the first, but really I'm the last. By writing I can live in ways that I could not survive. I've only had children with two fathers. Lulu's had children by what, eight? People sometimes ask me, Did you really have these experiences? I laugh, Are you crazy? I'd be dead. I'd be dead fifty times. I don't write directly from my own experience so much as an emotional understanding of it.

I suppose one develops a number of personas and hides them away, then they pop up during writing. The exertion of control comes later. I take great pleasure in writing when I get a real voice going and I'm able to follow the voice and the character. It's like being in a trance state. Once that had happened a few times, I knew I needed to write for the rest of my life. I began to crave the trance state. I would be able to return to the story anytime, and it would play out in front of me, almost effortlessly. Not many of my stories work out that way. Most of my work is simple persistence. I've had some stories for twenty years. I keep adding to them word by word.

But if the trance happens, even though it's been wonderful, I'm suspicious. It's like an ecstatic love affair or fling that makes you think, It can't be this good, it can't be! And it never is. I always need to go back and reconfigure parts of the voice. So the control is working with the piece after it's written, finding the end. The title's always there, the beginning's always there, sometimes I have to wait for the middle, and then I always write way past the end and wind up cutting off two pages.

INTERVIEWER

Why do you do that?

ERDRICH

When I can't end a story, I usually find that I've actually written past the ending. The trick of course is to go back and decide where the last line hits.

INTERVIEWER

How do you keep all your characters straight?

ERDRICH

I used to try to keep them straight in my head, but I didn't really care if they got messed up. It didn't mean a lot to me if I got them wrong. I'd like to say it was out of some sense of aesthetics, or adherence to some tradition, but really I just didn't care. I wanted to get on with the story. If it weren't for Trent Duffy, the best copy editor in New York, everything would be inconsistent and I still wouldn't be worried about it. And, you know, there still are inconsistencies.

INTERVIEWER

But they're not deliberate?

ERDRICH

You mean are they there so that English and Native American literature scholars have something to work on? No.

INTERVIEWER

Why did you decide to add family trees to your books?

ERDRICH

I resisted for a long time, but then at readings people began to come up and show me their painfully drawn out family trees, so finally I was overcome by guilt. Delightfully, my dear Trent had kept track of the relationships. Now people come up to me and say how grateful they are that they don't have to write out the family trees themselves. It never seemed particularly important to me. In the Turtle Mountains, everybody is related because there are only so many families. Nobody sits down and picks apart their ancestry. Unless you want to date somebody.

How do your books come into being? Where do they start?

I have little pieces of writing that sit around collecting dust, or whatever they're collecting. They are drawn to other bits of narrative like iron filings. I hate looking for something to write about. I try to have several things going before I end a book. Sometimes I don't have something immediately and I suffer for it.

Why?

I feel certain that I'm never going to write again. I'm positive that it's over. The world seems boring. I can't enjoy anything. My family knows I'm moping. I'm not nice to live around, and I'm not a stellar cook. Nothing seems right. The worst times are ending a book tour and not having a book to return to. It's sheer emptiness.

But I guess that's an essential part of this entire process. You feel your mortality and there's nowhere to go. I walk more, which is good. Then I start rummaging around, thinking, It's all over, so what's there to lose? I go to our bookstore, and others, used bookstores, I talk to the booksellers and look around. I go back to things I didn't finish, but then, if I didn't finish it in the first place, it probably isn't really worth going back to. I go to a historical society and leaf through things. I'll take a drive in the car. Eventually something turns up. That's where I am now. I haven't really engaged with the next book in the same way that I engaged with *Shadow Tag* (2010). I suppose I could go back to my eternal science-fiction novel, though it is a failure.

Then why do you go back to it?

ERDRICH

It's irresistible, especially when I'm in free fall. Maybe in a decade I'll have finished it.

INTERVIEWER

Is it set in North Dakota?

ERDRICH

Yes. The North Dakota of the future!

INTERVIEWER

Do you ever feel like you're writing one long novel?

ERDRICH

All of the books will be connected somehow—by history and blood and by something I have no control over, which is the writing itself. The writing is going to connect where it wants to, and I will have to try and follow along.

INTERVIEWER

Is it true that you have control over the cover designs of your books? Writers aren't always afforded that privilege.

That's because the most clichéd Native images used to be suggested for the cover design, so I fought to have some say. On a foreign copy of *Tracks* there was a pair of massive breasts with an amulet hanging between them. Often, a Southwestern landscape appears. Or an Indian princess or two. A publisher once sent me a design for *Master Butchers Singing Club* (2003) that was all huge loops of phallic sausages. They were of every shape and all different textures, colors, sizes. I showed it to my daughter and we looked at it in stunned silence, then we said, Yes! This is a great cover! I have twenty copies left of that edition, and I'm going to keep them. Sometimes I'll show one to a man and ask what he thinks of it. He'll put it in his lap and look at it for a while and the strangest look will cross his face. He'll look sideways at the women in the room, and he'll point and say, I think I see myself in that one.

Do you revise already-published work?

At every opportunity. Usually, I add chapters that I have written too late to include in the original. Or I try to improve the Ojibwe language used in the book. As I learn more or I consult my teachers, I learn how much I don't know. Ojibwe is something I'll be a lifelong failure at—it is my windmill. I've changed *Love Medicine* quite a lot, and I wanted to revise *The Blue Jay's Dance* (1995). For one thing I wanted to take out the recipes. Don't try the lemon-meringue pie, it doesn't work. I've received letters.

I can't wait to change *Four Souls* (2004). There are some big mistakes in that.

Like what?

I'm not saying. It is absurd and filthy—and this is a family publication. But I also feel the ending is too self-consciously poetic, maybe sentimental. I wouldn't end it that way now. I am engaged these days in rewriting *The Antelope Wife* (1998) substantially—I always had a feeling it began well and got hijacked.

Many of the books are hijacked by a child in trouble.

When I had to go on my first book tour—those are the lowest points in my life, the times just before a book tour, when I have to leave my children—I was sitting on a plane next to a psychiatrist. I said to her, I've just written this book and it has another abandoned child in it. Another loveless person abandons another child in the beginning. What is it about abandonment? This psychiatrist, who had a deep, scratchy voice, said, My dear, we are all abandoned.

Abandonment is in all the books—the terror of having a bad mother or being a bad mother, or just a neglectful mother, letting your child run around in a T-shirt longer than her shorts.

Every summer you drive several hours north to visit the Turtle Mountains, sometimes also Lake of the Woods. Why?

Actually, I do this all year. These places are home for me. And I like to travel. Driving takes hold of the left brain and then the right brain is freed—that's what some writer friends and I have theorized. But I can't always stop when I get an idea. It depends on the road—North Dakota, no traffic. When I'm driving on a very empty stretch of road I do write with one hand. It's hardly legible, but still, you don't want to have to stop every time.

Of course, if you have a child along, then you do have to stop. By having children, I've both sabotaged and saved myself as a writer. I hate to pigeonhole myself as a writer, but being a female and a mother and a Native American are important aspects of my work, and even more than being mixed blood or Native, it's difficult to be a mother and a writer.

Because of the demands on your time?

No, and it's not because of hormones or pregnancies. It's because you're always fighting sentiment. You're fighting sentimentality all of the time because being a mother alerts you in such a primal way. You are alerted to any danger to your child, and by extension you become afraid of anybody getting hurt. This becomes the most powerful thing to you—it's instinctual. Either you end up writing about terrible things happening to children—as if you could ward them off simply by writing about them—or you tie things up in easily opened packages, or you pull your punches as a writer. All deadfalls to watch for.

Having children also makes it difficult to get out of the house. With a child you certainly can't be a Bruce Chatwin or a Hemingway, living the adventurer-writer life. No running with the bulls at Pamplona. If you value your relationships with your children, you can't write about them. You have to make up other, less convincing children. There is also one's inclination to be charming instead of presenting a grittier truth about the world. But then, having children has also made me this particular writer. Without my children, I'd have written with less fervor. I wouldn't understand life in the same way. I'd write fewer comic scenes, which are the most challenging. I'd probably have become obsessively self-absorbed, or slacked off. Maybe I'd have become an alcoholic. Many of the writers I love most were alcoholics. I've made my choice, I sometimes think—wonderful children instead of hard liquor.

INTERVIEWER

Were you ever in danger of becoming a drunk?

ERDRICH

Likely, but for the gift of the Rudolf Hotel. I got hepatitis. That saved me.

INTERVIEWER

On your journeys do you visit with members of the reservation and hear their stories?

ERDRICH

You'd think so. That would make sense. But I never hear stories that go into my work, although place description might. Just germs of stories, and most of those I hear from my father. I've internalized my father to such a degree that sometimes he has only to start a few sentences and my mind races off. Same with my mother. She once told me a story about a boy secretly playing a violin and it was only a few sentences, but it became "Shamengwa" (2002). Bits of narrative always cling to a title, like magnetism. I love titles. I have lists of titles that I haven't gotten to. *Tales of Burning Love* (1996) and *Shadow Tag* were there for the longest time.

The closest thing to a complete story that went into my work was a bank robbery. My dad's great on bank robberies. He was telling me a story about a woman taken hostage during a holdup. She was being used as a hostage shield, and a deputy shot her in the hip. She became "Naked Woman Playing Chopin" (1998).

INTERVIEWER

Some people refer to your writing as magical realism. Is that another pigeonhole?

ERDRICH

I have six brothers and sisters, and nearly all of them work with Ojibwe or Dakota or other Native people. My youngest brother, youngest sister, and brother-in-law have worked with the Indian Health Service for a total of more than forty years. My second-oldest brother works in northern Minnesota sorting out the environmental issues for all of the Ojibwe Nations

382

throughout the entire Midwest. Their experiences make magical realism seem ho-hum. It's too bad I can't use their experiences because everyone would know who they are, but believe me, my writing comes from ordinary life.

INTERVIEWER

A man nursing a baby in *The Antelope Wife*?

ERDRICH

What's strange about that? There are several documented cases of male lactation. It's sometimes uncomfortable for me to read that scene in front of mixed audiences. Men get upset. But I think it's a great idea. It would solve about half of the world's problems.

INTERVIEWER

A violin washing ashore in an empty canoe in *The Plague of Doves*?

ERDRICH

It made the story.

INTERVIEWER

When you're writing and a character or situation starts to approach the supernatural, do you think twice about writing it?

ERDRICH

I'm not aware of the supernatural in the same way, so I can't tell when it starts to approach. Maybe it goes back to childhood, still spoiled by the Old Testament. Maybe it's Catholic after all, this conviction that there are miracles and things like violins appearing in a canoe. To me that was possible. I love it when a story begins to write itself, and that particular story did. The piece in *The Plague of Doves* where the men are taking on a surreal journey—there's nothing magical in the least about it. "Town Fever" (2006) is based on a historical trip that ended up in Wahpeton. There is now a stone that commemorates their near starvation. It fascinated me that they began right down at the river here in what became Minneapolis, where I go every week or so. With their ox-pulled sleighs, they traveled what is now Interstate 94. So I knew the exact route they took, and my description was based on reality. Daniel Johnston, who wrote the account, recorded that the party had bowel troubles and so took "a remedy." Then it only remained for me to look up what remedy there was at the time, and it was laudanum. They were high on opium the whole time. Then I read *The Pursuit of Oblivion* and became interested in what it is like to be high all the time. And last week you saw me reading *Methland*. You must think I'm obsessed with drugs.

INTERVIEWER

Do you discuss your books with other writers?

ERDRICH

I talked to Gail Caldwell quite a bit about *Shadow Tag* and *The Last Report on the Miracle at Little No Horse* (2001). She describes this wonderful state when there's "fire in the room." When there's a fire burning in the room, and it's illuminated and warm, you can't stop reading. With *Shadow Tag*, she told me when the fire was in the room. And she was kind when the fire went out, which a number of times it did.

At what point do you show a manuscript to your editor?

Terry Karten has been my editor since *Last Report*. I have no rule about when to show her something. I trust her, and often we talk about books I'm thinking about before I do show the work to her. She is ruthlessly honest, has superb instincts, and is a true book person. There are probably very few relationships like this left in the publishing world. I have also worked with Jane Beirn all of my writing life—another person of the highest caliber. I don't know what I would do without her.

What do you do when you can't make something work?

I walk—I usually have a little pen and some note cards with me. But one day I didn't and I was halfway around the lake when the words started to appear, the end of *Shadow Tag*. The words rained into my mind. I looked up and saw my sister Heid's car on the road around the lake, and I ran over to her, flagged down her car, and said, Give me a pencil and paper! Quick, quick, quick! Please. I still have the piece of paper that she gave me taped into my notebook.

If not with a title, how did you begin working on what you're working on now?

That began with digging shoots and saplings out of the foundation of my parents' house. I was quite aware that this was the beginning of something. Driving from Wahpeton to Minneapolis, I started writing it in my head and I had to pull over and start writing. I pulled over because I had my youngest child in the car.

I figured I was all washed up when I learned I was going to have another baby at forty-six. I thought, Oh, the hell with it. I'm never going to get out of this. But before she was born, I had all of this pent-up desperation and I wrote *The Master Butchers Singing Club*. I'd always wanted to write that book. I wrote the first part of the book by hand, but because I was pregnant I started writing my first draft on the computer. My baby was getting bigger and bigger, and my arms were stretching farther and farther to reach over her to the keyboard.

Were you concerned that the quality of your writing would suffer?

It's a touchstone for me to have everything written down by hand.

Do you transfer your writing to the computer yourself?

ERDRICH

I don't let anybody touch my writing.

INTERVIEWER

And do you revise at that point?

ERDRICH

I revise as I type, and I write a lot by hand on the printouts so they feel repossessed. I have always kept notebooks—I have an obsessive devotion to them—and I go back to them over and over. They are my compost pile of ideas. Any scrap goes in, and after a number of years I'll get a handful of earth. I am working right now out of a notebook I used when I wrote *The Blue Jay's Dance*.

INTERVIEWER

You wrote in that book about moments in which suicide was appealing.

ERDRICH

Postpartum depression, but I beat that thought down. Certainly after Michael's death it became clear that I wouldn't kill myself to save my life. At that point I realized that the main thing a parent has to do is stay alive. It doesn't matter how rotten you are, or if you fail. A failed parent is better than a dead parent. A failed parent at least gives you someone to rail against. A former army psychiatrist said something that struck me. He said that there are people who will kill themselves no matter what, and there are people who won't do it no matter what. There are people who can go through an endless level of psychological pain, and still they will not kill themselves. I want to be that last person.

You wrote *The Crown of Columbus* with your husband, Michael. How was that different from the experience of writing your other books?

I've not spoken much about what it was like to work with Michael, partly because I feel that there's something unfair about it. He can't tell his side of the story. I have everything that we once had together. It touches me that he left me as his literary executor. I think he trusted that I would be good to his words, and I have tried to do that. So it's difficult to set the record straight because it would be my view, the way I see it. Still, he controlled our narrative when he was living. I am weary of all of the old leftover assumptions, and what else, really, do people have to go on?

I would have loved for Michael to have had his own life as a writer and not covet my life as a writer. But he couldn't help himself. So in agreeing to write *The Crown of Columbus* I really made a deal, at least in my thoughts, that if we wrote this one book together, then we could openly work separately—as we always did in truth, of course. I wanted to make him happy, you know. He was the kind of person whom people want to make happy. People did this all the time, they tried to make him happy, but there was a deep impossibility within him and he couldn't really be happy. Or he couldn't be happy alone. So I'd had the idea for *The Crown of Columbus*. I'd done the research and I said, This is the project. We can do it together because you can write your part and I can write mine and both of our names will be on the cover.

I haven't ever read the published book. I've never watched the movie of *The Broken Cord* (1989) either. There are just certain things that I've never been able to get close to again. I haven't been able to revisit most of the year 1997. I hoped that *The Crown of Columbus* would be what Michael needed in order to say, Now it is enough, we truly collaborated. Instead, it became the beginning of what he wanted for every book. When he told me he wanted both of our names on every book now, something in me—the writer, I guess—couldn't bear it any longer, and that was the beginning of the long ending. We're talking only of our writing relationship, as distinct from the tangle of our family.

INTERVIEWER

Why do you think he wanted and needed so badly to see himself as a writer?

ERDRICH

Perhaps because I loved writing so much and he loved me. Perhaps because he was a very good writer. Or perhaps—I don't say this in a negative or judgmental way, because this is the case with writers whether they admit it or not—Michael also adored everything that went with the identity. He adored meeting other writers, adored being part of a literary world. He would answer everyone who wrote to him, beautiful letters, every single person. I don't take much pleasure in being the writer. That's what my bookstore is for. So that people can visit a version of the writer, and incidentally, visit a real bookstore. I can't talk to people, so—

You can't talk to people?

Still socially awkward. Once I was in a bookstore in New York and a very short man reached up and patted me on the top of my head and said, "I think you're a good little writer." So I patted him on the head and said, "Thank you. You're a good little reader." Then I thought, I can't take this anymore. It's just what I tried to get away from in Wahpeton, being a good little anything.

How did the relationship with Michael break down?

There were signs from the beginning, but I ignored them or even exhaustedly encouraged them. He took over as the agent for *Love Medicine*. After it won an award and *The Beet Queen* was published, we went to New York for an interview with the *New York Times*. I was walking out the door to meet the interviewer, and I noticed that he was dressed up, too. So I asked him where he was going. He said, I'm going to be in the interview. And I said, No, they asked me. And he said, What do you mean—I can't come? So it was both of us from then on. As long as he was content with being in on the interview and saying what he needed to say, I wasn't that unhappy. Actually, I was tired. *Love Medicine* and *Jacklight* were published in 1984, and I had a baby. *The Beet Queen* was published in 1985, and I bore my second daughter in that year. What kind of woman can do that? A tired woman who lets her husband do the talking because she has the two best things—the babies and the writing. Yet at some point the talking infected the writing. I looked into the mirror and I saw Michael. I began to write again in secret and put together a novel that I didn't show him.

INTERVIEWER

Was he a good agent?

ERDRICH

He was a terrific agent. He had the energy for it, and the excitement about the book world. He was a very good and generous editor, too. Not to mention a teacher.

INTERVIEWER

A journalist once asked you what advice you would give someone trying to write a novel. You said, "Don't take the project too seriously." Is that what you would say today?

ERDRICH

I think I meant that grand ideas kill first efforts. Begin with something in your range. Then write it as a secret. I'd be paralyzed if I thought I had to write a great novel, and no matter how good I think a book is on one day, I know now that a time will come when I will look upon it as a failure. The gratification has to come from the effort itself. I try not to look back. I approach the work as though, in truth, I'm nothing and the words are everything. Then I write to save my life. If you are a writer, that will be true. Writing has saved my life.

How?

I needed a way to go at life. I needed meaning. I might have chosen something more self-destructive had I not found writing.

Do your daughters help you when you write your books for children?

They are great editors—they read and react. When my older daughters were little, I used to tell them the story of a little girl marooned alone on an island, everyone else had died. My daughters wanted that story over and over, so finally I wrote it down and showed it to a friend who said, This is the anti–Little House on the Prairie! Of course, Little House on the Prairie is foundational literature. Everyone refers to it. But the series has an appalling view of how the American settlers went into an empty world. There was no one there, so Pa set out his claim. The Indians are always slinking off and Ma's holding her nose. But I do love the parts about making sausage.

I thought I would write about the other side, the people who were in that empty space, the people who were forced ahead of the settlers and what happened to them. The path taken by these people in the Birchbark books roughly mirrors the path the Ojibwe side of my family took crossing from Madeline Island, over what is now Minnesota, up to Lake of the Woods and over to the Turtle Mountains. So far in the series, I've reached Lake of the Woods.

INTERVIEWER

How is writing novels for children different from writing them for adults?

ERDRICH

One of the jobs I had in the old days was writing for children's textbooks. I followed a mathematical formula to choose big words and little words in combination to make each sentence. A maddening challenge for a young writer. Writing for children now, I pare back description, stick to action, humor, trouble, triumph. Of course there also has to be death, but not too much. I have to watch that. I can't become Cormac McCarthy for the middle reader.

INTERVIEWER

Do you ever fall into the wonderful writing trance when you're working on nonfiction?

ERDRICH

Nonfiction is always a grind for me. A great deal of research goes into the fiction, but when the research is for nonfiction all the pleasure is dulled. And no, I never fall into a trance.

INTERVIEWER

Are you still writing poetry?

ERDRICH

I stopped thinking like a poet back when I started writing narrative poems. Occasionally I get some poetry, and I'll write poetry for as long as I can. But it is as though I've been temporarily excused by the novel, and it wants me back. So I usually put whatever poetry I would have written into the novel. I only keep a few of my poems as poems.

INTERVIEWER

Why?

ERDRICH

It usually turns out that the poem was connected to the prose in a subterranean way. If I am writing a novel, it casts an aura around me and I get ideas for it, descriptions, words, phrases, at all times. I'm always jotting in notebooks I keep with me. That delight of immersion in a book is as good as a trance. For a while, the book is so powerful that I can follow the thread even through my chaotic daily existence, with children at all hours, school, dinner, long calls to my daughters, my ever demanding house, barking dogs, and the bookstore.

INTERVIEWER

You said before that your bookstore is a way you have of meeting with other people. Is the business still working?

ERDRICH

Birchbark Books is still here! In fact, doing well. But I'm not a business person. At first I looked at the bookstore as a work of art that would survive on its own artfulness. Now I get that it's a business, but it is also much more. Any good business is about its people. Marvelous people work at Birchbark Books.

That's why it's still alive. Walking into a huge book-store feels a bit like walking into Amazon.com. But walking into a small bookstore, you immediately feel the presence of the mind that has chosen the books on the shelves. You communicate intellectually with the buyer. Then, if you're lucky, you meet another great reader in person—our manager, Susan White, ready with ideas for you. People need bookstores and need other readers. We need the intimate communication with others who love books. We don't really think we do, because of the ease that the Internet has introduced, but we still need the physical world more than we know. Little bookstores are community services, not profitable business enterprises. Books are just too inexpensive online and there are too many of them, so a physical bookstore has to offer something different. Perhaps little bookstores will attain nonprofit status. Maybe one fine day the government will subsidize them, so they can thrive as nonprofit entities. Some very clever bookstore, probably not us, is going to manage to do that and become the paradigm for the rest.

INTERVIEWER

What do you do to differentiate your store?

ERDRICH

We attract writers, especially Native writers, and we host literary events, which means, again, the book-store is more than a business—it is an arts organization. We support a number of Native artists, basket makers and jewelers and painters. We sell medicines grown by a Dakota family—sage, sweetgrass, bear root. My sister Heid and I launched an affiliated nonprofit press that will publish in the Ojibwe and Dakota languages. With a small bookstore, you get to encourage your eccentricities. It's quite a wonderful thing, this bookstore. I thought it would be a project for my daughters and me, some work we could do together, and that has happened. Each daughter has worked in the store.

There's something very wrong in our country—and not just in the book business. We now see what barely fettered capitalism looks like. We are killing the small and the intimate. We all feel it and we don't know quite why everything is beginning to look the same. The central cores of large cities can still sustain interesting places. But all across our country we are intent on developing chain after chain with no character and employees who work for barely livable wages. We are losing our individuality. Killing the soul of our landscape. Yet we're supposed to be the most individualistic of countries. I feel the sadness of it every time I go through cities like Fargo and Minneapolis and walk the wonderful old Main Streets and then go out to the edges and wander through acres of concrete boxes. Our country is starting to look like Legoland.

INTERVIEWER

Do you find any shortage of good books being published these days?

ERDRICH

Writing is better than ever. As for the book as an object, it's like bread. It is such a perfectly evolved piece of technology that it will be hard to top. A hardcover book is a beautiful and durable piece of work. The paperback—so low-tech and high-tech at the same time—is also a great piece of technology because you don't mind passing it along. It is inexpensive. Even if you drop it in the bathtub, you haven't really lost much. You can leave a paperback somewhere and buy a used one for the price of a loaf of bread. You can't pass on an electronic reader, you can't page back in the same way, you can't write in it—you've lost the tactile sense of being able to fold it over, rip it up, feel its weight. I also like that you can throw books across the room, as people have done with mine. Plus, you don't need a power source. The whole absence of touching and feeling a book would be a loss, though I think there are a number of readers who really only want the text, so they'll adopt electronic books. Ultimately it's just another form of publishing, so I'm not against it. I don't feel that sense of alarm and threat that some writers seem to feel about e-books.

INTERVIEWER

Is writing a lonely life for you?

ERDRICH

Strangely, I think it is. I am surrounded by an abundance of family and friends, and yet I am alone with the writing. And that is perfect.

(2010)

Maxine Groffsky

THE ART OF EDITING NO. 3

Interviewed by Jeff Seroy

For the first two decades of its existence (1953–73), *The Paris Review* was a transatlantic operation. It was printed in Europe. It was distributed mainly in America. And it was edited in both places, by George Plimpton—who moved back to New York in 1956—and by a series of Paris editors, who also oversaw the physical production of the magazine. These Paris editors were a distinguished group: over the years they included Robert Silvers, Nelson Aldrich, and Frederick Seidel, among others. But the person who held the job longest, and left the biggest stamp on the *Review*, was Maxine Groffsky, who worked in the rue de Tournon office from 1965 until it closed in January 1974.

Although Groffsky went on to become a well-known literary agent, until now she has never spoken in depth about her time at the *Review*. When the editors and I proposed this interview, she was skeptical. Once she agreed, however, she prepared herself, rereading her correspondence in the *Paris Review* archive at the Morgan Library and visiting the office to pore over old issues. I spoke with her twice, in August and September of last year, at the dining table of the sunny, art-filled apartment high above Washington Square she shares with her husband, Win Knowlton.

In person, Groffsky was vivacious and warm and, as regards this text, exacting. The transcripts of our meetings went through several months of revision in her hands. They also grew by many pages, as Groffsky patiently wrote and rewrote in response to follow-up questions and as new memories surfaced about this relatively unknown—but very fertile— period in the *Review*'s history.

INTERVIEWER

First, how did you come to be Paris editor of *The Paris Review?*

MAXINE GROFFSKY

Through the downtown art world and Random House publishers—but it's a long story.

INTERVIEWER

That's why we're here.

GROFFSKY

Swell. Just before graduating from Barnard College in 1958, I had a blind date who took me to a party in a loft. It was Elaine de Kooning's studio and the party was for James Schuyler and the publication of his novel *Alfred and Guinevere*. I met a painter there who told me about a jazz club, the Five Spot, that was opening a place in the Hamptons just for the summer. I didn't know anything about the Hamptons or jazz, and I didn't know what I wanted to be when I grew up, but I knew that I didn't want to work in the city that summer. So I went downtown to a joint on the Bowery to see Joe Termini, co-owner of the Five Spot, asked to be one of the waitresses for the season in the country, and was hired.

The place in the Hamptons was in a white clapboard house on the Montauk Highway in Water Mill. Frank O'Hara and Bill de Kooning were at the opening-night party, along with the poets and artists who had convinced Termini to try such a drastic change of locale. The Hamptons weren't ready for the Five Spot—the old-money, country-club set wasn't interested in jazz, and summer-rental swingers hadn't yet appeared. Even the painters couldn't drink enough to make the place profitable, but it stayed open until Labor Day. When the season was over, I returned to the city with a boyfriend, Larry Rivers, and a new life south of Fourteenth Street.

I took secretarial jobs during the day and went to New York University at night and by the end of the semester knew that graduate school and academe were not for me. Whenever I was midtown, I stopped in to visit Joan Geismar, a friend from Barnard who worked at Random House in the old Villard Mansion on Madison Avenue—it's part of the Palace Hotel now. Joan was the lowest person on the editorial totem pole, but she had her own office—built expressly for her job—in a corner of the impressive marble foyer. She logged in, read, and sent back the unsolicited manuscripts. Thousands a year. Joan was leaving Random House, and I thought it would be a good place to work. She was to pick her successor, so I had a perfunctory interview with her boss, Albert Erskine. "Can you type?" "So-so." "Can you take shorthand?" "No." "Welcome to Random House."

Bennett Cerf and Donald Klopfer, the young cofounders of the firm in 1925, were still at the helm and set the convivial atmosphere. Bennett was a celebrity—a regular panelist on the popular TV show *What's My Line?* Donald was quieter, a lovely gent who brought in baskets of tomatoes from his garden and left them on the reception desk for all comers. Albert, editor in chief and the most handsome, distinguished man in publishing, was William Faulkner's editor.

INTERVIEWER

Were there any women editors?

GROFFSKY

At that time, young women were hired as secretaries or copy editors but were not promoted to editor. Only one woman was a full-fledged editor—Lee Wright, two generations older and a tough cookie. She was in charge of crime fiction. Lee used the executive bathroom next to my office while the copy editors went down to the Ladies in the basement. One day, Lee was passing by and I asked if I could use the executive bathroom. She replied, "I don't see why the fuck not!" And so we did, all of us.

INTERVIEWER

Did you want to be an editor yourself?

I wasn't particularly ambitious or thinking about a career. When I left work at five and headed to my studio apartment—not much bigger than my office—it was into another world. There were painters and openings and parties in lofts with live jazz, and readings by the New York School and Beat poets—and Merce Cunningham, the Living Theatre, and John Cage concerts. One night I appeared onstage at the Village Gate in an evening of avant-garde Japanese music and poetry. The featured event was "Of a Grapefruit in the World of Park," a poem written, narrated, and staged by Yoko Ono. I was asked by the composer of "Sonans Objectivis" to wear a bathing suit while I performed his piece. The *New York Times* reviewer loved the music but found me "an incongruous visual note." Nonetheless, the next day there was a star pasted on my office door.

I know some people downtown assumed I was just a party girl, but I did get up early each morning. I liked going to work at Random House and I started to do more—that is, I read and reported on manuscripts submitted by agents, and learned to proofread and copyedit. A month before I left Random House, I finally read an unsolicited manuscript that I thought we should publish. It was Cormac McCarthy's first novel, *The Orchard Keeper*. He had sent it to Random House because we published Faulkner and it was the only publisher he knew.

INTERVIEWER

What was the connection between Random House and *The Paris Review*?

GROFFSKY

I should mention first that my office was across from the elevator and several steps from the grand staircase that led up to the big shots on the second floor. It was a very social location. I soon met William Styron, Terry Southern, and Harold Humes, who had novels coming out with Random House. I didn't connect them with *The Paris Review* until a colleague in our editorial department took me to my first party at George Plimpton's, on East Seventy-Second Street, and they were all there. In fact, the three of them had been part of the group living in Paris in the early fifties that founded the magazine. In the first issue, there was a manifesto by Styron and a short story by Southern, and Humes was at least nominally the magazine's first managing editor.

George and I became friends, occasionally going out, usually with others—no hint of romance—to Elaine's or to some new "in" place like Smalls Paradise in Harlem.

INTERVIEWER

Did George ask you to take over the Paris office?

GROFFSKY

Nothing like that yet, I have to get to Paris first—I told you it was a long story.

INTERVIEWER

Go right ahead!

GROFFSKY

In early 1962, I was proofing a first novel by Harry Mathews called *The Conversions* and I thought it was fabulous, my favorite novel published by Random House. Although Harry and his wife, the artist Niki de Saint Phalle, lived in Paris, I'd met them in the Hamptons the summer before. By the time I read his proofs, Harry and Niki were splitsville, and Larry and I were, too. I announced to friends that I was going to have an affair with Harry when he showed up for his book publication in June.

"How can you have an affair with him? You don't even know him!"

"I read his book, I know him."

Which was sort of true. I knew that he was a great prose stylist, was fantastically inventive, and had a stunning intelligence. He was also a hunk.

We met again at his publication party and that was that. I was smitten. He was going back to France in two weeks, and I didn't know what I would do if he didn't ask me to join him. But he did—over blintzes at Ratner's, a kosher dairy restaurant on Second Avenue. I went to Bennett and asked him for a three-month leave of absence, and he said I could come back whenever I wanted. So I ran off to Paris with Harry. This is simply amazing to me now.

After a day or two in Paris, we left on a kind of honeymoon. First to Turin, Italy, to pick up Harry's new car, a Lancia and a real beaut. Then we drove to the magnificent eighteenth-century Villa Balbianello, on a promontory above Lake Como. The villa had belonged to Butler Ames, who left it to the enjoyment of his many nieces and nephews. Harry and George had known each other since grammar school, and George published an excerpt from *The Conversions* in issue no. 27, but it was his sister, Sarah, a poet and painter living in Paris, who had invited us. We arrived in the late afternoon and everyone was still at the lake, so we strolled down a lovely shaded path and met, walking up, three dowagers in long flowery dresses and a very sunburned rotund man in black bathing trunks carrying an inner tube. Adlai Stevenson. We stayed several glorious days at the villa and then went on to the French Riviera. Villefranche-sur-Mer was the last stop on that dreamy trip.

I'm sure I thought we would get married and live happily ever after, but that was not in the cards for us. Love at first sight- -or first reading—has to contend with the real world at some point. It wasn't until several weeks after we returned that I woke up and realized that, although I was wild about Harry, I had no life in Paris. No friends, no job, not even a room of my own. And only high-school French. I was confused and miserable at times and wondered what the hell I was doing there, but after several months, I decided to try to make a life in Paris with Harry.

I told Bennett that I wasn't coming back to Random House, and I found all kinds of freelance jobs in the *International Herald Tribune*. The oddest was selling an E-Type Jaguar for a lazy rich kid. The most amusing was working for the screenwriter Harry Kurnitz—he wrote *Witness for the Prosecution* with Billy Wilder—who lived at the Hotel George V. I typed letters to Frank Sinatra and sent flowers to movie stars. Kurnitz was ailing, but he was a pleasure to be with. "I would rather eat it than step in it," he announced when served chocolate mousse at the Duke and Duchess of Windsor's, in the Bois de Boulogne. My earnest jobs were translating simple plays and editing all kinds of nonfiction written in

English. I was also in-house editor on Harry's new novel, *Tlooth*.

INTERVIEWER

Did you become part of an expatriate literary community?

GROFFSKY

There were no expat circles left in Paris, though there were several notable writers—John Ashbery and Harry, who were great friends, and Mary McCarthy and James Jones, who were not. I am confident this foursome was never in a room together. There had been several groups of Americans and Brits in Paris when the first issue of *The Paris Review* appeared in the summer of 1953, but by the time George returned to New York in 1956, the other founders of the magazine and many of their friends had already gone home.

INTERVIEWER

If they all went home, why did the *Review* maintain an office in Paris?

GROFFSKY

Decades later, George wrote that he kept the Paris office "the better to find and publish material largely out of the mainstream of literature"—to be in touch with cutting-edge writers all over Europe. That may have been the original intention. I'd always assumed we kept the office in Paris for financial reasons, because it was considerably cheaper to print abroad, and, I dare add, for sentimental reasons, too. At any rate, the Paris office was always in charge of all production.

When George first met his successor, Robert Silvers, he described him in a letter to Peter Matthiessen as a young man who "will do well ... He wants to make publishing his career." After Silvers, the Paris editors were Nelson Aldrich, Blair Fuller, Frederick Seidel, and then Patrick Bowles, a South African poet who had worked closely with Samuel Beckett on the translation of *Molloy* into English. In the early sixties, while I was finding my way in Paris, the magazine was more or less hidden in a dingy office on the Right Bank.

INTERVIEWER

Well, you are getting closer to *The Paris Review* now.

GROFFSKY

Absolument. I went to New York annually—the best airfare was for twenty-one days—and stayed at the Hotel Chelsea. When I saw George at his apartment in the spring of 1964, he complained that after an impressive first year in the job, Bowles had stopped paying attention. He ignored important queries, the copyediting and proofing were careless, and there were significant cost overruns at the printer. Issue no. 31, the tenth-anniversary issue, was the final straw. George was so horrified by the number of typos and other errors he found in a hand-sewn advance copy that he telegrammed to stop the presses. Too late.

INTERVIEWER

And so he offered you the job?

GROFFSKY

Yes, he did—but I didn't take it! Even though I was

by then accustomed to French ways and loved living in Paris—making the rounds each day of my neighborhood food stores, sitting in cafés, hopping onto the back of a bus, reading in the Luxembourg Gardens, simply strolling anywhere—I was still uncertain about staying on.

INTERVIEWER

But why?

GROFFSKY

Harry and I were the uncertainty. We were considered a couple on both sides of the Atlantic and lived an interesting and rather glamorous life, but if the relationship ended, and at times it came perilously close, I was out of there. So I suggested to George that he hire Lawrence Bensky, a friend from Random House who was then in Paris, reading and improving his French. Larry took over for issue no. 33 and we worked together from the start—literally, since I found the artist Alain Jacquet who did the cover, a boldly colored nude that startled George at first but proved to be a crowd-pleaser.

INTERVIEWER

So you went to work in the dingy office.

GROFFSKY

Not at all. We had a great gift from the publishing gods. Or rather, from the eminent French publisher Gallimard. George was good friends with Colette Duhamel, a lovely Parisienne who was affiliated with Gallimard and arranged for us to have space in one of their buildings on the Left Bank. Our two small rooms were in a charming cobblestoned courtyard on rue de Tournon, a beautiful street that leads up to the Luxembourg Gardens. We were a few doors down from Café de Tournon, where George and his friends used to hang out, so it was a homecoming of sorts. And, get this, it was rent free. No matter there was no heat or running water. I went out and got a portable gas heater, and the Tournon provided our water. The post office—our lifeline to the world— was next to the Tournon.

INTERVIEWER

How did you put the issues together?

GROFFSKY

The logistics were ridiculously complicated. There were two offices in New York—George worked out of his apartment in Manhattan and Lillian von Nickern, known as Nicky, handled the back-office work at her home in Queens. Our poetry editor, Tom Clark, was in Bolinas, California. There were two distributors in the States and one in the UK. We also had an advertising man in London. All the copy for an issue was painstakingly gathered in Paris for final editing and design instructions, then mailed off to our printer in Nijmegen, Holland. The printer set everything into type and returned three sets of proofs. Two were for proofreading—although we proofread everything in Paris, many authors had to see proofs no matter where they were. The third was for layout and design. We cut with scissors and pasted with glue all the stories, poems, interviews, and front and back matter onto a maquette—blank sheets of paper the size of a *Paris Review* page—

which was sent to the printer along with the corrected proofs. Of course everything went airmail, but it still took forever, and things really did get lost in the mail. For the final stages of production, we had to go to Holland.

INTERVIEWER

Why Holland?

GROFFSKY

The first two printers of the magazine had been in Paris, but in 1958 Silvers found an excellent printer in Holland, G. J. Thieme, that did a much better job and charged less. Even so, by June 1965, when Larry and I went to the plant with issue no. 34, *The Paris Review* owed Thieme several thousand dollars. It took two trains and about eight hours to reach Nijmegen, the oldest city in Holland and renowned for its university. We spent all day in a pleasant but windowless room going over proof after proof. It was mind-numbing work.

INTERVIEWER

But hadn't everything already been proofread?

GROFFSKY

Never everything. Don't forget about mail delays. And since the magazine was printed in Monotype, there was always the possibility that making a correction would lead to more errors. With Monotype, each printed page is composed of thousands of pieces of metal called slugs—one slug for each letter of the alphabet, punctuation symbol, numeral, or blank space. The slugs were assembled on a thick piece of cardboard and tied together with string. Slugs might slip away, and words or simply a few letters at the corners of a printed page would mysteriously disappear when these cardboards were carried by apprentices from one part of the plant to another.

Also, we had brought with us last-minute material from New York—the interview and some advertisements—that had to be set into type. This was not unusual. After six or seven days, we signed off on the final proofs. When we returned from the printer, Larry went to Greece for the summer, and I went to meet up with friends at the Settimana della Poesia in Italy.

INTERVIEWER
What was that?

GROFFSKY
Something new at the Spoleto Festival—a week-long gathering of dozens of poets from around the world, among them Pablo Neruda, Charles Olson, Pier Paolo Pasolini, Stephen Spender, Ezra Pound, and Yevgeny Yevtushenko. We had just interviewed Yevtushenko, so I brought along a stack of publicity posters for issue no. 34 and put them up all over town. This was a great place to drum up business and to find artists and writers for the magazine. John Ashbery and Bill Berkson were also participants, and other friends from New York stopped by—the writer Kenward Elmslie and the artist Joe Brainard. There were poetry readings scheduled throughout the day. In the evenings we went dancing at a small disco with great music—Olson was a nifty dancer.

Pound read toward the end of the week, but he did not appear on the stage of the theater. He read from his seat in a box that happened to be below me, so I only heard a mumble that seemed to be coming from a tomb. The next day I actually saw Pound at a short concert given by the great percussionist Max Neuhaus, who traveled the world with a ton of metal, wood, and other materials that he would arrange in a kind of sculptural edifice and "play" for sound. The audience, except for Pound, was standing in a circle around Neuhaus and his construction as he performed a beautiful, delicate piece by Morton Feldman. Seated on a simple wooden chair a foot away from Neuhaus, his guardians close at hand, Pound was a wraithlike figure. After the concert, Olson grabbed my arm and took me over to meet him. Pound attempted to stand up to greet me—old-fashioned manners—but his alarmed keepers started shouting, "Don't stand up! Don't stand up! Don't let him stand up!" and kept tugging him back down. Later, Neuhaus asked me, "Who the fuck was that old man?"

I left Spoleto in great spirits. Back in Paris, I had to deal with a situation in the office—Larry's attitude toward his job and his colleagues was increasingly tenuous, and I was doing more and more of the Paris editor's work. George knew this, and I finally wrote to him in July 1966 that I wanted the title and the salary that went with the job and asked him to please straighten things out. In September, Larry flew to New York. I have no idea what transpired there, but by October he had left the magazine and I was Paris editor.

INTERVIEWER

Did you have a staff?

"Staff" is much too formal. From the very beginning of the magazine, there were always assistants in the Paris office. In my day, some lived in Paris and others were just hanging around for several months. They came by to learn about publishing, for fun, or as a pretext to stay abroad. We had no money for salaries, but we could acknowledge their help on the masthead. Paula Wolfert was the person who stayed the longest and did the most work. She lit up the office. She had two children and a husband who was writing the Great American Novel. Nothing came of his effort, but Paula became one of the premier food writers in the world.

We didn't have office hours per se, but there was a notice on our door that somebody was usually there in the afternoons. During the height of hippie pilgrimages to Kathmandu and other meaningful destinations in Asia, we were a stop in the West for writers. There were requests for money, but we had none to spare. Former editors and associates also came by. Styron would sit down and ask, How are we doing on subscriptions?—and really want to know. I shouldn't have been surprised that they all still cared. Being back on the rue de Tournon was a nostalgic trip for them, as it is now for me. Styron once took me to a party at Gloria and James Jones's place on the Île Saint-Louis. I'd not met them before, but even with their spectacular view over the Seine, the evening seemed more New York than Paris, with hard liquor and boisterous drunks gathered around their bar, one woman brandishing a knife and announcing what she'd do to her husband if he ever screwed around. When George's friends and acquaintances

traveled to Paris, he'd send them our way. I sometimes took visitors to the Tournon for a coffee or for
a walk into our park. Can you imagine having the
Luxembourg Gardens up at the corner? I wrote to
George early in my Paris editor days, "Mr. Sports
Illustrated stopped by the office. I gave him the A-2
treatment, drinks but no dinner. (Do I have to spend
the evening with the people you send by the office?)"

INTERVIEWER
Did George ever visit the office himself?

GROFFSKY
George came over only once during my tenure, en
route to Africa for a wildlife-preservation group, and
we went to dinner at La Coupole. George thought
it was great that a French poet we'd just published
climbed over the banquette to say hello, but that was
nothing compared to a greeting he received later at
Régine's, the swinging nightclub in Montparnasse.
We were on the dance floor when a gorgeous
blonde—Ursula Andress, the original Bond girl—
came rushing over and threw herself at George.

When I first met George, in the late fifties, he
was a popular man about town in New York—great
looking, smart, charming, talented, and extraordinarily generous and amiable. By this time, he had
become a world-class celebrity. He appeared in movies, TV shows, and commercials, emceed events,
supported causes, hung out with the Kennedys, you
name it. But he was foremost an excellent writer and
editor. One could say he put the literary interview on
the map, as well as participatory journalism, a field
in which he excelled. He should not be taken less

seriously by literary highbrows because his essays and books are so entertaining.

INTERVIEWER
What was the hardest part of working together?

GROFFSKY
The waiting. The interviews were the keystone of *The Paris Review* and the most difficult part of any issue, editorially and logistically. George was solely responsible for them, but he was often overextended and simply did not have enough time for his work on the magazine. He did, after all, have to earn a living. I could start editing and designing an issue before all of the manuscripts arrived in Paris—that was usually the case—but I could not print an issue without an interview, even if it meant delaying publication for weeks or even months. I preferred working to a lot of downtime, but at least I didn't have to wait around in the office. I traveled. And if necessary, everything I needed to make an issue, or complete one—manuscripts, proofs, maquette pages—fit into a leather-and-canvas satchel I carried with me on trips.

INTERVIEWER
What made the interviews so complicated?

GROFFSKY
They had to be done from scratch, starting with the pairing of subject and interviewer. Once the interviewing was finished, all sorts of questions arose. Was the transcription accurate? If there was a translation, was it good? Had the interviewer worked on

the text before it was sent on to George? Where, for that matter, was George? He had taken the two-part Pablo Neruda manuscript to Los Angeles where he was staying for three weeks at the Beverly Hills Hotel while filming a documentary. He wrote me that he had carefully worked on Part 1 and wanted to send it to me, but he couldn't find it. "I fear a Beverly Hills chambermaid either threw it away or took it home to read. Only Part 2 survives, but there's a copy in NY." Followed by, "I discovered Part 1 under the goddam curtains where it had slipped."

Gerard Malanga, the poet and Andy Warhol groupie, interviewed Charles Olson, and the transcription was done by someone, perhaps stoned, who simply made up anything that he didn't understand or hear, or that he felt like. When discovered, this caused considerable delay. For some reason, Ted Berrigan held onto the Jack Kerouac manuscript for four months.

INTERVIEWER

Where did you go while you were waiting for the interviews?

GROFFSKY

All over Europe. Once to the South of France to see the Merce Cunningham Company dance at the Fondation Maeght in Vence. When we stopped for lunch en route, Harry teased me for not leaving my "precious" *Paris Review* satchel in the car and carrying it to our table in the restaurant. During the meal, our car was broken into and everything in it was taken.

Most memorably, in the summer of 1967, I went with Harry to Rome for a four-week stay with

Brigitte Bardot and Gunter Sachs, a super playboy before he married the film star and a really good guy. He had rented a villa on the Appia Antica to work on his film script with Harry. Our neighbors up the road were Jane Fonda and Roger Vadim, who were shooting *Barbarella* at Cinecittà. Harry and Gunter spent mornings writing a script involving a wager, a seduction, and a woman who loved her panther— Harry was being paid, of course—and I worked on the proofs and manuscripts I'd brought with me. Brigitte pouted—the sex kitten was a pill in real life. We did get work done, and Gunter even flew me back to Paris to pick up more material for the next issue. But it was hardly Yaddo, and by noon la dolce vita prevailed. The villa usually had about eight guests, and in the evenings Harry and I went our separate way into town, as did the others.

One exceptional evening, Gunter asked Harry and me to stay in. His marriage wasn't going so well and he thought a lovely dinner at home, just the four of us, would be helpful. What an idea. We'd barely sat down when Brigitte picked a fight about Vuitton luggage and ran off from the table. After dinner we were having a drink in the living room and trying to cheer up Gunter when the doorbell rang. It was Vadim. We heard the exchange—"Come on in, where's Jane?" "Jane has a headache, where's Brigitte?" "Brigitte has a headache." Picture these two guys, and their movie-star wives sulking in their bedrooms.

What was the financial situation of the *Review* in those days?

The magazine was usually broke, and my salary and office-expense checks were often late. Some bounced. I continued freelance editing and scouting to supplement a salary of about two to three hundred dollars a month. We scrimped on supplies, used the lightest onionskin stationery, and delayed changing the typewriter ribbon. Correspondence from our office may have caused eye strain.

I had just signed off on printing an issue with a John Berryman interview when I received a telegram from George that Berryman had killed himself. I admit my first thought was that we should get an in memoriam ad from his U.S. publisher, but it was too late. George hoped there would be some way to acknowledge his death, so I had to make a long-distance call to Holland to see if our printer could possibly add Berryman's dates to the title page of the interview. That call was an extravagance. Most people did not make long-distance, much less transatlantic calls. It was incredibly expensive and simply not done. I don't think I made ten personal transatlantic calls during a dozen years in Paris. Telegrams were used for speedy communication and for emergencies. The few times I called George collect from the office it was for shock effect—to prompt action on missing interviews or fiction.

George was always thinking of ways to raise money to pay the ever growing debt to our printer and other creditors. His two most successful fund-raisers were our annual party, the Revel, still going strong, and the poster series, famous artists creating lithographs for us to sell that included the words *The Paris Review*.

Did the *Review* take money from the CIA?

GROFFSKY

In the early days of the magazine, in the early fifties? The Shadow knows. If we'd been getting money in the midsixties, I would have splurged on typewriter ribbons. I do know that when I sold interview reprint rights to magazines funded by the Congress for Cultural Freedom—a CIA front in Paris and the best-known secret in Europe—they paid the same amount we'd charge anybody else. Usually a whopping thirty to forty dollars. There weren't that many requests from the Congress magazines, and on one occasion we had to dun the Congress for payment.

INTERVIEWER

What changes did you make to the *Review* as Paris editor?

GROFFSKY

I thought the magazine had an old-fashioned, tired look. Since there was no art editor or design firm, and since the selection of art for covers and portfolios, not to mention the layout and design, were always done in the Paris office, I could pretty much try whatever I pleased. I went for bold covers that would catch the eye and for a cleaner, more modern look. I changed to a sans serif typeface for covers and some of the inside pages. Later, I took the new look much too far by removing from our covers almost all text about contents. This was misguided, to say the least. After all, our magazines were not destined for art galleries but for bookstores and newsstands, where info on the covers might have helped sales.

Since we thought of ourselves as a transatlantic magazine, I was concerned that most of our contributors were from the States. The easiest solution was to find European artists—no translators necessary—so my covers and art portfolios were mostly done by artists from abroad. Wherever I traveled, I was on the lookout for new painters and for new advertisers. Translations of French texts were not a problem since Harry was my in-house translator, but I never found the right combo of text and translator for other languages.

My Europe-first campaign went by the wayside when it came to John Ashbery, Kenneth Koch, and James Schuyler, who had never appeared in the magazine. They knew how much I admired their work and they began sending poems our way. I published everything they sent and even went so far as to change the "Fiction" rubric in our table of contents to "Prose" in order to publish "The System" by Ashbery and "Life, Death and Other Dreams" by Schuyler. I am proud of their legacy in my issues.

INTERVIEWER

Did you have any other goals as editor?

GROFFSKY

From the time George returned to New York in 1956, the *Review* had come out only two or three times a year. Since we were supposed to be a quarterly, I wanted to put out four issues. That was a goal I accomplished only twice in seven years, most dramatically when Nicky sent an impassioned letter from New York that we had to publish four issues in the current year or lose our second-class mailing privileges. An increase in postage costs would have sunk us. This was desperation. Since Thieme planned and allocated press time, we couldn't just waltz into the plant and say, We have to print now, but that seemed to happen. I felt as though I had commandeered the presses. Everyone pitched in. Thieme provided me with daily updates of boats scheduled to leave from Rotterdam for New York and the deadlines for getting our shipment out of the plant and trucked to the port—and we made one! Our issue arrived at the docks in New York before the end of the year. Who could have predicted a strike by the longshoremen? Our magazines stayed on board until January. Fortunately, Nicky worked things out with the U.S. Postal Service. As usual, George still had to meet with a U.S. customs inspector and go over the contents of the issue to make sure there was no offensive material—"bad" words or "dirty" pictures.

INTERVIEWER

You mentioned that you and George often disagreed about fiction. Why is that?

GROFFSKY

Taste. We disagreed about particular stories and took turns getting on the "I don't presume to be the arbiter of taste, but ... " high horse, or the other one, "We don't necessarily love each other's selections, but our readers profit when there is no party line ... "—to quote from our letters. This was not a traditional-writing versus contemporary-writing divide. George was just as interested in avant-garde writing as I was, but he didn't do anything about it—he was too busy. I had the zeal and contacts and could follow through. We were at times an Odd Couple of editors, but we both cared deeply about the magazine.

INTERVIEWER

Besides Ashbery, Koch, and Schuyler, who were some of the other contributors you were bringing to the magazine?

GROFFSKY

When John Cage came to France with Merce Cunningham, he told me about his *Diary: How to Improve the World (You Will Only Make Matters Worse)*. I jumped at the chance to publish an excerpt and felt the same way when I heard about Jim Carroll's *Basketball Diaries*. Some of my favorite selections are still the artist-writer collaborations "An Anecdoted Topography of Chance," by Daniel Spoerri and Emmett Williams of Fluxus, and *The Power Plant Sestina*, by Joe Brainard and Kenward Elmslie, along with Niki de Saint Phalle's text and drawings in *Letter to Diana*.

INTERVIEWER

Were there writers you and George both admired?

GROFFSKY

Certainly. Harry and James Salter immediately come to mind.

George was a fan of Harry's work and first published him in the *Review* while I was still at Random House—before I'd read a word of his. Over the years I published Harry's prose and poetry, along with his translations of French poets, and prose by his friend Georges Perec. I tested the limits of George's enthusiasm in issue no. 51 when I printed Part 1—forty-five magazine pages—of Harry's third novel, *The Sinking of the Odradek Stadium*. It is composed of letters between Zachary McCaltex, a librarian in Miami, and his wife, Twang Panat-tapam, from Pan-Nam in Southeast Asia, who is learning English and whose mother tongue was made up by Harry. George wrote about that excerpt, "Harry's stuff is marvelous. I always find myself reading it with a curious fixed smile of delight." Such a perfect response to Harry's work—especially since I planned to publish the entire novel in four installments.

Jim's novel *A Sport and a Pastime* was published in 1967 by Doubleday under the Paris Review Editions imprint. Up to five books a year were selected by George and an editorial board in New York for this venture—the *Review* would make some money and Doubleday would get some estimable books. Jim's book had a rave review in the *Times*, and *Kirkus Reviews* called it "as erotic a novel as any since Henry Miller even where it is as lyrical as it is lubricious." We were amazed that it didn't sell.

I first met Jim when he stopped by the office in August 1968. He had just finished preproduction and was going to Provence the next day to direct Charlotte Rampling and Sam Waterston in *Three*, a film he had written based on a story by Irwin Shaw. Over the years, Jim and I became friends and pen pals. He had sent submissions to George, but when it took forever to hear back or the manuscripts were "lost," he started sending stories to me and cautioned, "You expect a great deal from me, I see, perhaps that's best. Please don't kill the good while waiting for the excellent however." He knew that if I said no to a story, he had a second chance with George and it would most likely be accepted.

Jim was one of the first friends I told that I was thinking about leaving *The Paris Review*.

INTERVIEWER
Why did you want to leave?

GROFFSKY
I'd been running the Paris office for almost six years, much longer than any of my predecessors. Now it was my turn to think about a job with a real salary and career prospects. George had sent over two stories with a note that "these won't exult your heart, but it's the best we have on hand... We're slackening off here—perhaps because I can't find enough energy with all the other things I'm doing." He was running out of steam for the *Review*. We both were. To complete this dim picture, the dollar was sinking and our printing costs rising. We economized. We cut some issues by thirty-two pages and skipped art portfolios, but our debts still grew.

By 1973, Harry and I, the couple, were faltering, too, but there were still some trips and good times. We met friends at Mardi Gras in Nice, then on to Palermo where we stayed at the Grande Albergo e delle Palme in homage to Raymond Roussel. Later that spring, Sarah invited us again to the Villa Balbianello. This time it rained for most of our stay, and the lake vistas were gray and melancholy compared to the brilliant summer days in 1962.

At the end of July, I wrote George that I felt Thieme would not compose another issue until we paid our bills. His response was a thoughtful analysis of our predicament, with three possible courses of action. We could try to raise money and hope that the dollar would strengthen—"The consensus on this choice is skepticism." We could close the Paris office and move our production to New York— "What we would lose, naturally, is the international flavor, which ... I have always thought to be an indispensable quality of the enterprise." Or, George wrote, "We could close up shop altogether. We've been at it for twenty years, which is a long time... There is not as much energy and dedication as we have enjoyed in the past. It may indeed be that a new guiding hand is needed if we do decide to continue."

To me, it was clear that we should close the Paris office, which is what I told George. "You have always been *The Paris Review*, and I think the decision whether the magazine moves, changes hands, or simply stops is absolutely yours. I suppose it would be wisest economically to close shop here. (I'm sure you've noticed the re-evaluation of the guilder.) About new guiding hands, it's impossible for me to think of the magazine without you. New guiding hands should be a new, another magazine.

"If you decide to print another issue at Thieme, and you want me to do it, you can count on me. I'm very happy to do one more issue, but after that I'll be turning in my rue de Tournon key... I have loved working on *The Paris Review*... It's very sad to 'resign' after all these terrific years, but I'm sure you'll understand my desire to do new work. Please write soon and let me know what you plan to do."

What new work did you have in mind?

Film editing. Paris was movie heaven, and I didn't need perfect French in a cutting room. I took an intensive course in film production the year before and had been looking for any kind of work. In September, the day after I sent George my letter of resignation, I drove to Normandy with a small film crew. Anatole Dauman, producer of films by Resnais, Godard, and Bresson, offered me a production-assistant job on *Contes immoraux* by Walerian Borowczyk, a writer-director much admired by cinephiles. No pay, but great experience, perhaps a credit on-screen. Does this sound familiar? There were eight of us on location for a week—Borowczyk, the young unseasoned cast of two, a cameraman and his assistant, a soundman, a jack-of-all-trades, and me. I was supposed to be apprentice to the script girl but there was no script girl, so I did that, too.

La Marée, the first of the *Contes immoraux*, is the story of a young man who has spent many summers with his sweet cousin at their aunt's château on the Normandy coast. In our short film, he carefully plans an excursion to the beach so that they will be trapped by the incoming tide, and then she docilely obeys his wishes—a blowjob! That's it. Mind you, this story was adapted from a work by the Goncourt winner André Pieyre de Mandiargues. There we were on the third or fourth day of shooting. The wind was fierce and it was very cold and our poor girl was naked, or almost, and turning blue. The young man remained fully clothed in jeans, T-shirt, sweatshirt, and a stupid little hat—I don't think he even unzipped. Everyone was extremely busy when I happened to look around and was horrified to see the tide rushing in. We made it out of there just in time, but the bad weather continued. We finished shooting the rest of the film in a room off the kitchen of our hotel, the couple on a very large table, and pebbles and sand, too.

Borowczyk is still widely recognized as an important filmmaker, considered by some a genius and others a pornographer—or both. According to his obit in the *New York Times*, "To many critics, *Contes immoraux* marked the start of Mr. Borowczyk's slide into complete depravity." How was I to know? The movie is now a cult classic, and I do have a screen credit.

INTERVIEWER
Did you go to work on a new movie?

GROFFSKY
No, I had declined an offer—with pay—to work in Sweden on the second *Contes immoraux* featuring Picasso's daughter and fifty naked girls. I was still on rue de Tournon. Of course, George decided to close the Paris office and to publish in the States, but two months after his decision I was still waiting to hear where he wanted me to ship everything. Incidentally, it was December and I hadn't received my final paycheck due at the end of October or money to pay for the move.

Moping around the office one afternoon, a question popped into my head—Am I going to spend the rest of my life in France? The answer was an emphatic "No!" and I knew that this was the time for me to go home.

When I told Harry about my decision, it wasn't a big surprise and we both pretended that it was not the end of the affair. We took our final trip together, a swan song. We drove to Burgundy and visited friends at the Domaine de la Romanée-Conti, for both of us the Olympus of French vineyards. That was my last great taste of France.

On January 10, 1974, Transports et Transit Maritimes Associés came to the rue de Tournon and took away three large metal trunks—two green and one orange, each insured for twenty-five hundred francs—and I closed the Paris office of *The Paris Review* for good.

(2017)